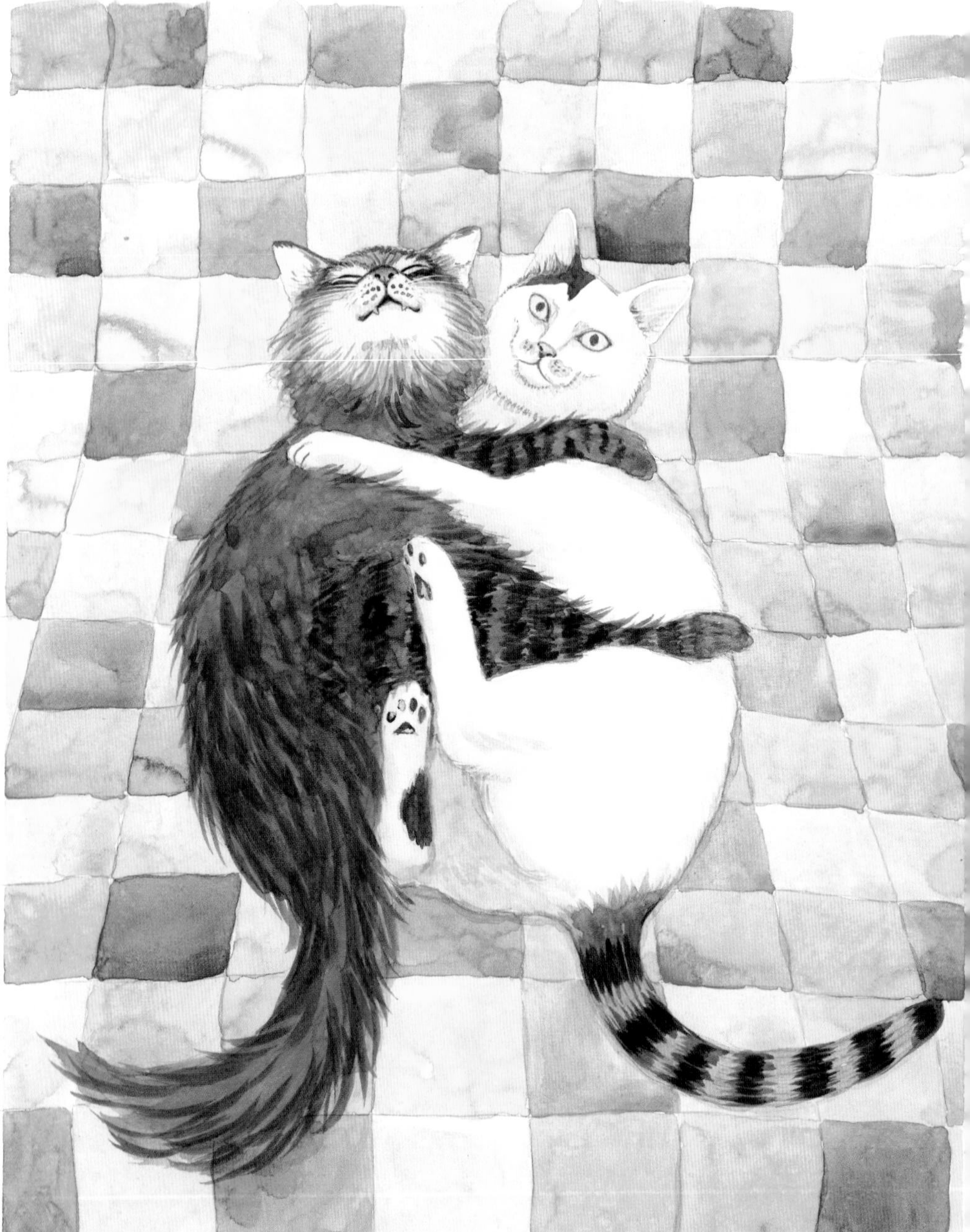

JUNJI ITO'S CAT DIARY:

YON & MU

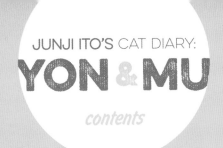

JUNJI ITO'S CAT DIARY:
YON & MU

contents

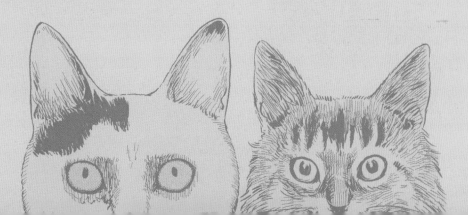

Chapter 1: MU APPEARS

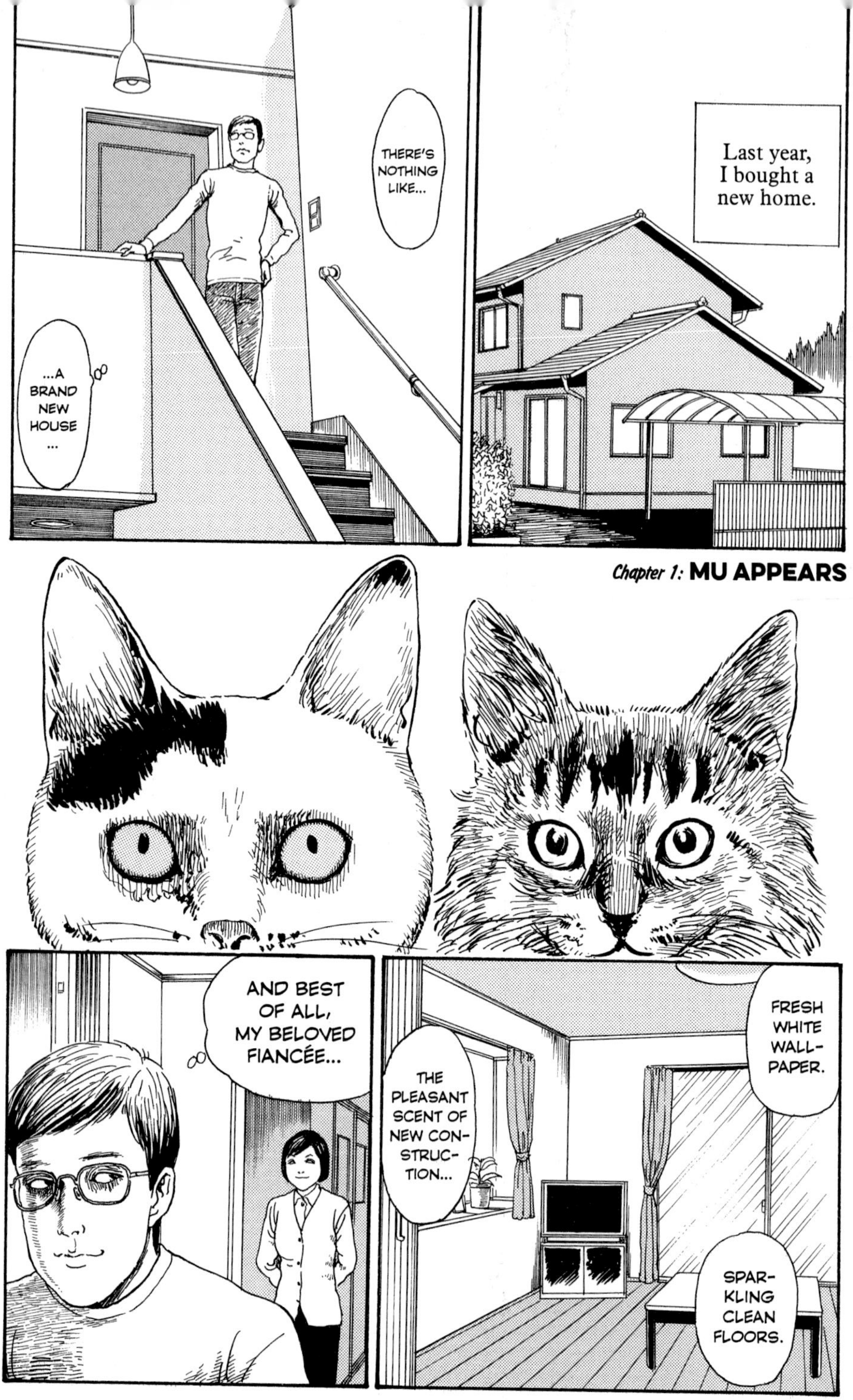

Last year, I bought a new home.
THERE'S NOTHING LIKE...
...A BRAND NEW HOUSE...
FRESH WHITE WALL-PAPER.
THE PLEASANT SCENT OF NEW CON-STRUC-TION...
SPAR-KLING CLEAN FLOORS.
AND BEST OF ALL, MY BELOVED FIANCÉE...

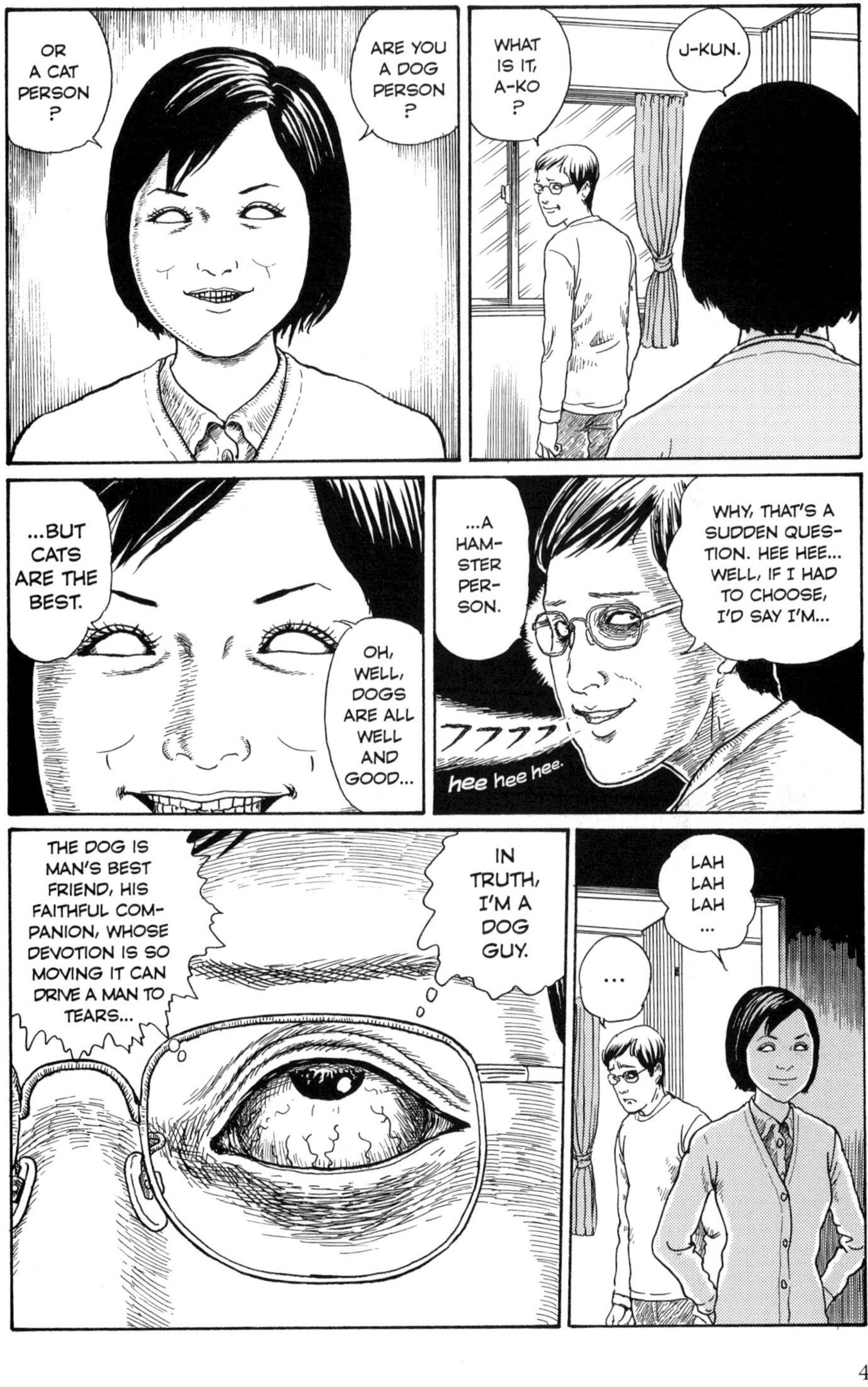

J-KUN.
WHAT IS IT, A-KO?
ARE YOU A DOG PERSON?
OR A CAT PERSON?
WHY, THAT'S A SUDDEN QUESTION. HEE HEE... WELL, IF I HAD TO CHOOSE, I'D SAY I'M...
...A HAMSTER PERSON.
hee hee hee.
OH, WELL, DOGS ARE ALL WELL AND GOOD...
...BUT CATS ARE THE BEST.
LAH LAH LAH ...
...
IN TRUTH, I'M A DOG GUY.
THE DOG IS MAN'S BEST FRIEND, HIS FAITHFUL COMPANION, WHOSE DEVOTION IS SO MOVING IT CAN DRIVE A MAN TO TEARS...

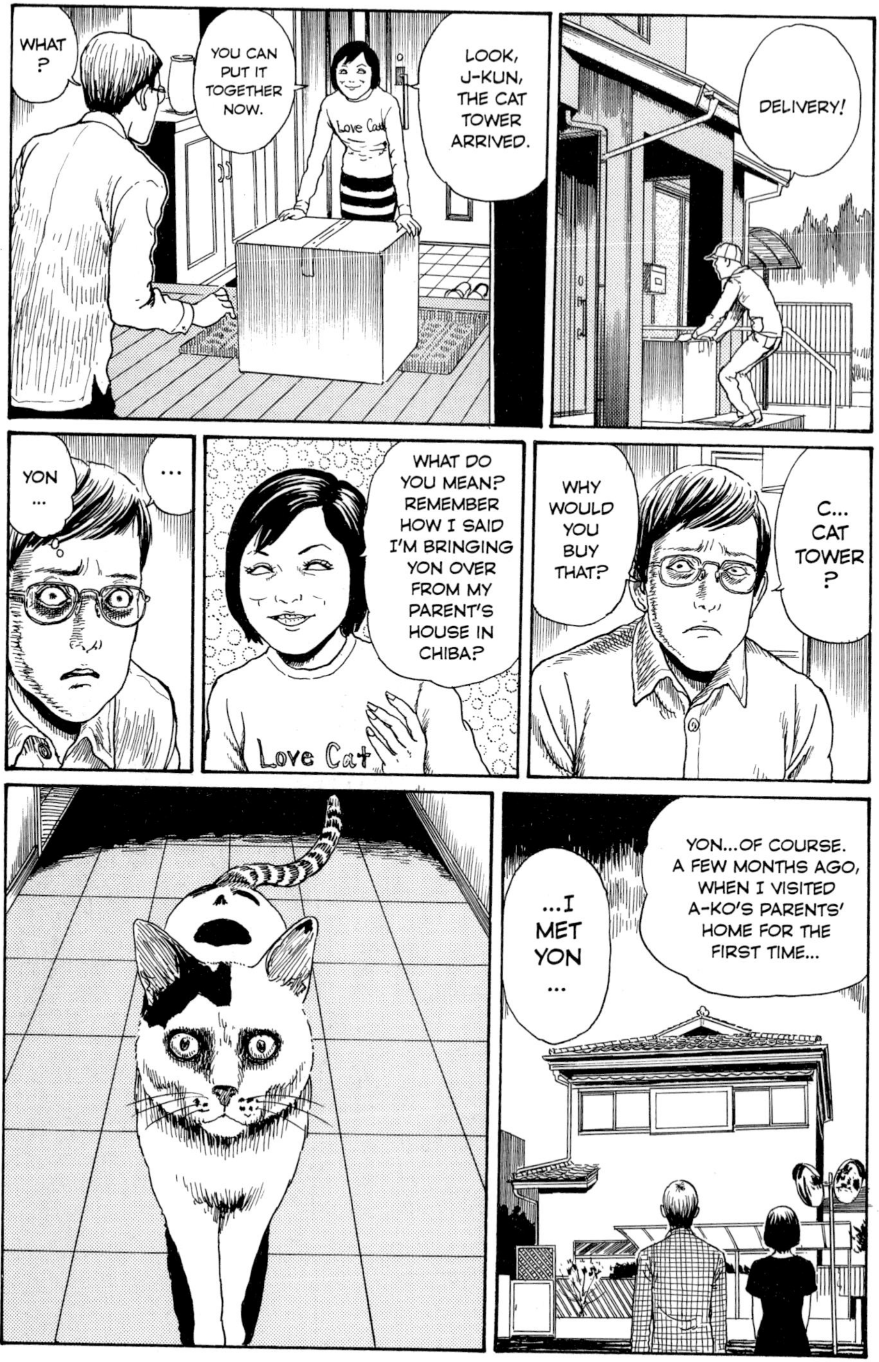
DELIVERY!
LOOK, J-KUN, THE CAT TOWER ARRIVED.
YOU CAN PUT IT TOGETHER NOW.
Love Cat
WHAT ?
C... CAT TOWER ?
WHY WOULD YOU BUY THAT?
WHAT DO YOU MEAN? REMEMBER HOW I SAID I'M BRINGING YON OVER FROM MY PARENT'S HOUSE IN CHIBA?
Love Cat
...
YON ...
YON...OF COURSE. A FEW MONTHS AGO, WHEN I VISITED A-KO'S PARENTS' HOME FOR THE FIRST TIME...
...I MET YON ...

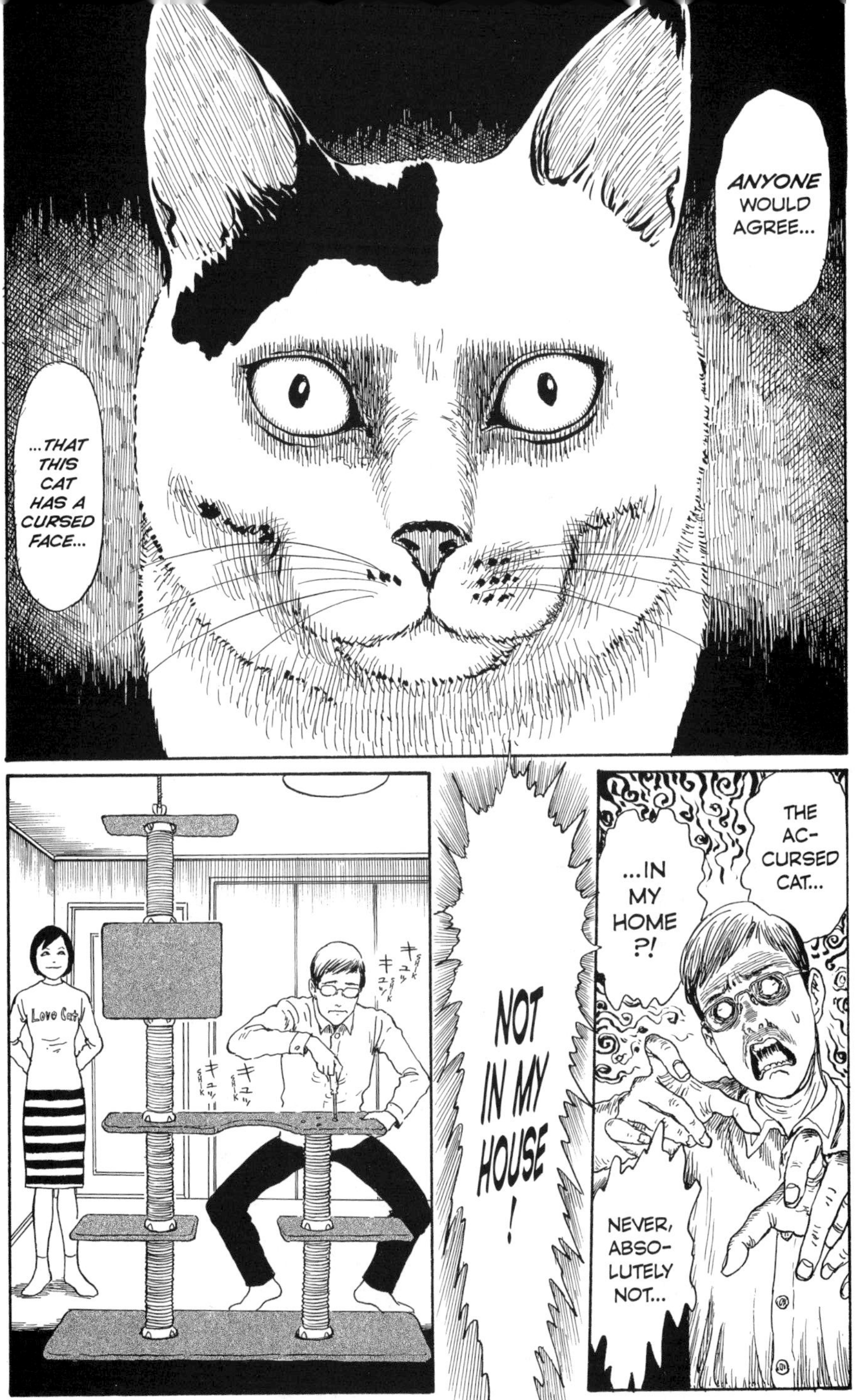
ANYONE WOULD AGREE...
...THAT THIS CAT HAS A CURSED FACE...
THE AC-CURSED CAT...
...IN MY HOME ?!
NEVER, ABSOLUTELY NOT...
NOT IN MY HOUSE !
キュッ SHIK キュッ SHIK
キュッ SHIK キュッ SHIK

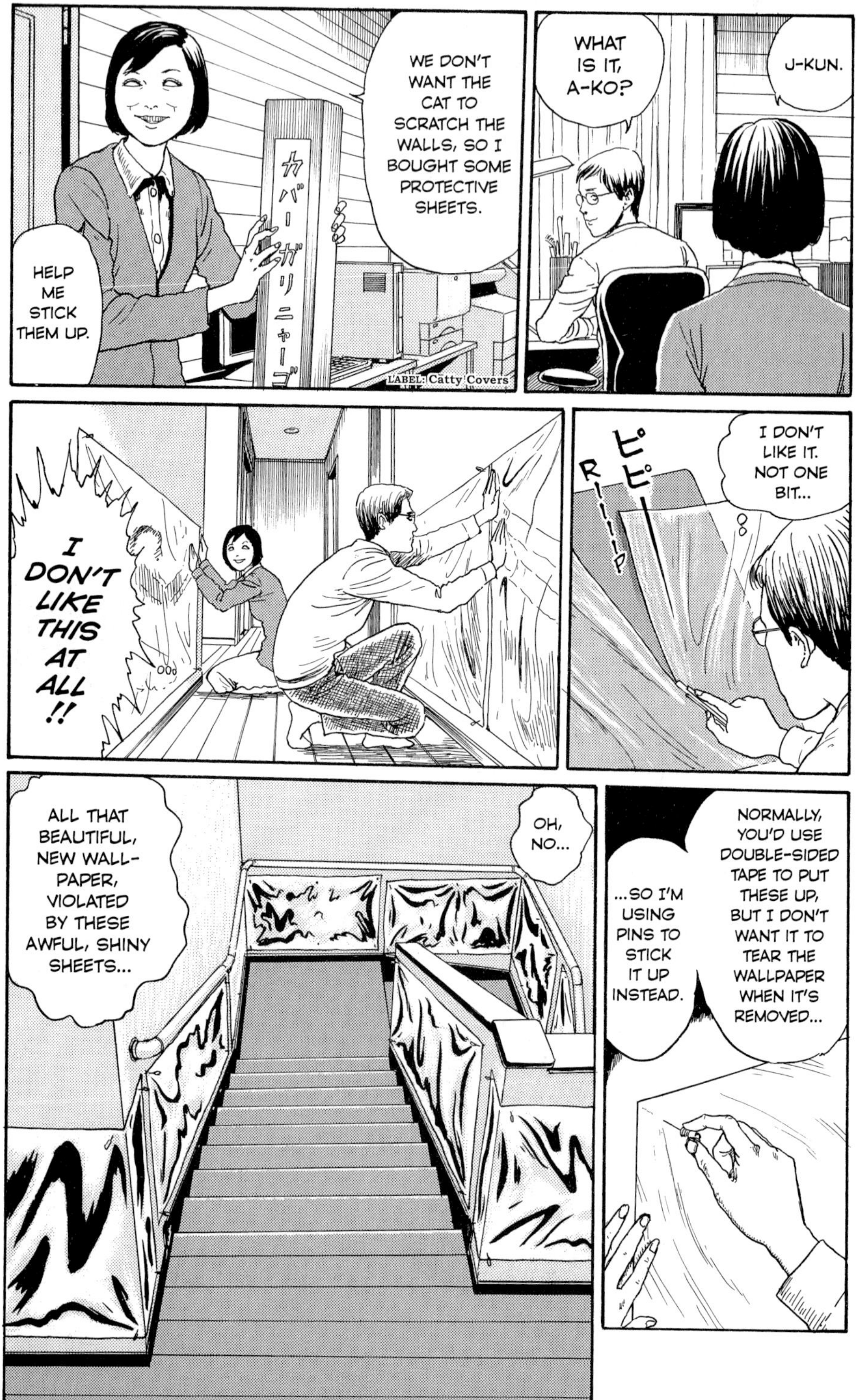
J-KUN.
WHAT IS IT, A-KO?
WE DON'T WANT THE CAT TO SCRATCH THE WALLS, SO I BOUGHT SOME PROTECTIVE SHEETS.
カバーガリニャーゴ
HELP ME STICK THEM UP.
LABEL: Catty Covers
I DON'T LIKE IT. NOT ONE BIT...
ピピー
R-I-I-I-P
I DON'T LIKE THIS AT ALL!!
NORMALLY, YOU'D USE DOUBLE-SIDED TAPE TO PUT THESE UP, BUT I DON'T WANT IT TO TEAR THE WALLPAPER WHEN IT'S REMOVED...
...SO I'M USING PINS TO STICK IT UP INSTEAD.
OH, NO...
ALL THAT BEAUTIFUL, NEW WALL-PAPER, VIOLATED BY THESE AWFUL, SHINY SHEETS...

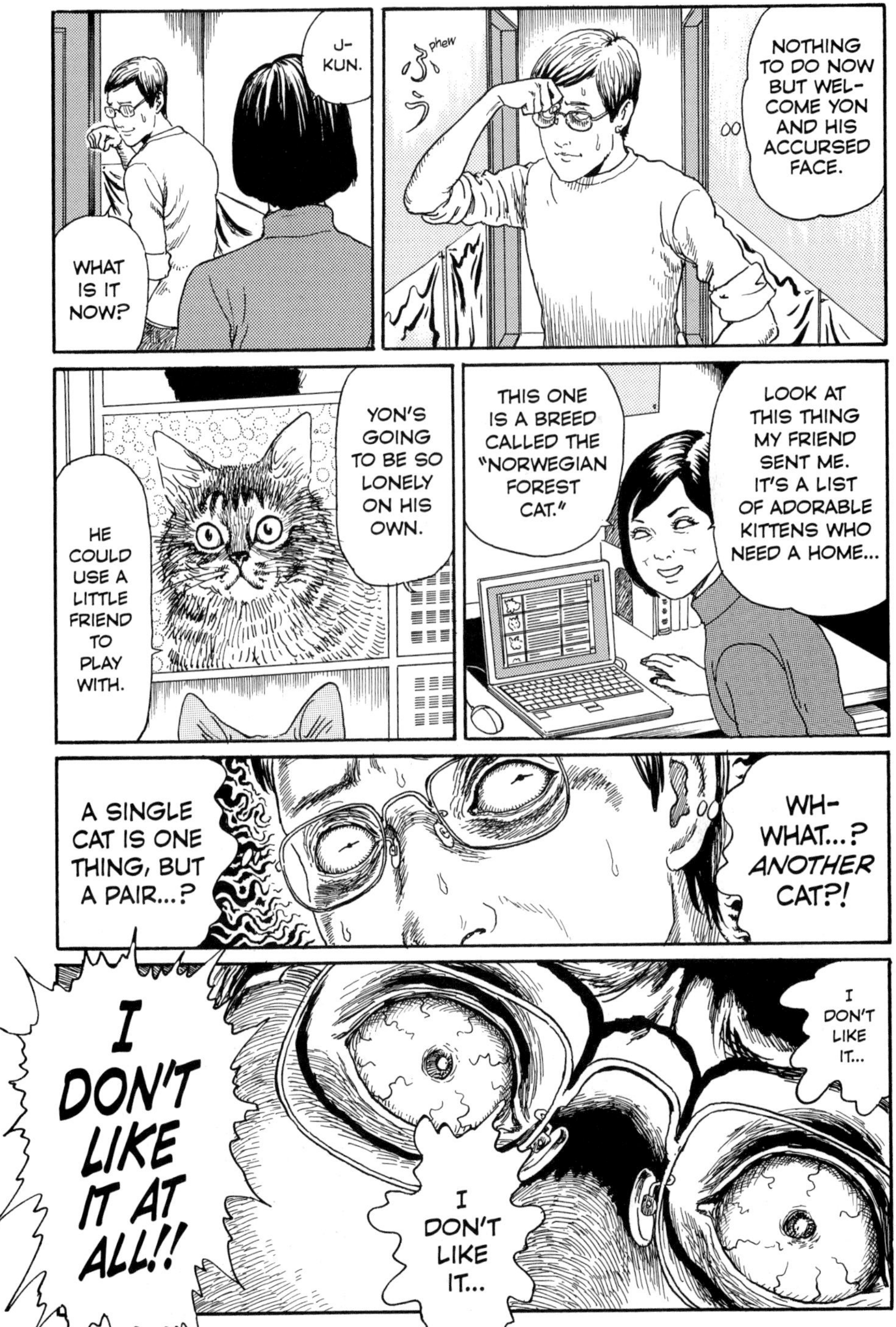
ふう
phew
NOTHING TO DO NOW BUT WEL- COME YON AND HIS ACCURSED FACE.
J- KUN.
WHAT IS IT NOW?
LOOK AT THIS THING MY FRIEND SENT ME. IT'S A LIST OF ADORABLE KITTENS WHO NEED A HOME...
THIS ONE IS A BREED CALLED THE "NORWEGIAN FOREST CAT."
YON'S GOING TO BE SO LONELY ON HIS OWN.
HE COULD USE A LITTLE FRIEND TO PLAY WITH.
WH- WHAT...? *ANOTHER* CAT?!
A SINGLE CAT IS ONE THING, BUT A PAIR...?
I DON'T LIKE IT...
I DON'T LIKE IT...
I DON'T LIKE IT AT ALL!!

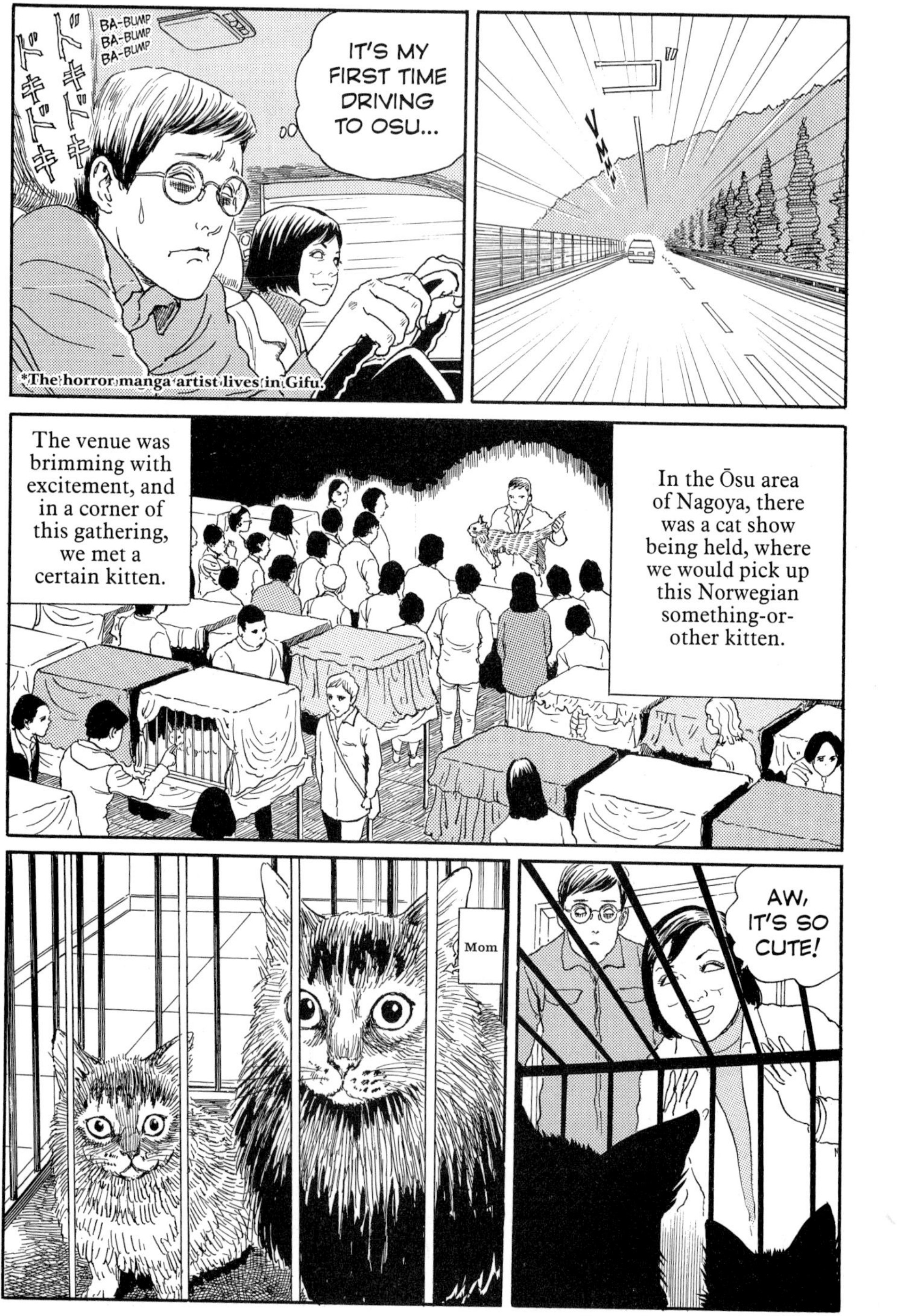
IT'S MY FIRST TIME DRIVING TO OSU...
BA-BUMP
BA-BUMP
BA-BUMP
*The horror manga artist lives in Gifu.
In the Ōsu area of Nagoya, there was a cat show being held, where we would pick up this Norwegian something-or-other kitten.
The venue was brimming with excitement, and in a corner of this gathering, we met a certain kitten.
AW, IT'S SO CUTE!
Mom

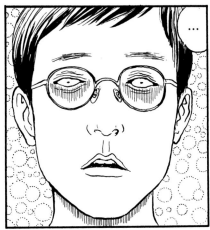

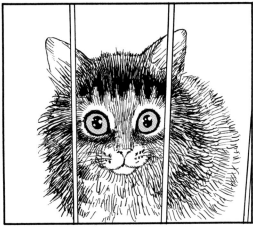

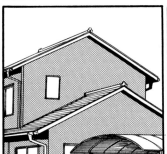

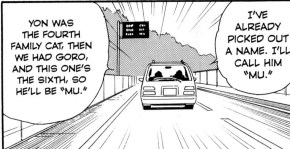

...
I'VE ALREADY PICKED OUT A NAME. I'LL CALL HIM "MU."
YON WAS THE FOURTH FAMILY CAT, THEN WE HAD GORO, AND THIS ONE'S THE SIXTH, SO HE'LL BE "MU."
コロン ROLL
コロン ROLL
THERE WE GO! THERE WE GO!
AWW, GOOD KITTY!

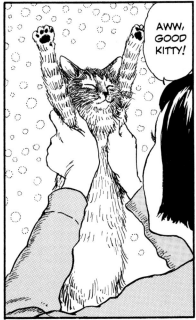

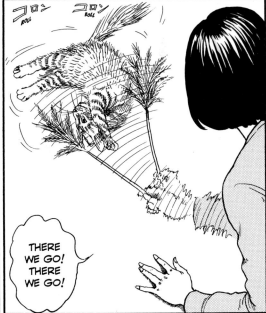

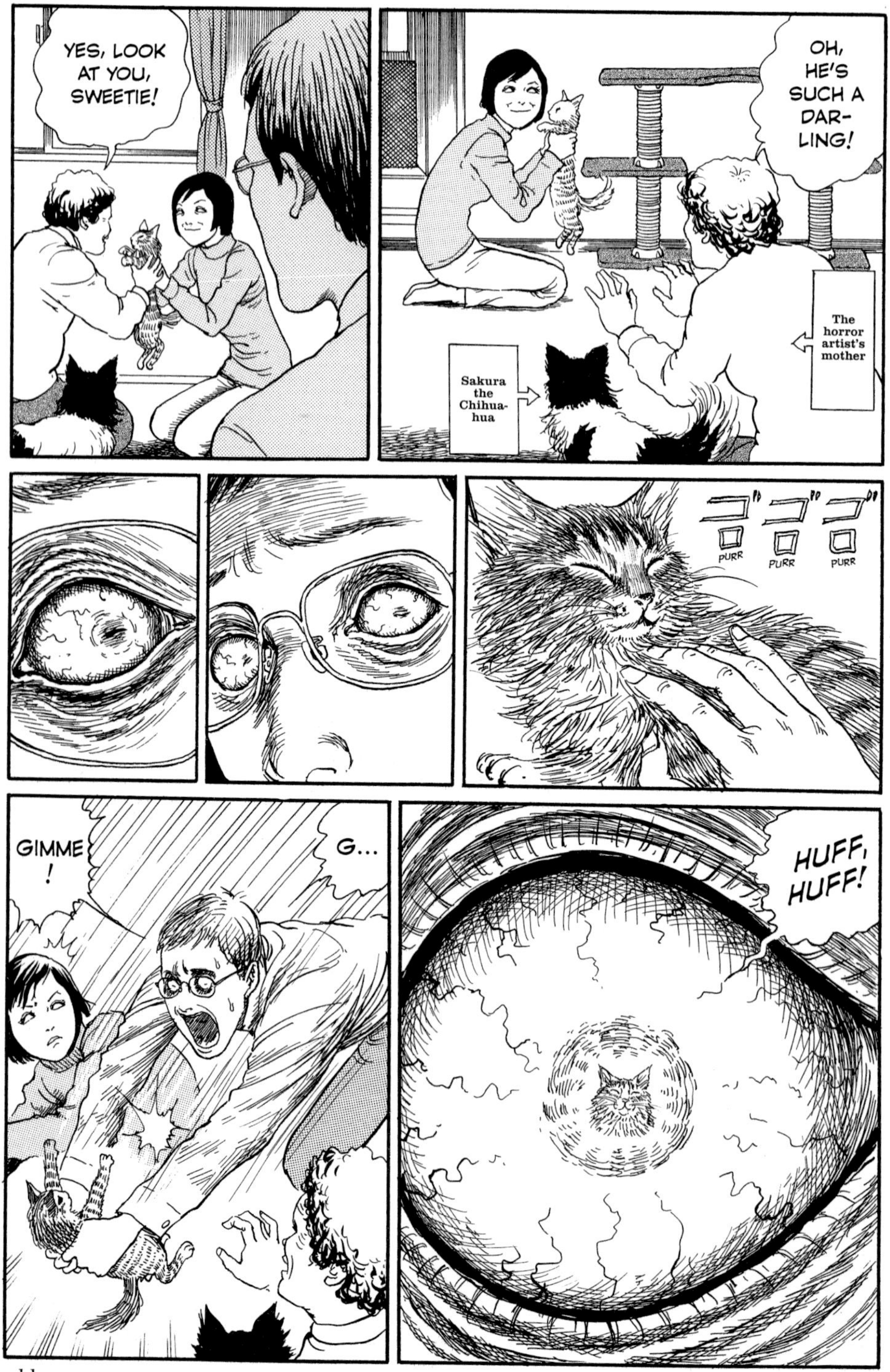

OH, HE'S SUCH A DAR-LING!
The horror artist's mother
Sakura the Chihua-hua
YES, LOOK AT YOU, SWEETIE!
ゴロゴロゴロ
PURR PURR PURR
HUFF, HUFF!
G...
GIMME!

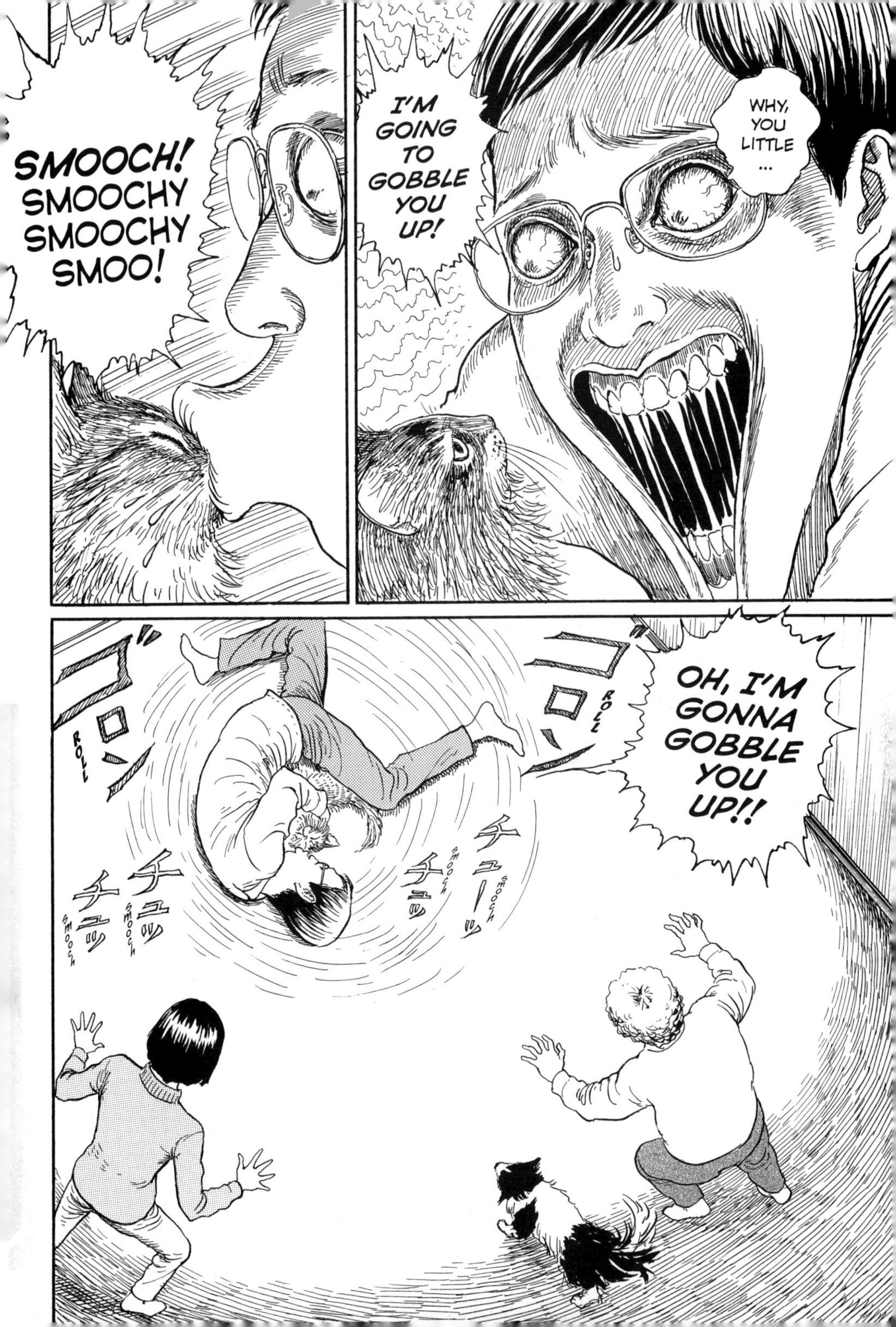
WHY, YOU LITTLE ...
I'M GOING TO GOBBLE YOU UP!
SMOOCH! SMOOCHY SMOOCHY SMOO!
OH, I'M GONNA GOBBLE YOU UP!!
ROLL
ROLL
SMOOCH
SMOOCH
SMOOCH

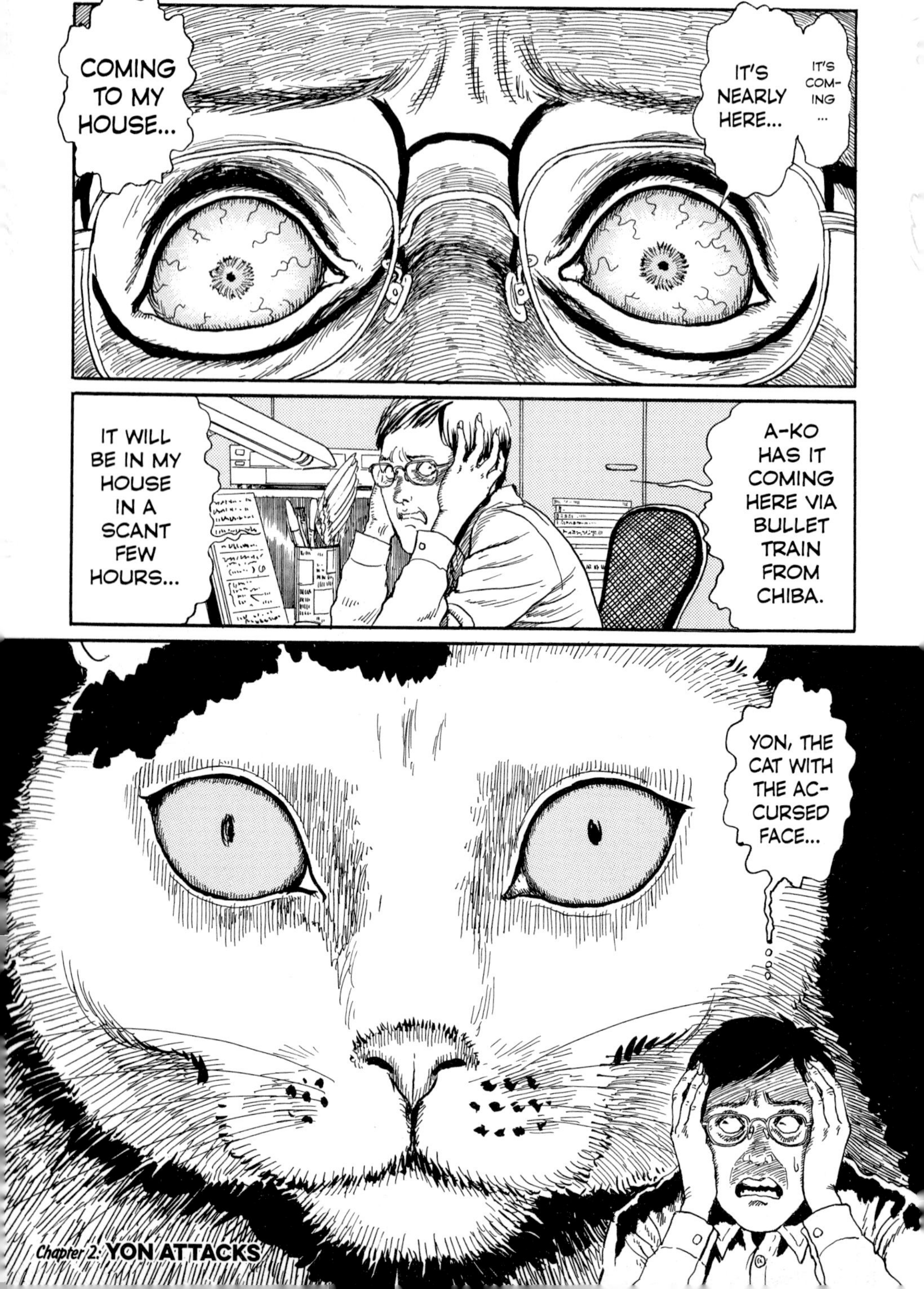
IT'S NEARLY HERE...
IT'S COMING...
COMING TO MY HOUSE...
A-KO HAS IT COMING HERE VIA BULLET TRAIN FROM CHIBA.
IT WILL BE IN MY HOUSE IN A SCANT FEW HOURS...
YON, THE CAT WITH THE ACCURSED FACE...
Chapter 2: YON ATTACKS

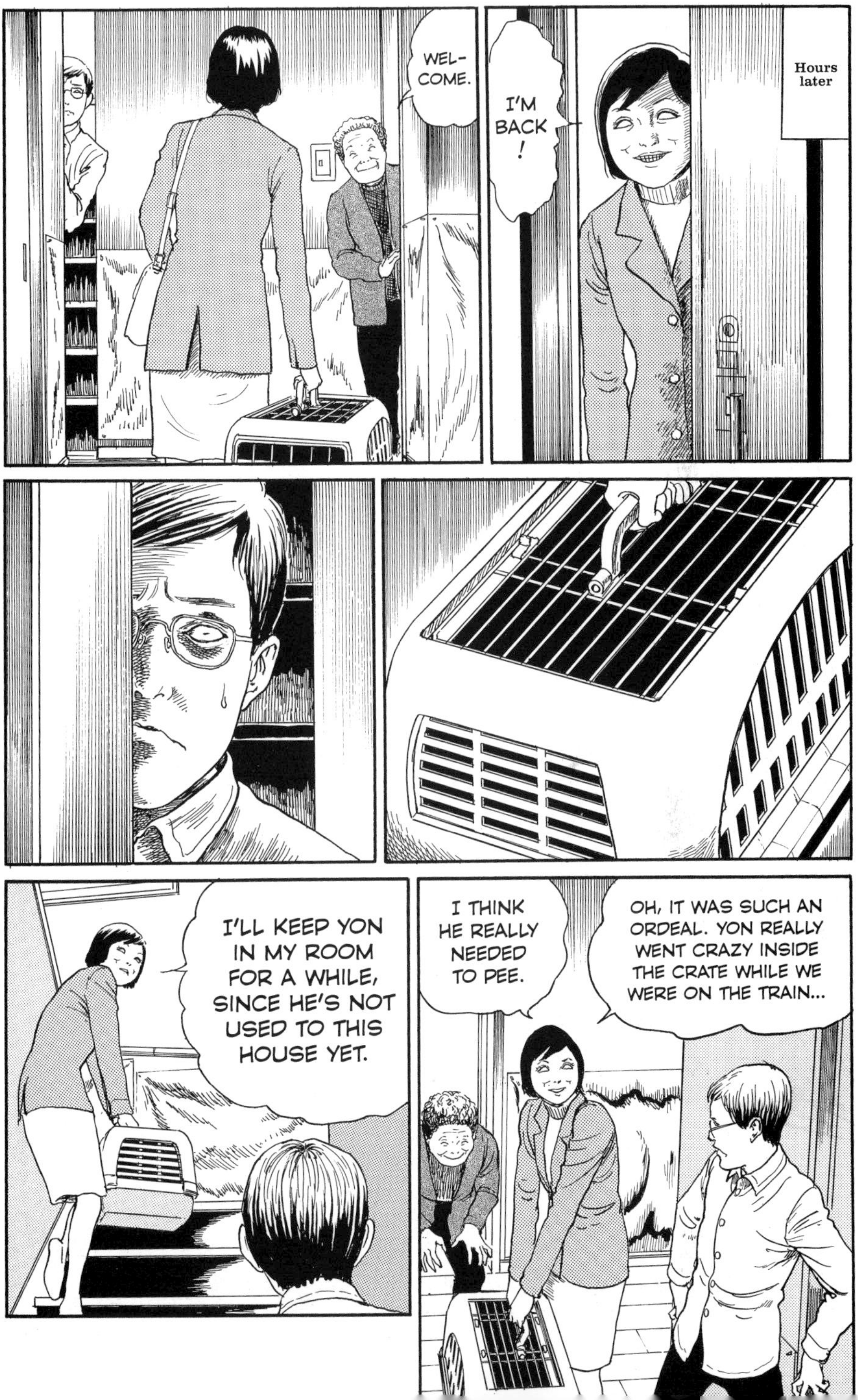
Hours later
I'M BACK!
WEL-COME.
OH, IT WAS SUCH AN ORDEAL. YON REALLY WENT CRAZY INSIDE THE CRATE WHILE WE WERE ON THE TRAIN...
I THINK HE REALLY NEEDED TO PEE.
I'LL KEEP YON IN MY ROOM FOR A WHILE, SINCE HE'S NOT USED TO THIS HOUSE YET.

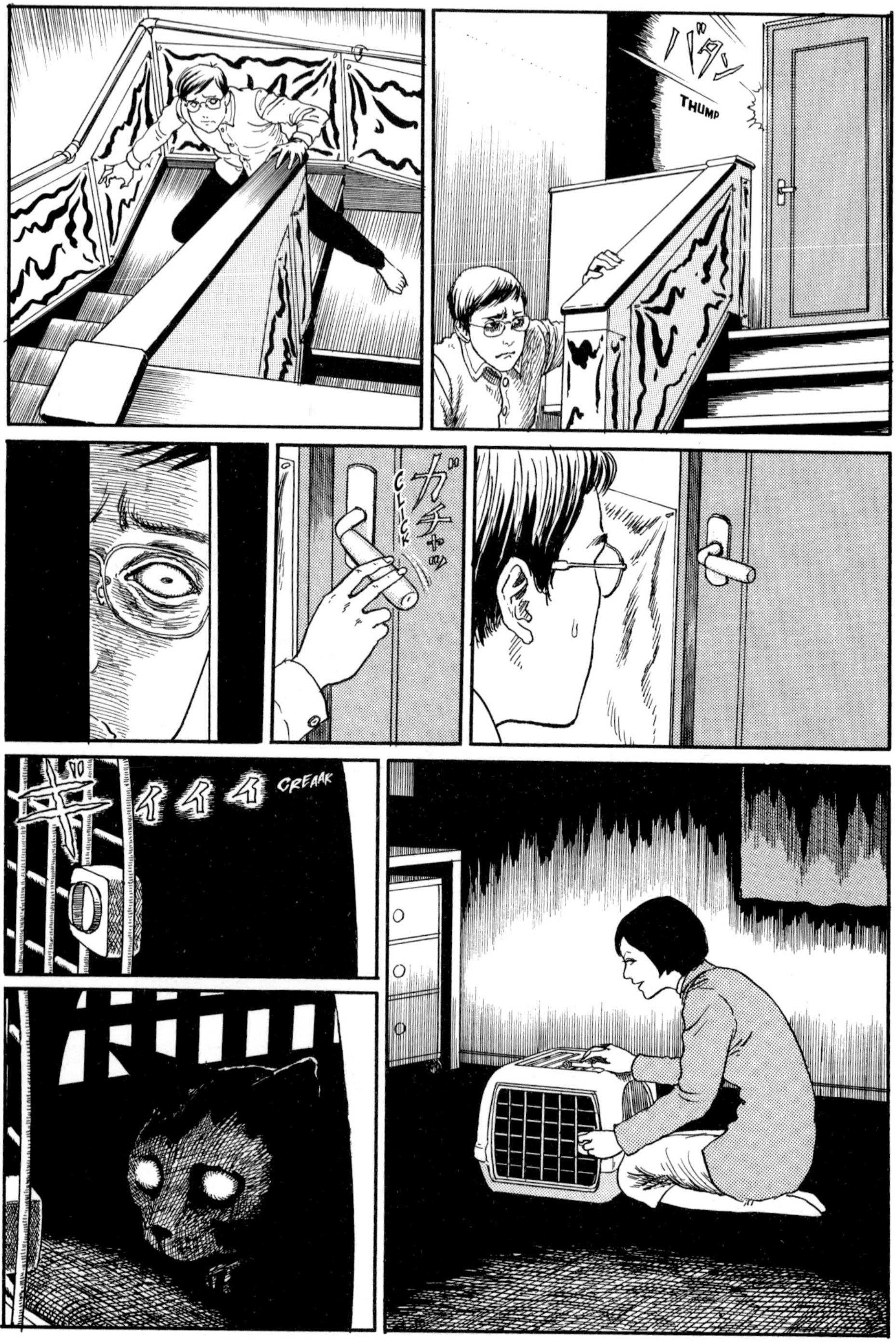
バタン
THUMP
ガチャッ
CLICK
ギイイイ
CREAAK

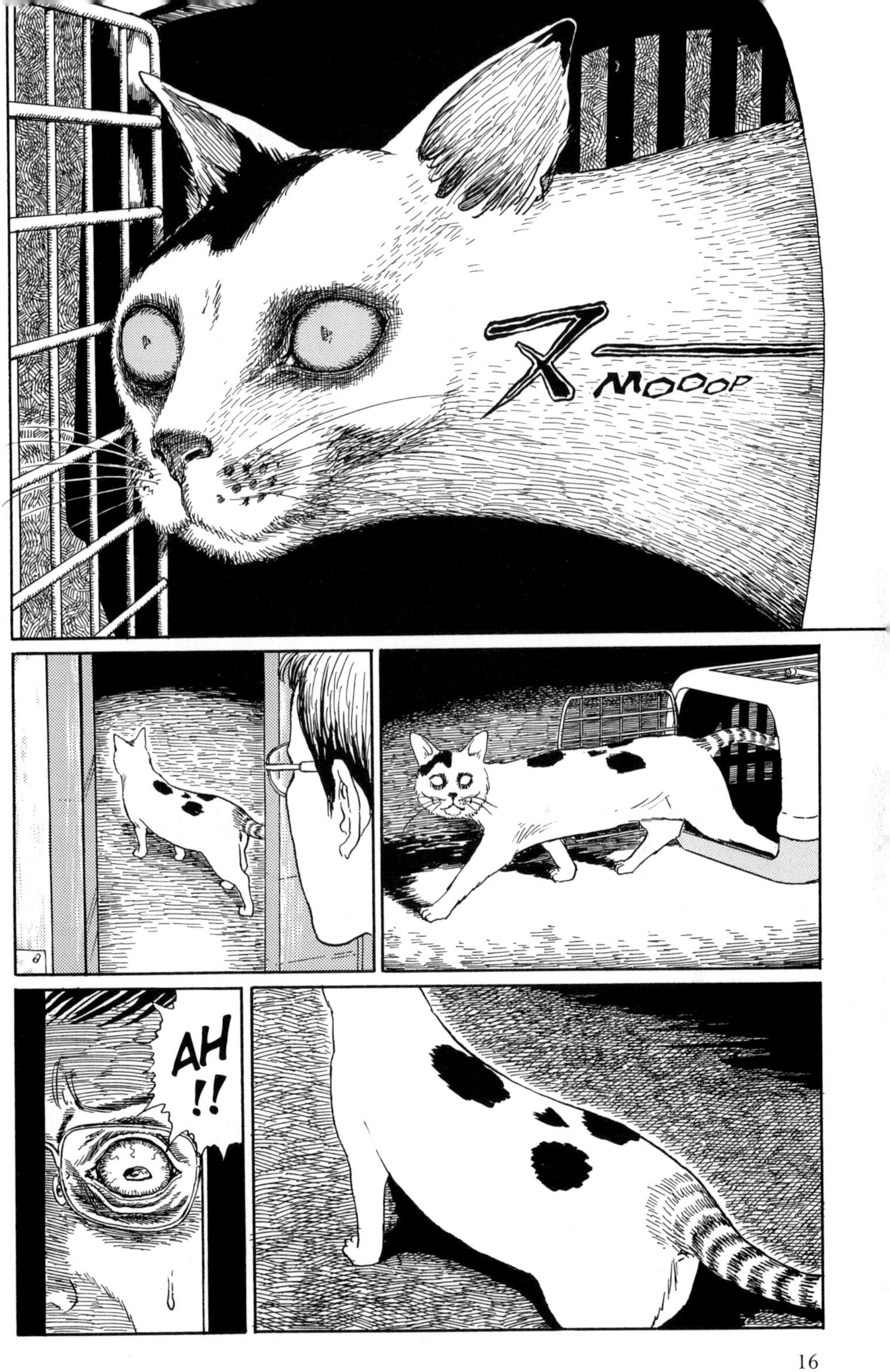
ヌ
MOOOP
AH
!!

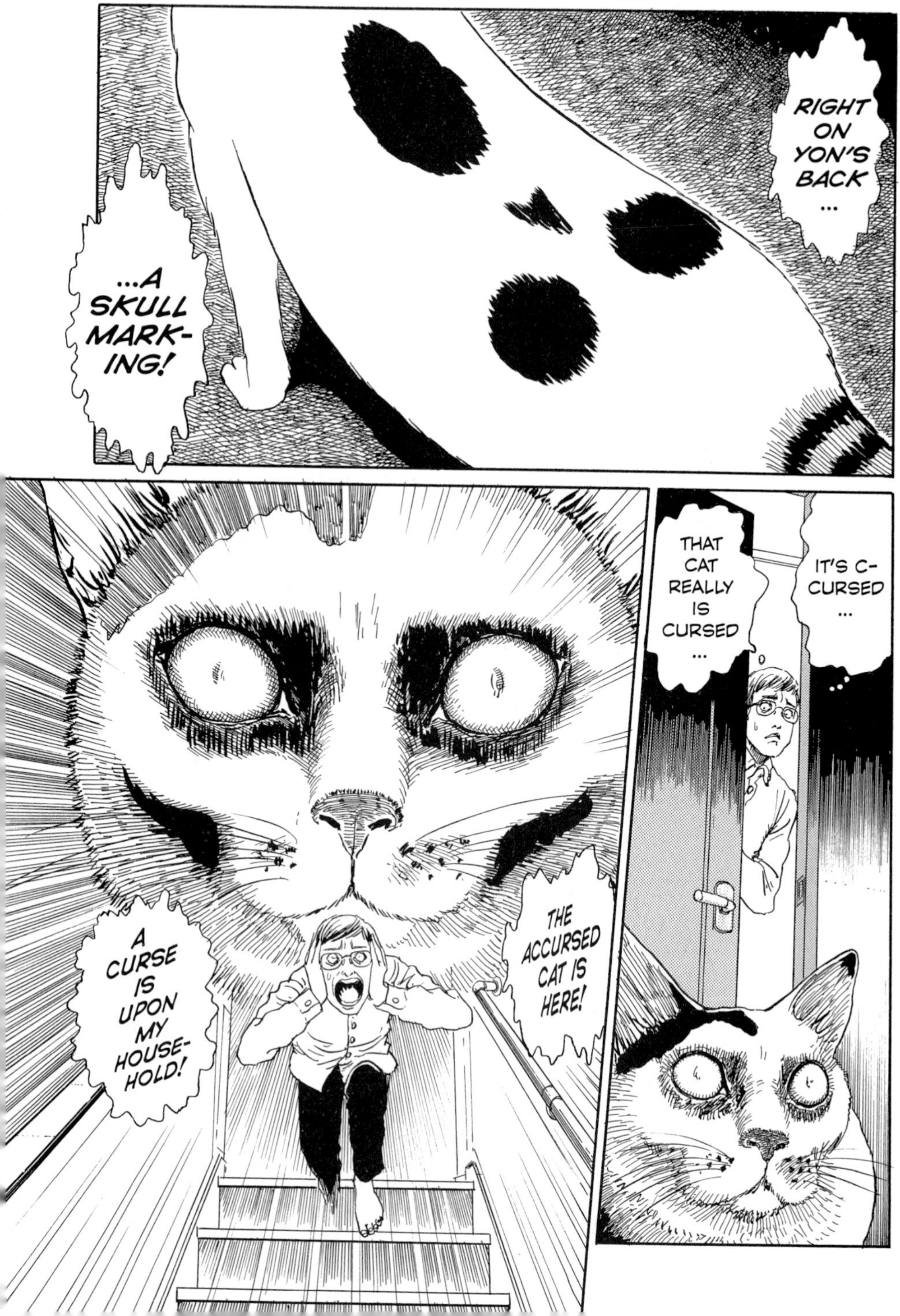
RIGHT ON YON'S BACK ...
...A SKULL MARKING!
IT'S C-CURSED ...
THAT CAT REALLY IS CURSED ...
THE ACCURSED CAT IS HERE!
A CURSE IS UPON MY HOUSEHOLD!

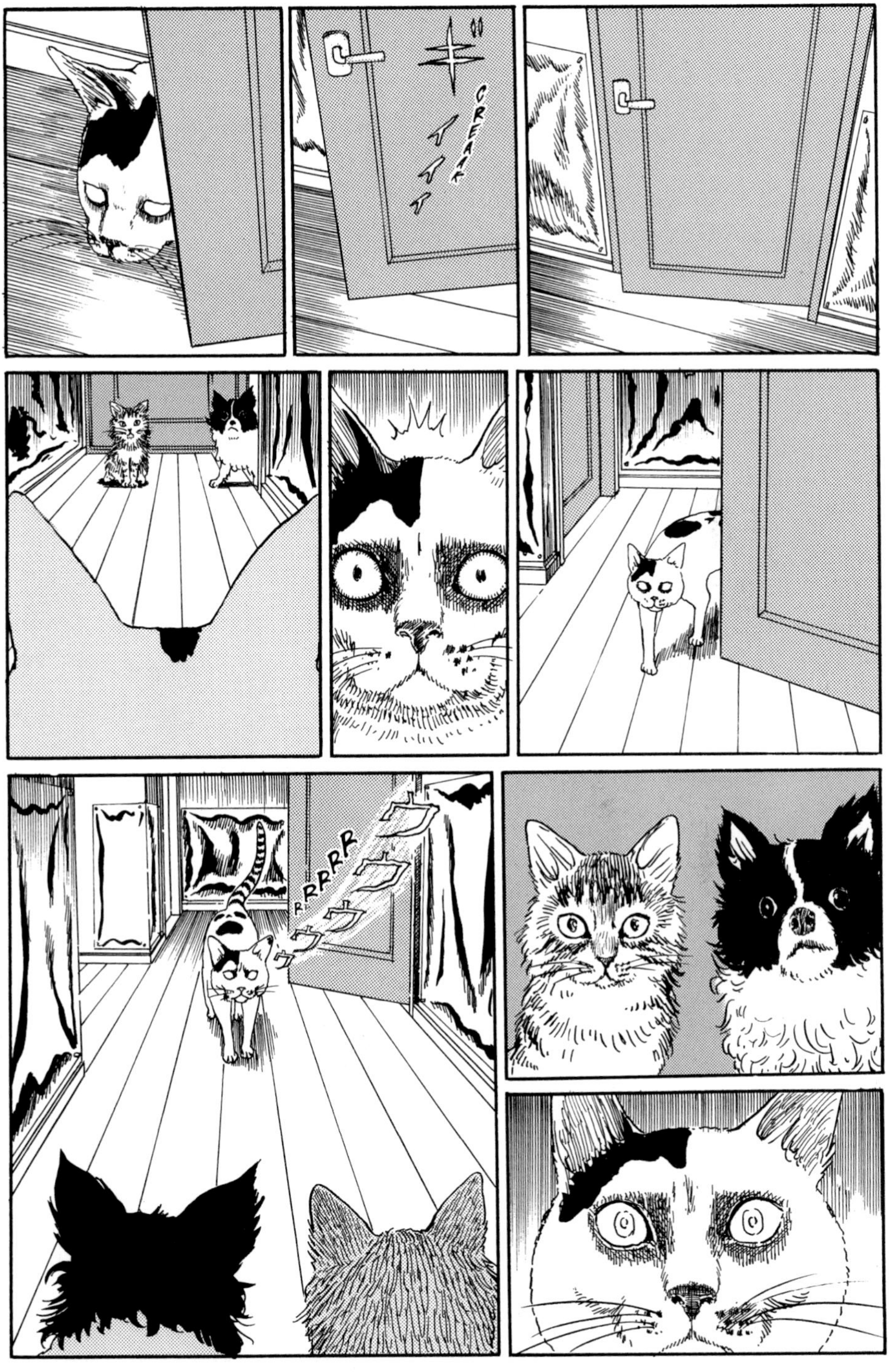
CREAK
RRRRR

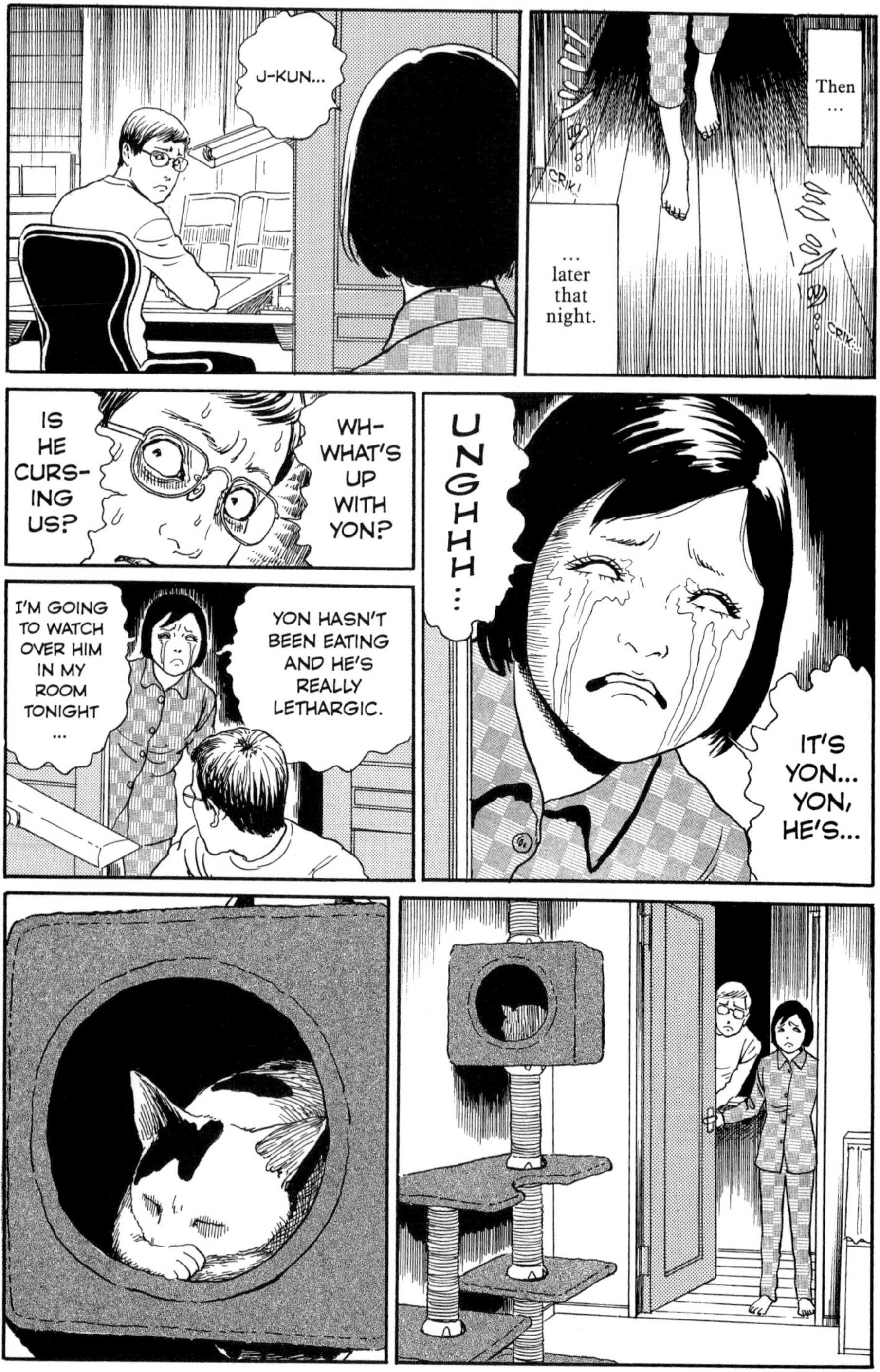
Then ...
CRIK!
... later that night.
CRIK...
J-KUN...
UNGHHH...
IT'S YON... YON, HE'S...
WH-WHAT'S UP WITH YON?
IS HE CURSING US?
YON HASN'T BEEN EATING AND HE'S REALLY LETHARGIC.
I'M GOING TO WATCH OVER HIM IN MY ROOM TONIGHT ...

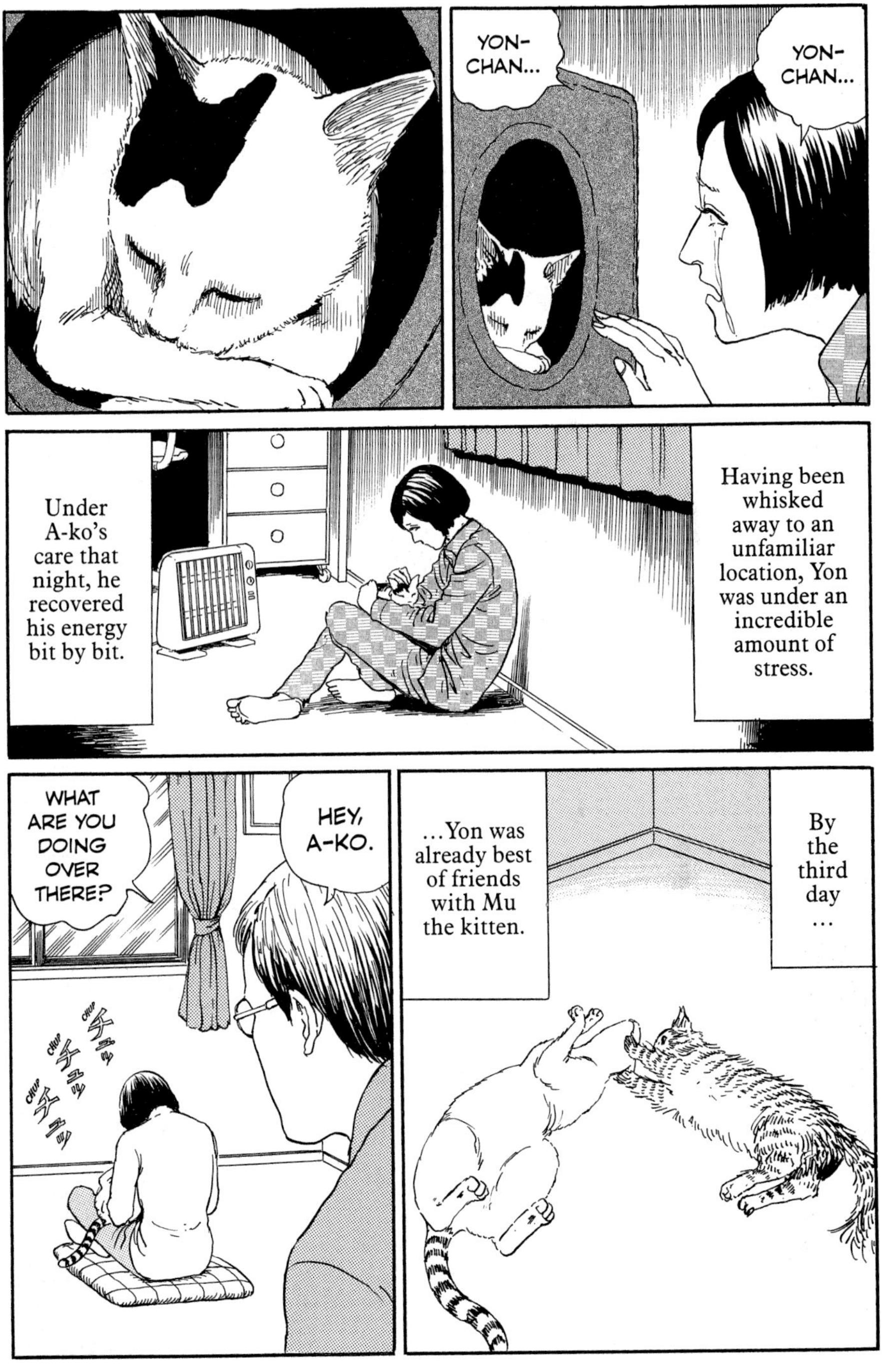
YON-CHAN...
YON-CHAN...
Having been whisked away to an unfamiliar location, Yon was under an incredible amount of stress.
Under A-ko's care that night, he recovered his energy bit by bit.
By the third day...
...Yon was already best of friends with Mu the kitten.
HEY, A-KO.
WHAT ARE YOU DOING OVER THERE?
CHUP チュッ
CHUP チュッ
CHUP チュッ

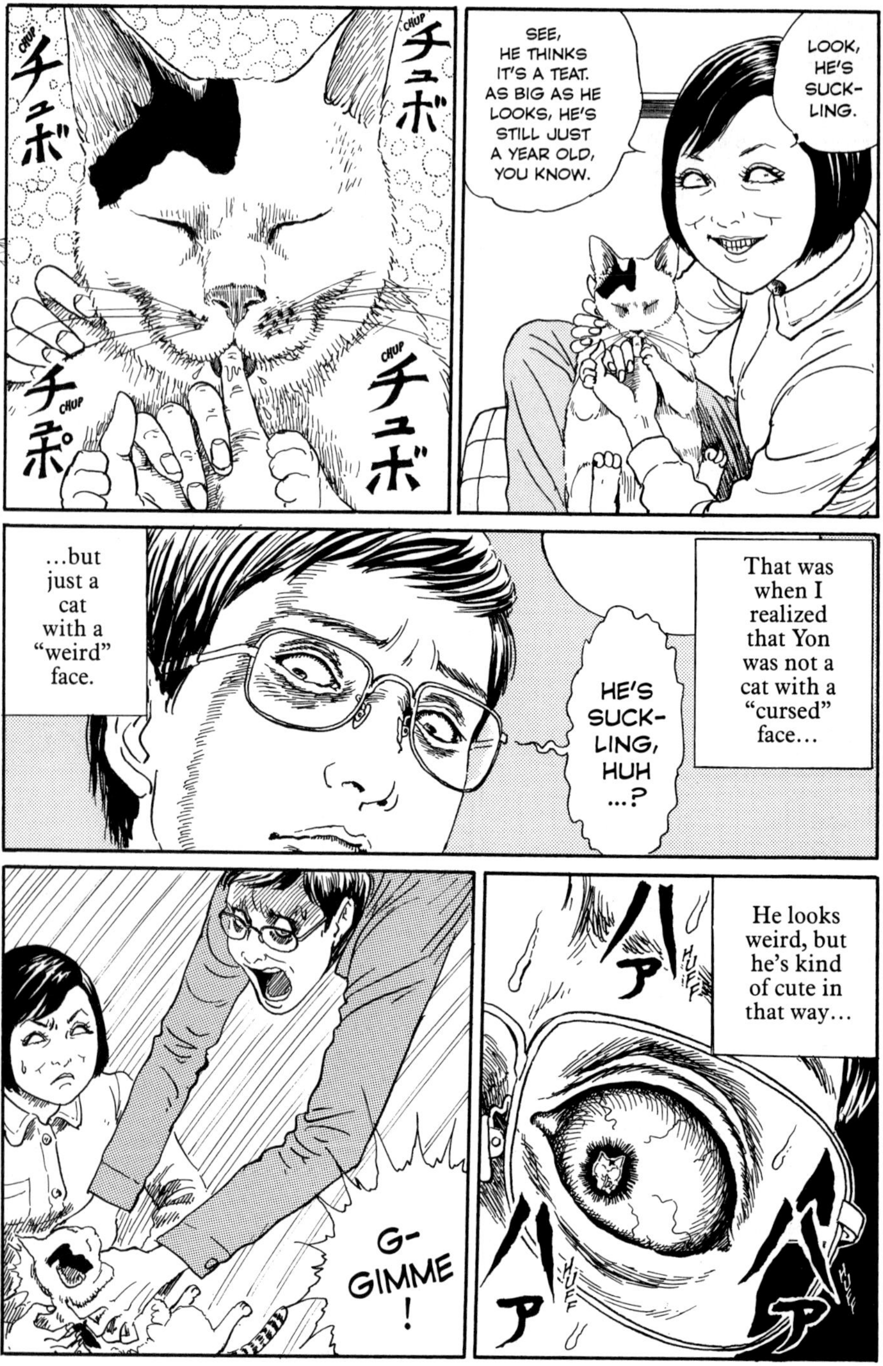
LOOK, HE'S SUCK-LING.
SEE, HE THINKS IT'S A TEAT. AS BIG AS HE LOOKS, HE'S STILL JUST A YEAR OLD, YOU KNOW.
CHUP
チュボ
CHUP
チュボ
CHUP
チュボ
CHUP
チュポ
That was when I realized that Yon was not a cat with a "cursed" face…
HE'S SUCK-LING, HUH …?
…but just a cat with a "weird" face.
He looks weird, but he's kind of cute in that way…
HUFF
ハァ
HUFF
ハァ
HUFF
ハァ
G-GIMME!

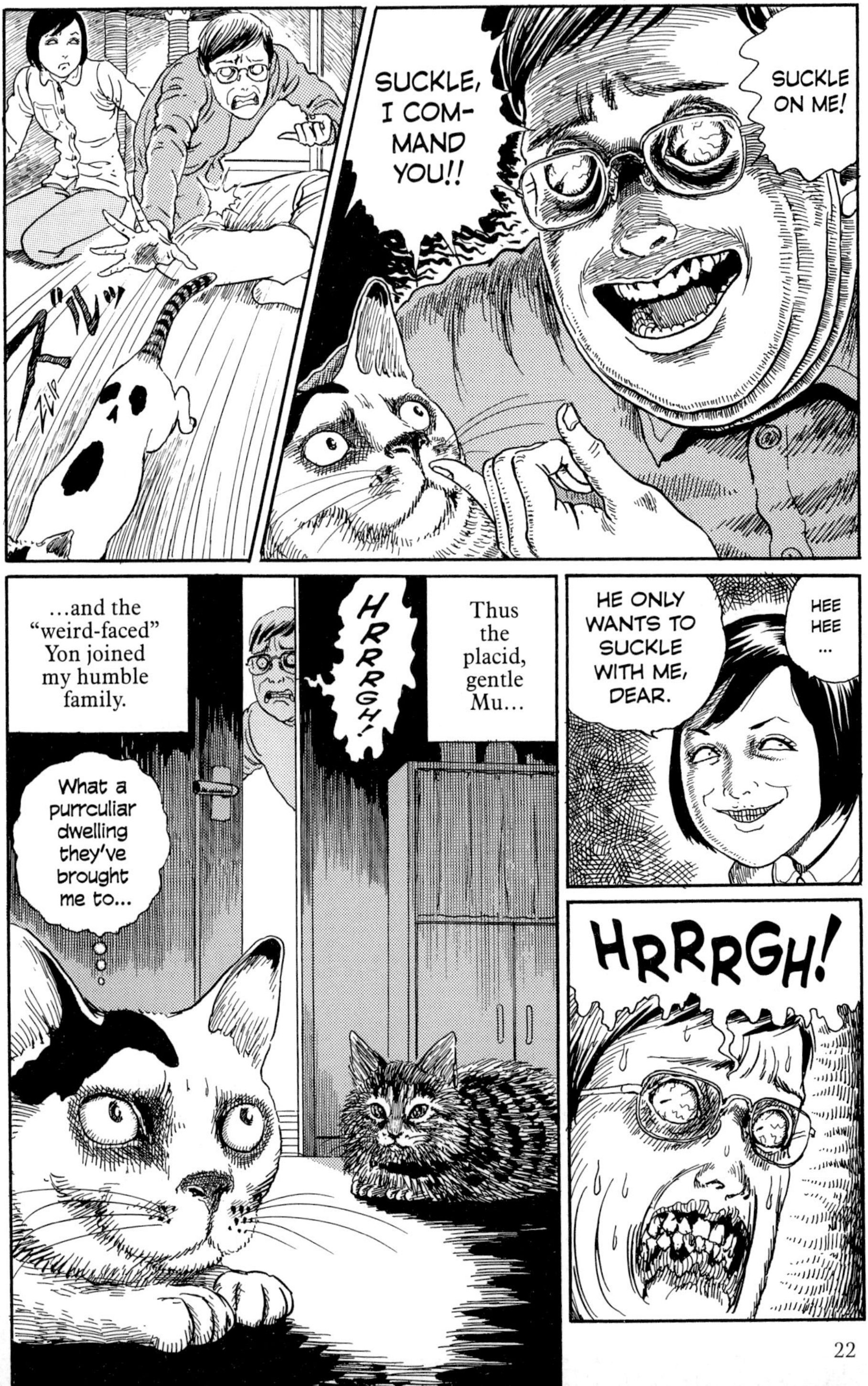
SUCKLE ON ME!
SUCKLE, I COMMAND YOU!!
ZIP
HE ONLY WANTS TO SUCKLE WITH ME, DEAR.
HEE HEE ...
HRRRGH!
Thus the placid, gentle Mu…
HRRRGH!
…and the "weird-faced" Yon joined my humble family.
What a purrculiar dwelling they've brought me to...

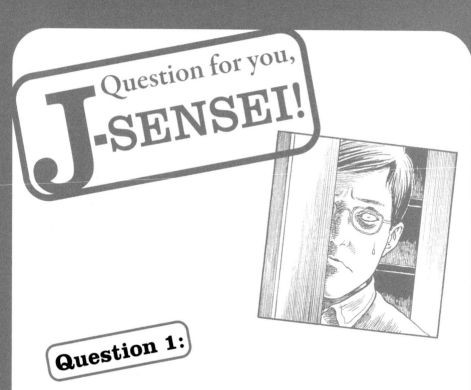

Question for you, J-SENSEI!

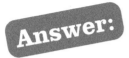
Question 1:

I understand you're the vice-chairman of your local town council. I hope you'll draw a side story for *Yon & Mu* called "The Vice-Chairman's a Horror Artist?!" By the way…what exactly does a town council vice-chairman do?

Answer:

Mostly, I just do accounting—making arrangements to gather council funds at the end of the month and managing income. I'm actually rather poor at calculating, so I have to be careful not to make mistakes. And as the chairman's assistant, I help out with town events and ceremonies. Recently, the council had a new year's party, and acting as the chairman's coordinator was a very busy job.

Question for you, J-SENSEI!

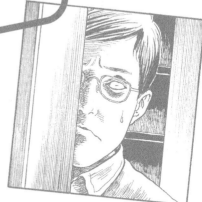

Question 2:

I've read that right after your debut as a manga artist, you had your mother and older sister help you with some work as assistants. Are the rumors true that they were even better at filling-in blacks than you?

Answer:

When I let them handle that task, they actually did it better than me. I'm particularly bad at pasting screentones, so my mother and sister would do a better a job. Now it's my wife and mother who help out.

Chapter 3: BATTLE OF THE CAT WAND!!

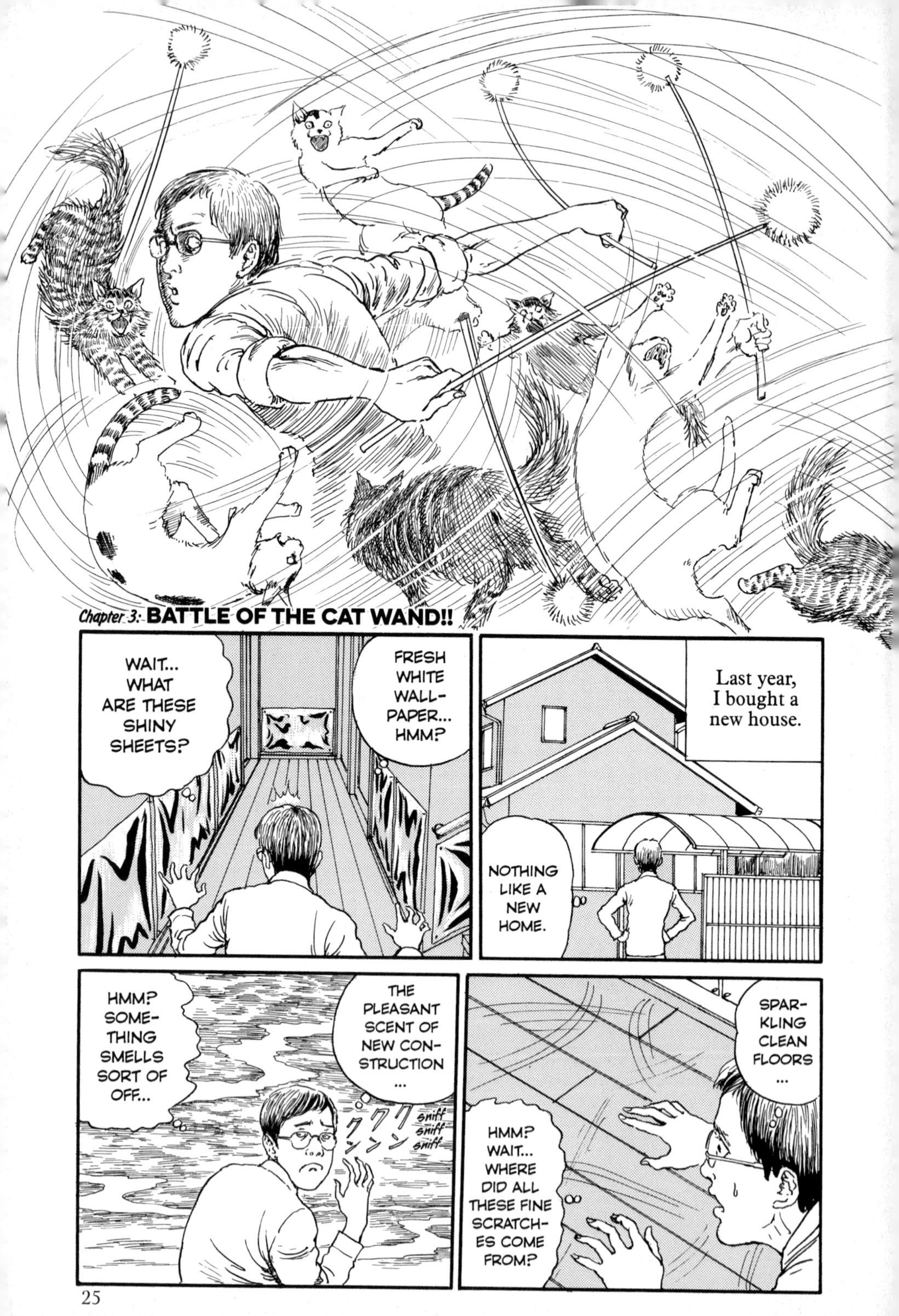

Last year, I bought a new house.
NOTHING LIKE A NEW HOME.
FRESH WHITE WALL-PAPER... HMM?
WAIT... WHAT ARE THESE SHINY SHEETS?
SPAR-KLING CLEAN FLOORS...
HMM? WAIT... WHERE DID ALL THESE FINE SCRATCH-ES COME FROM?
THE PLEASANT SCENT OF NEW CON-STRUCTION...
sniff sniff sniff
HMM? SOME-THING SMELLS SORT OF OFF...

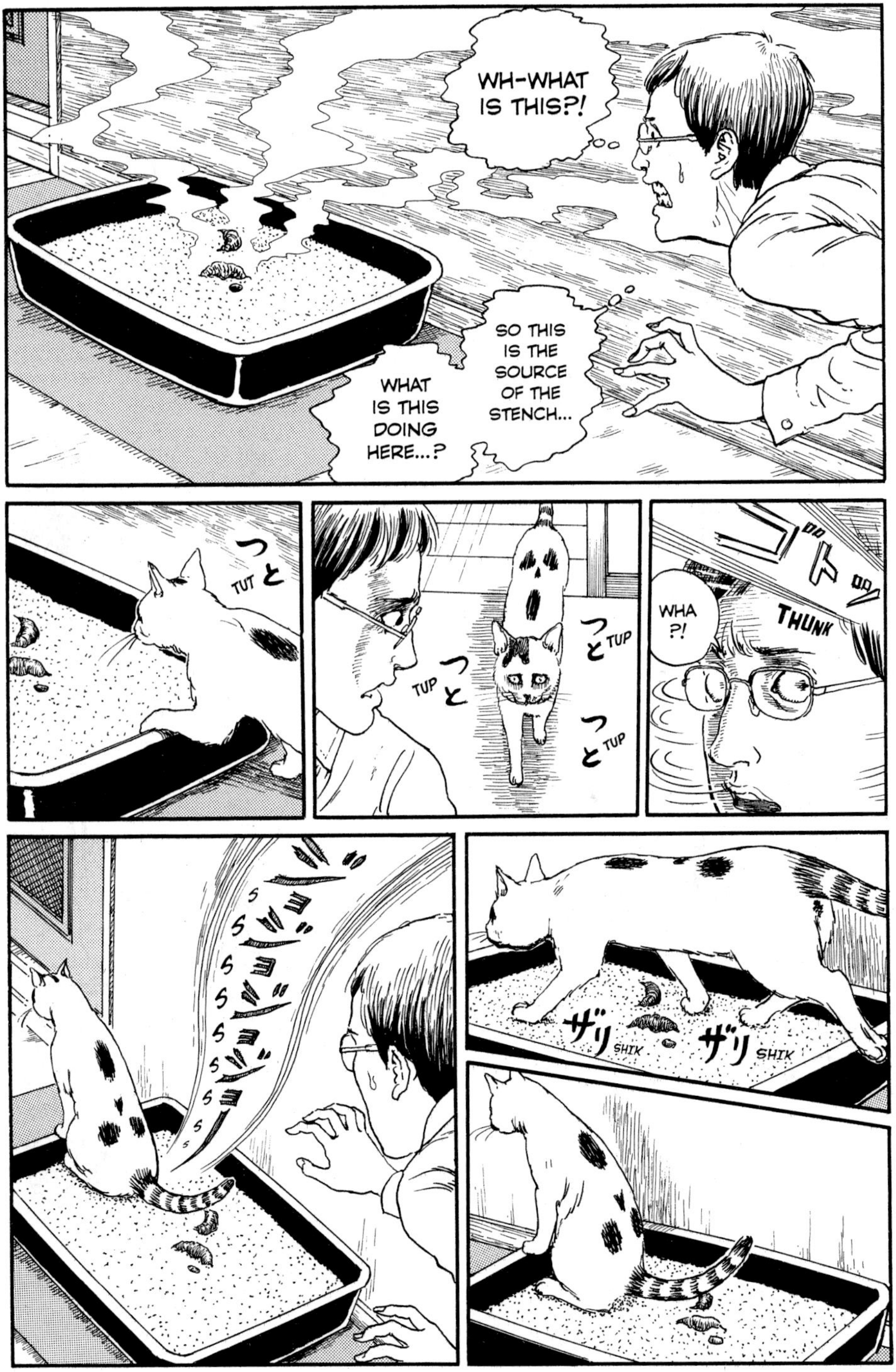
WH-WHAT IS THIS?!
SO THIS IS THE SOURCE OF THE STENCH...
WHAT IS THIS DOING HERE...?
ゴトッ
THUNK
WHA?!
つと TUP
つと TUP
つと TUP
つと
TUT
ザリ SHIK
ザリ SHIK

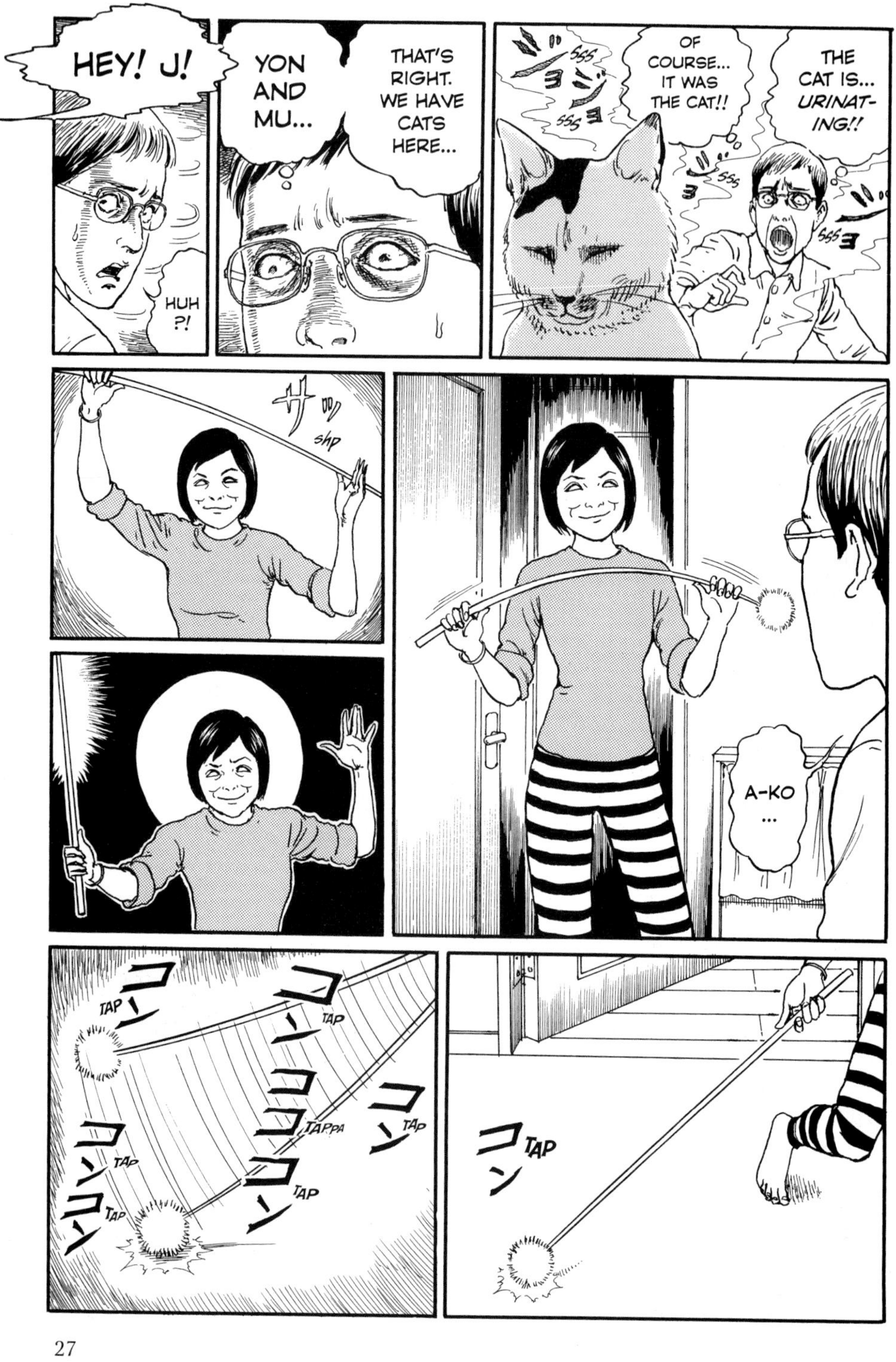
THE CAT IS... URINATING!!
OF COURSE... IT WAS THE CAT!!
SSS
THAT'S RIGHT. WE HAVE CATS HERE...
YON AND MU...
HEY! J!
HUH ?!
A-KO ...
shp
TAP
TAP
TAP
TAPPA
TAP
TAP
TAP
TAP

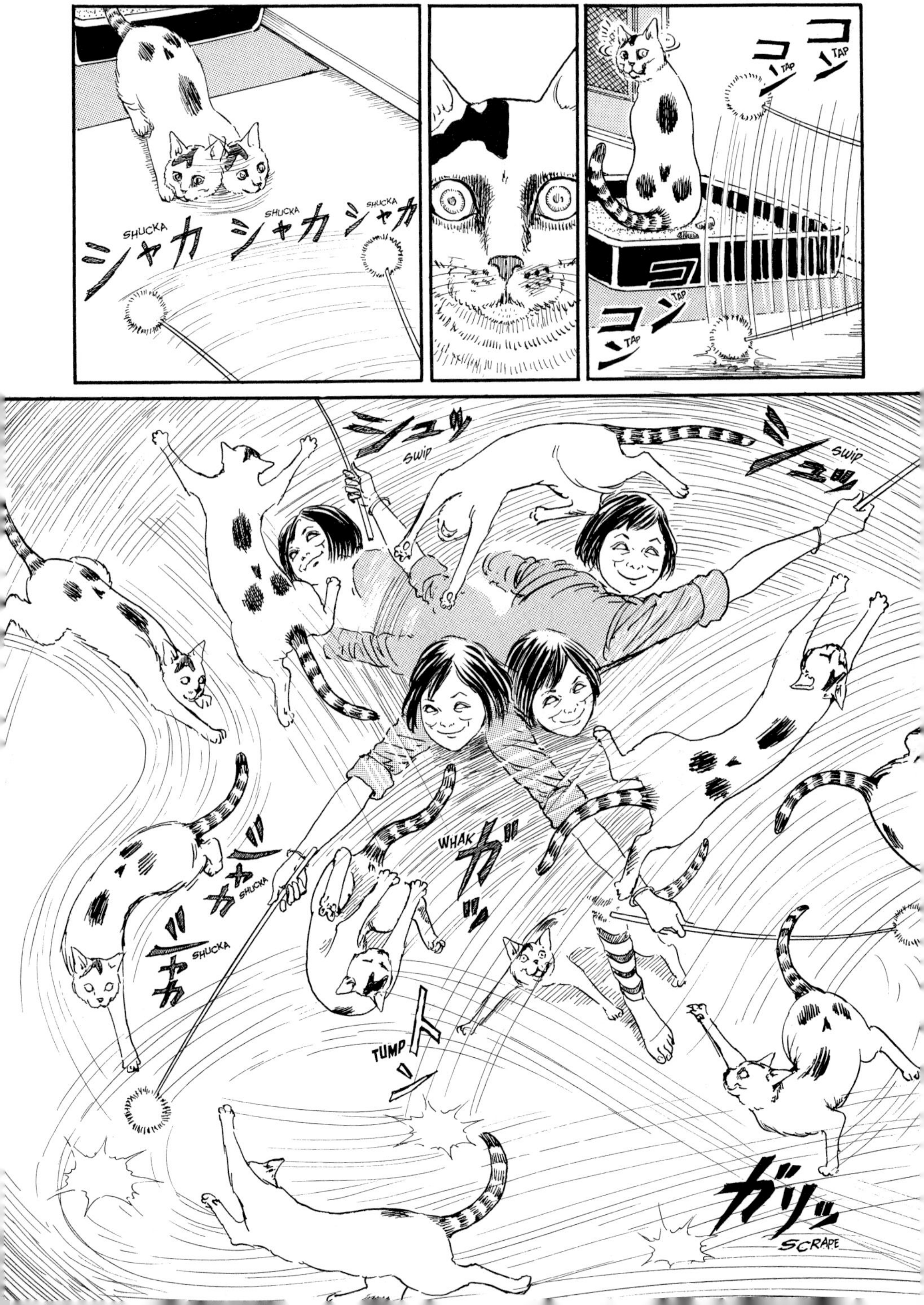
コン TAP
コン TAP
コン TAP
コン TAP
シャカ SHUCKA
シャカ SHUCKA
シャカ SHUCKA
シュッ SWIP
シュッ SWIP
ガッ WHAK
シャカ SHUCKA
シャカ SHUCKA
トン TUMP
ガリッ SCRAPE

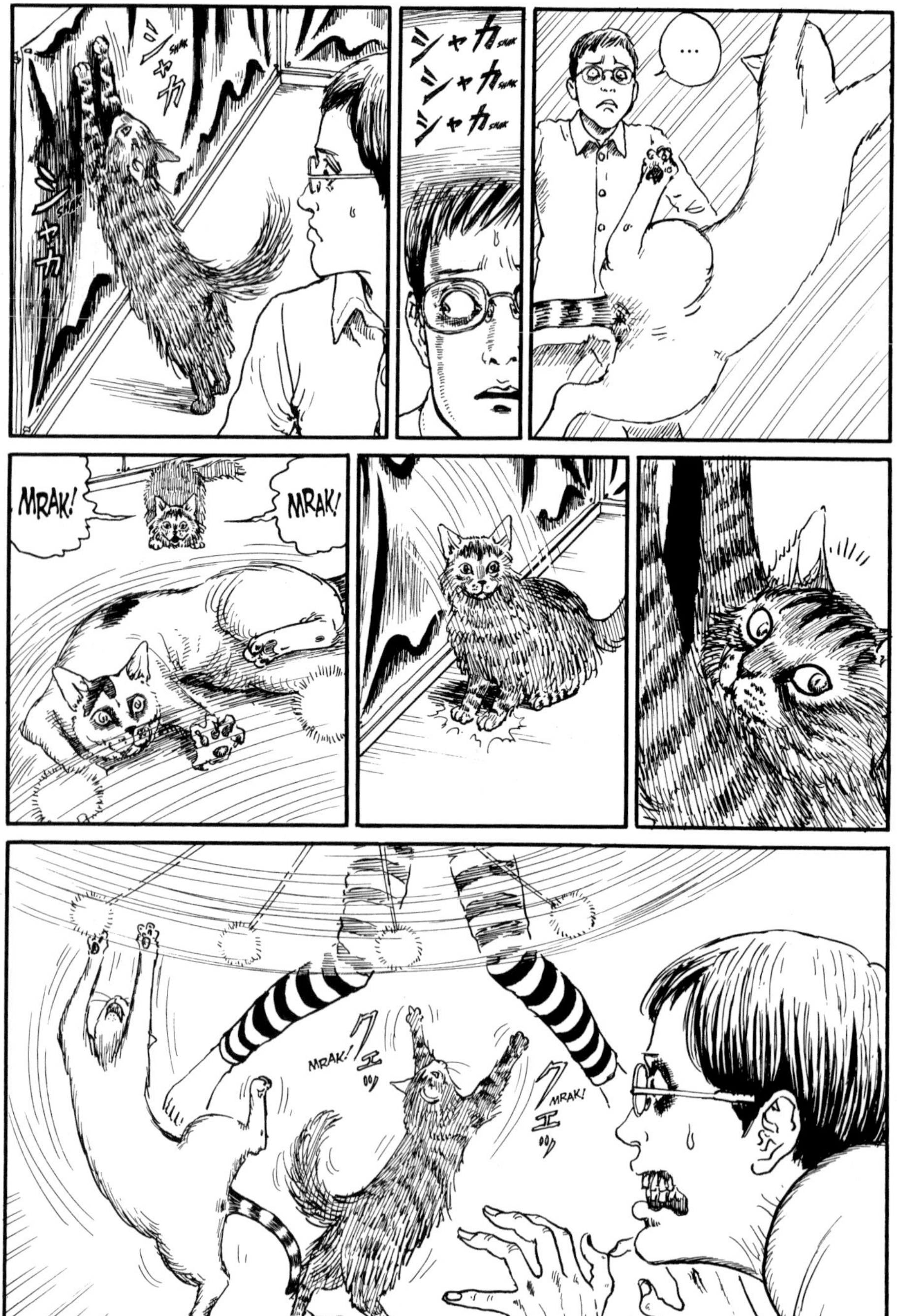
…
シャカ SHAK
シャカ SHAK
シャカ SHAK
シャカ SHAK
シャカ SHAK
MRAK!
MRAK!
クエッ MRAK!
クエッ MRAK!

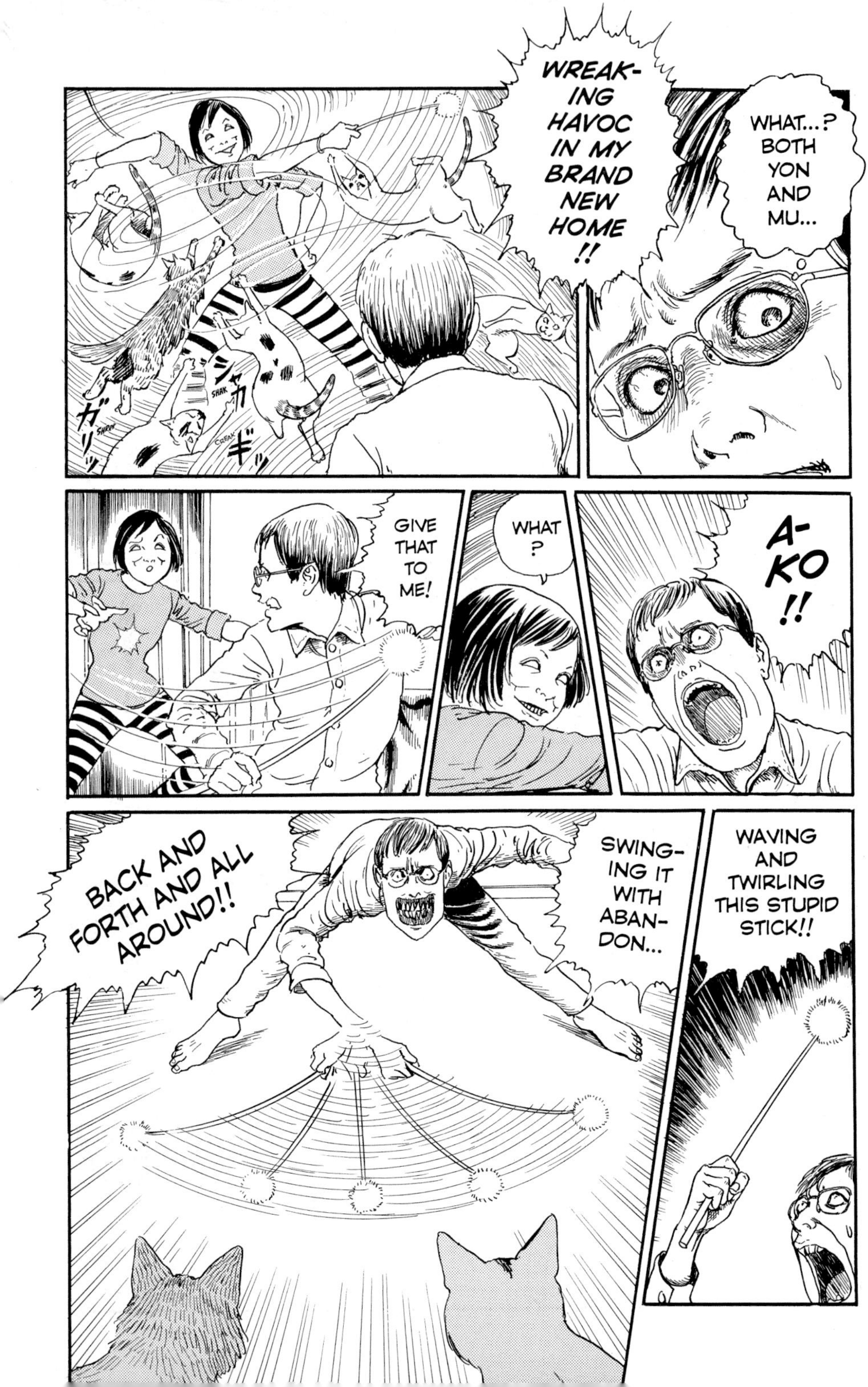
WHAT...? BOTH YON AND MU...
WREAKING HAVOC IN MY BRAND NEW HOME!!
シャカ
SHAK
ギッ
CREAK
ガリッ
A-KO!!
WHAT?
GIVE THAT TO ME!
WAVING AND TWIRLING THIS STUPID STICK!!
SWINGING IT WITH ABANDON...
BACK AND FORTH AND ALL AROUND!!

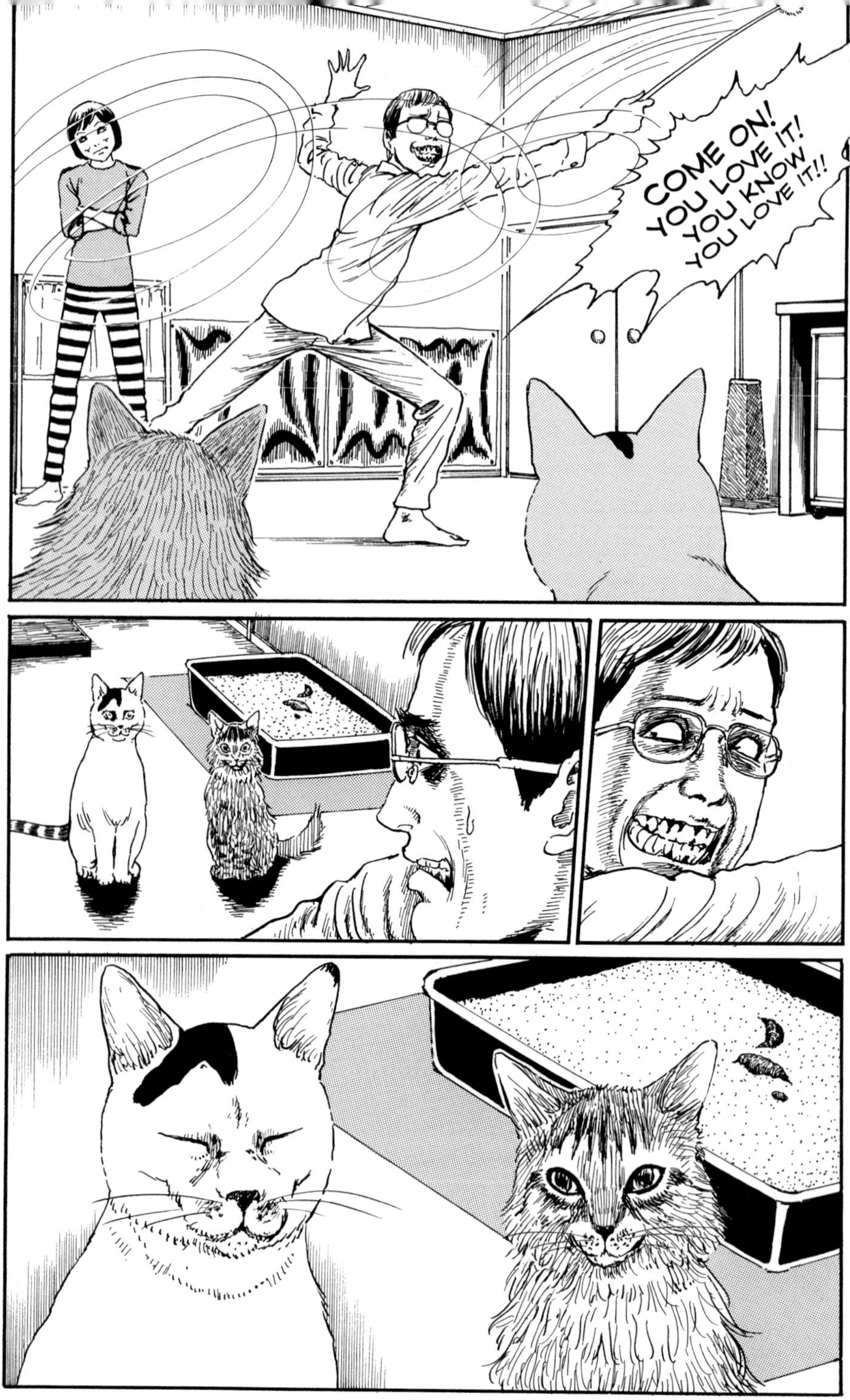
COME ON! YOU LOVE IT! YOU KNOW YOU LOVE IT!!

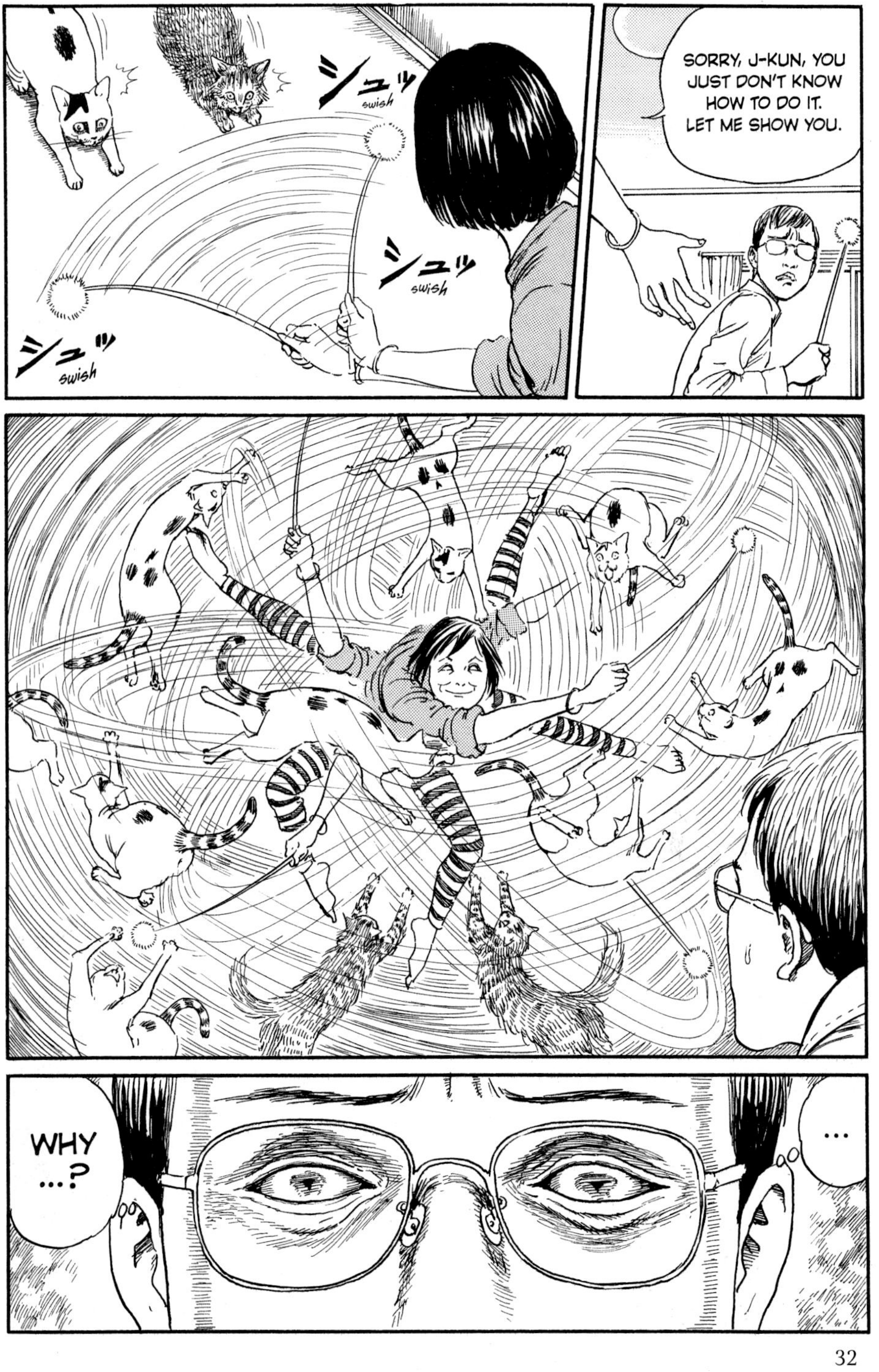
SORRY, J-KUN, YOU JUST DON'T KNOW HOW TO DO IT. LET ME SHOW YOU.
シュッ
swish
シュッ
swish
シュッ
swish
...
WHY ...?

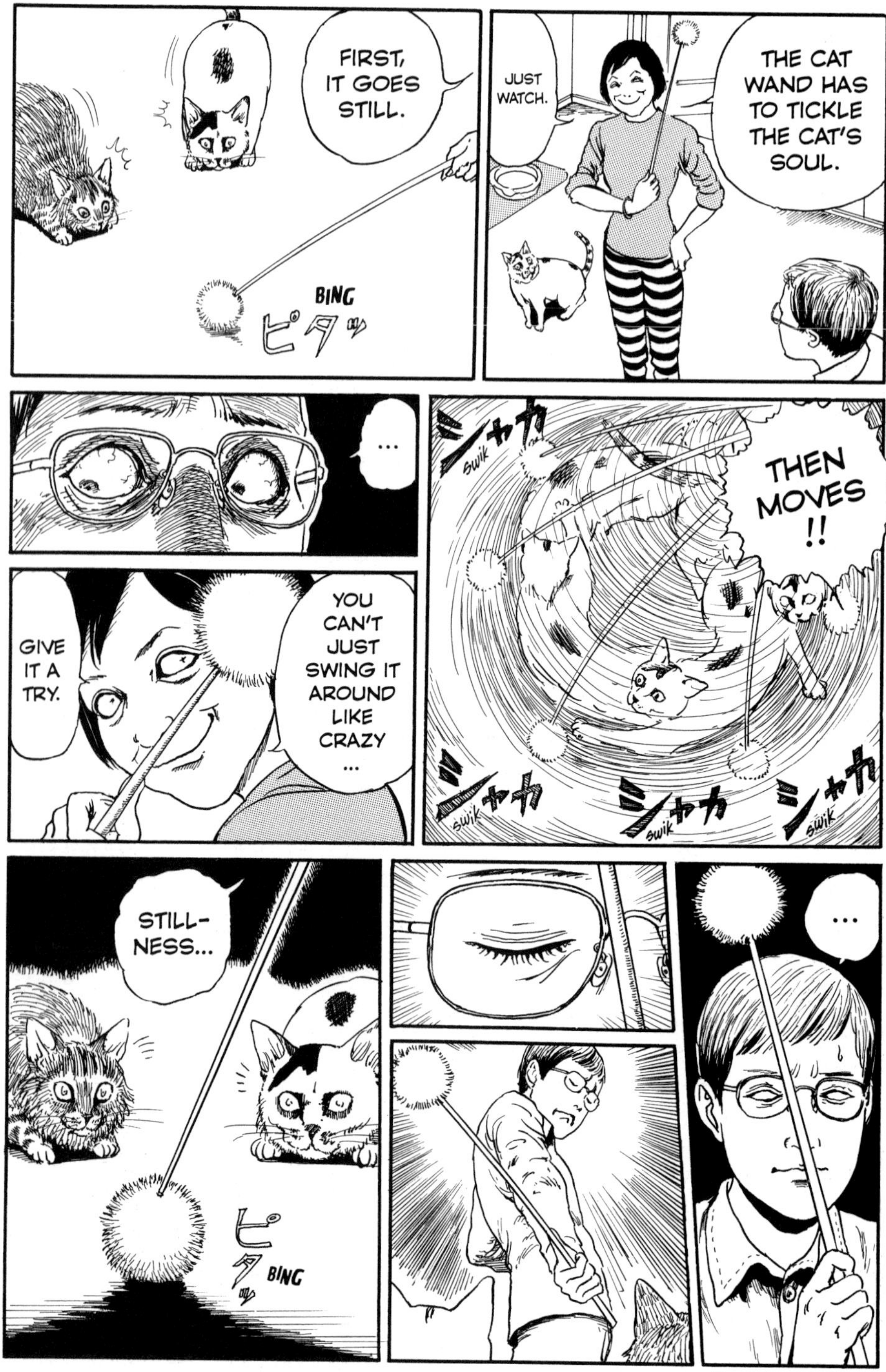

THE CAT WAND HAS TO TICKLE THE CAT'S SOUL.
JUST WATCH.
FIRST, IT GOES STILL.
BING
ピタッ
THEN MOVES !!
シャカ
swik
シャカ
swik
シャカ
swik
シャカ
swik
...
YOU CAN'T JUST SWING IT AROUND LIKE CRAZY ...
GIVE IT A TRY.
...
STILL-NESS...
ピタッ
BING

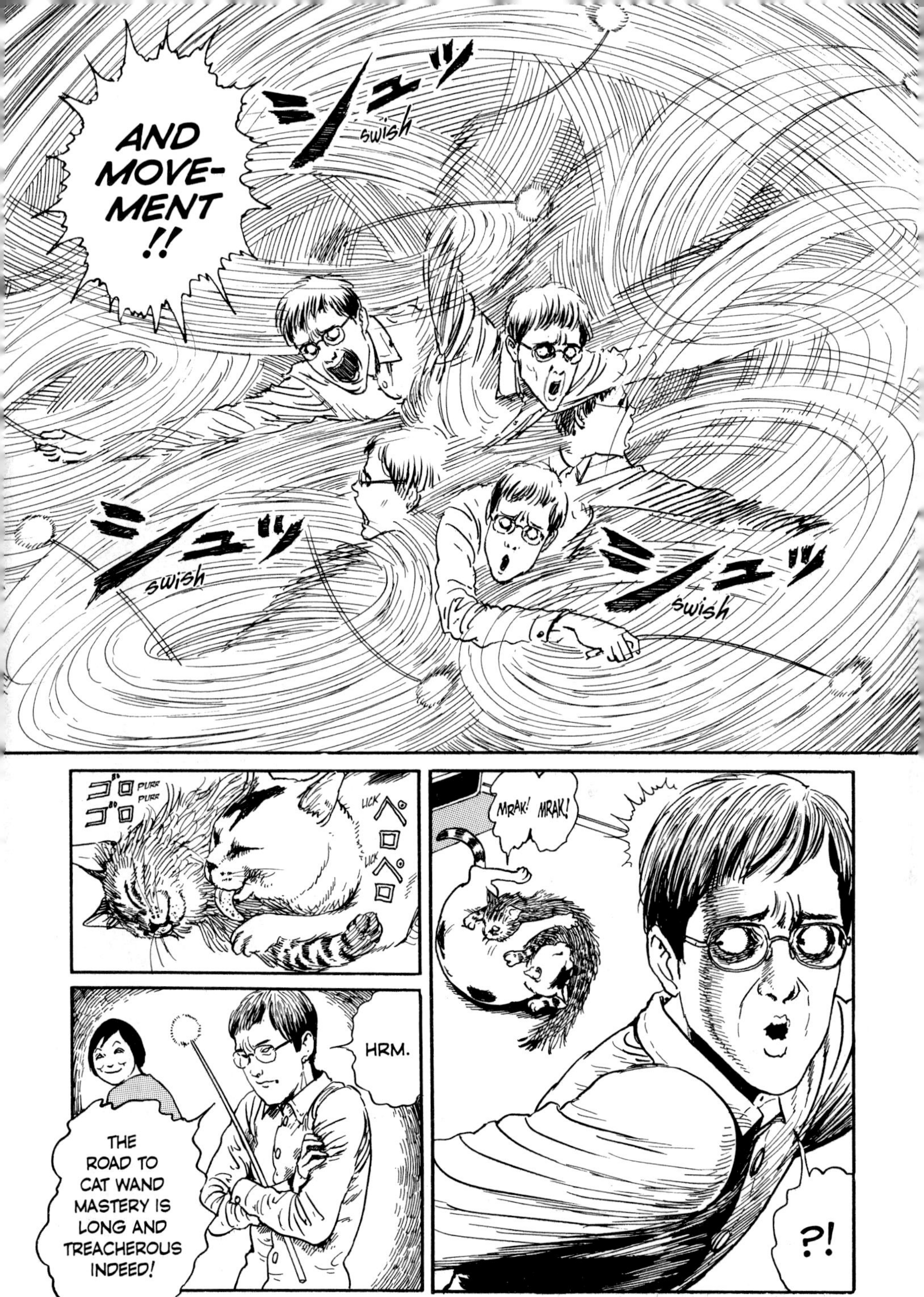
シュッ
swish
AND MOVEMENT!!
シュッ
swish
シュッ
swish
MRAK! MRAK!
?!
ペロペロ
LICK LICK
ゴロゴロ
PURR PURR
HRM.
THE ROAD TO CAT WAND MASTERY IS LONG AND TREACHEROUS INDEED!

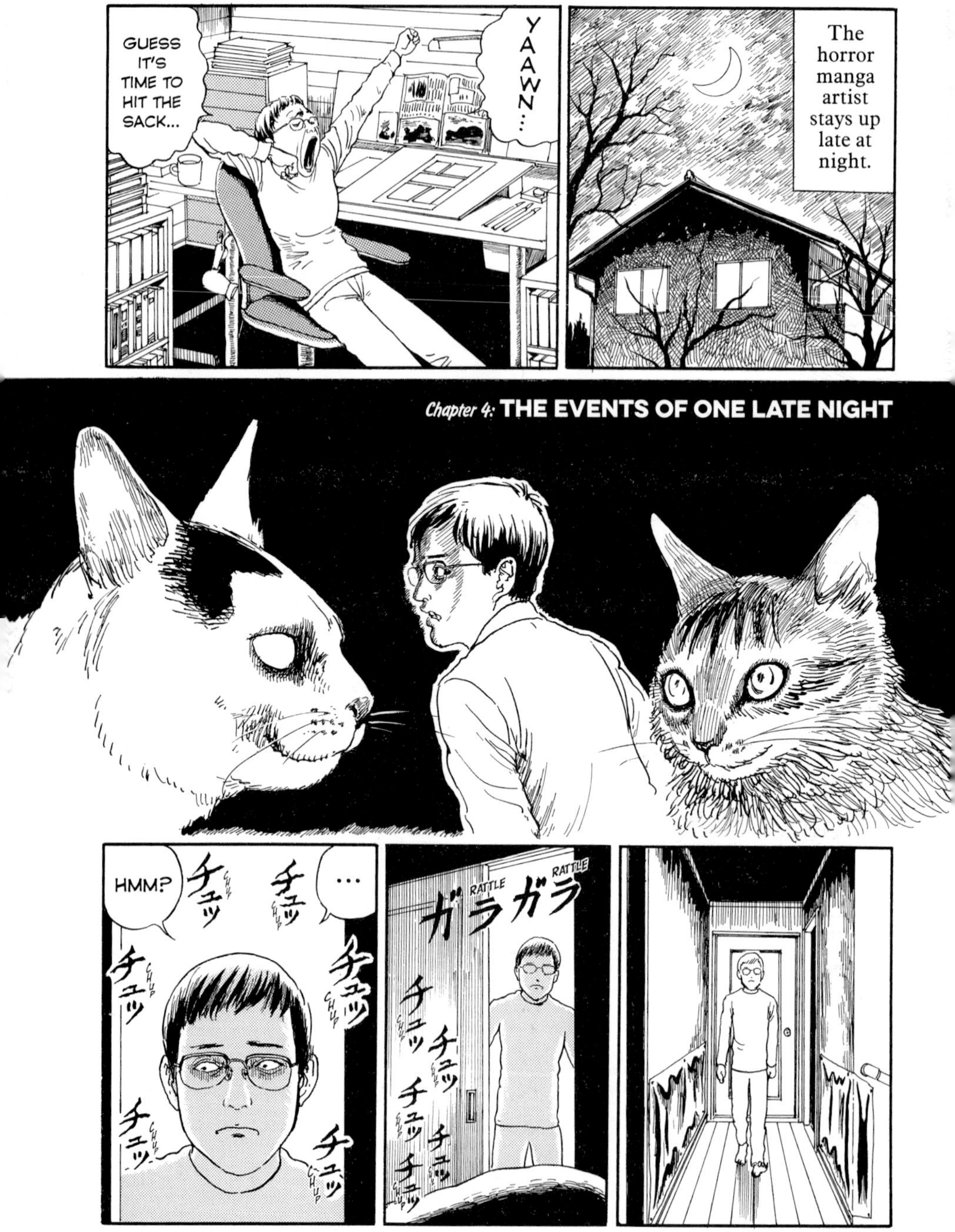
The horror manga artist stays up late at night.
YAAAWN...
GUESS IT'S TIME TO HIT THE SACK...
Chapter 4: THE EVENTS OF ONE LATE NIGHT
ガラガラ RATTLE RATTLE
チュッ CHUP
チュッ CHUP
チュッ CHUP
チュッ CHUP
チュッ CHUP
…
チュッ CHUP
チュッ CHUP
チュッ CHUP
チュッ CHUP
チュッ CHUP
チュッ CHUP
HMM?

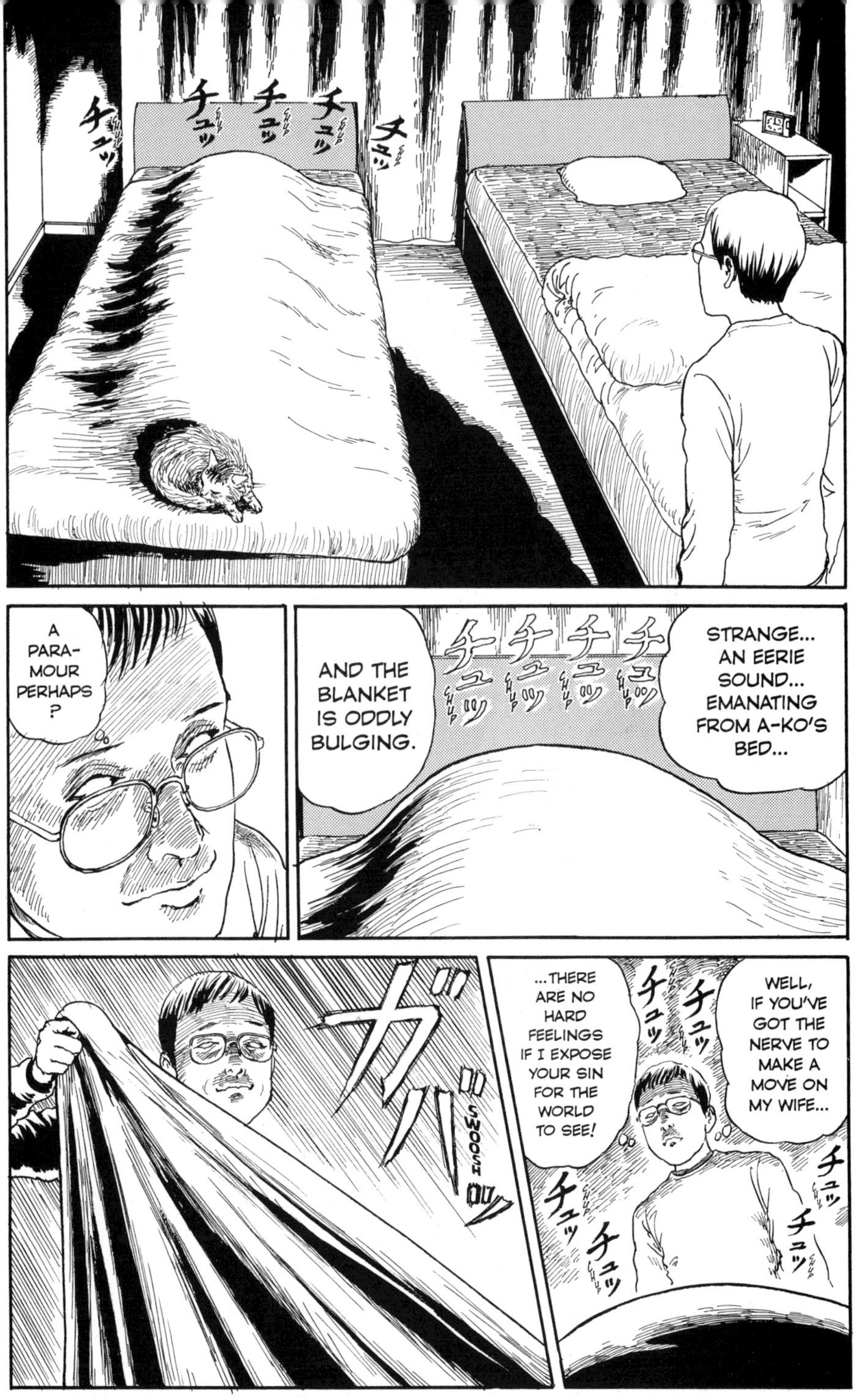

チュッ CHUP
チュッ CHUP
チュッ CHUP
チュッ CHUP
チュッ CHUP
STRANGE... AN EERIE SOUND... EMANATING FROM A-KO'S BED...
チュッ CHUP
チュッ CHUP
チュッ CHUP
チュッ CHUP
AND THE BLANKET IS ODDLY BULGING.
A PARA-MOUR PERHAPS?
WELL, IF YOU'VE GOT THE NERVE TO MAKE A MOVE ON MY WIFE...
...THERE ARE NO HARD FEELINGS IF I EXPOSE YOUR SIN FOR THE WORLD TO SEE!
チュッ CHUP
チュッ CHUP
チュッ CHUP
チュッ CHUP
チュッ CHUP
チュッ CHUP
ガバッ SWOOSH

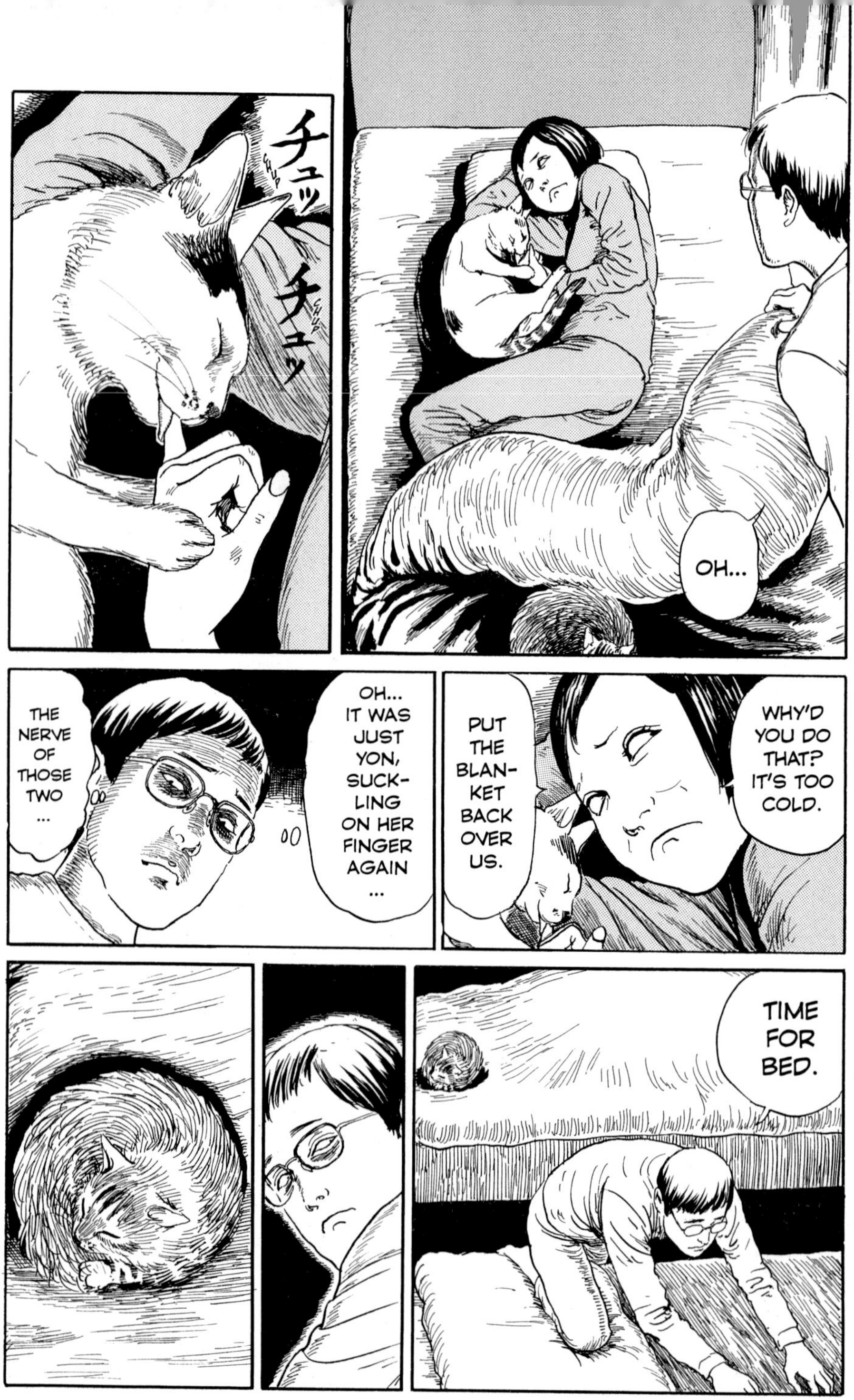
OH...
チュッ
CHUP
チュッ
CHUP
WHY'D YOU DO THAT? IT'S TOO COLD.
PUT THE BLAN-KET BACK OVER US.
OH... IT WAS JUST YON, SUCK-LING ON HER FINGER AGAIN ...
THE NERVE OF THOSE TWO ...
TIME FOR BED.

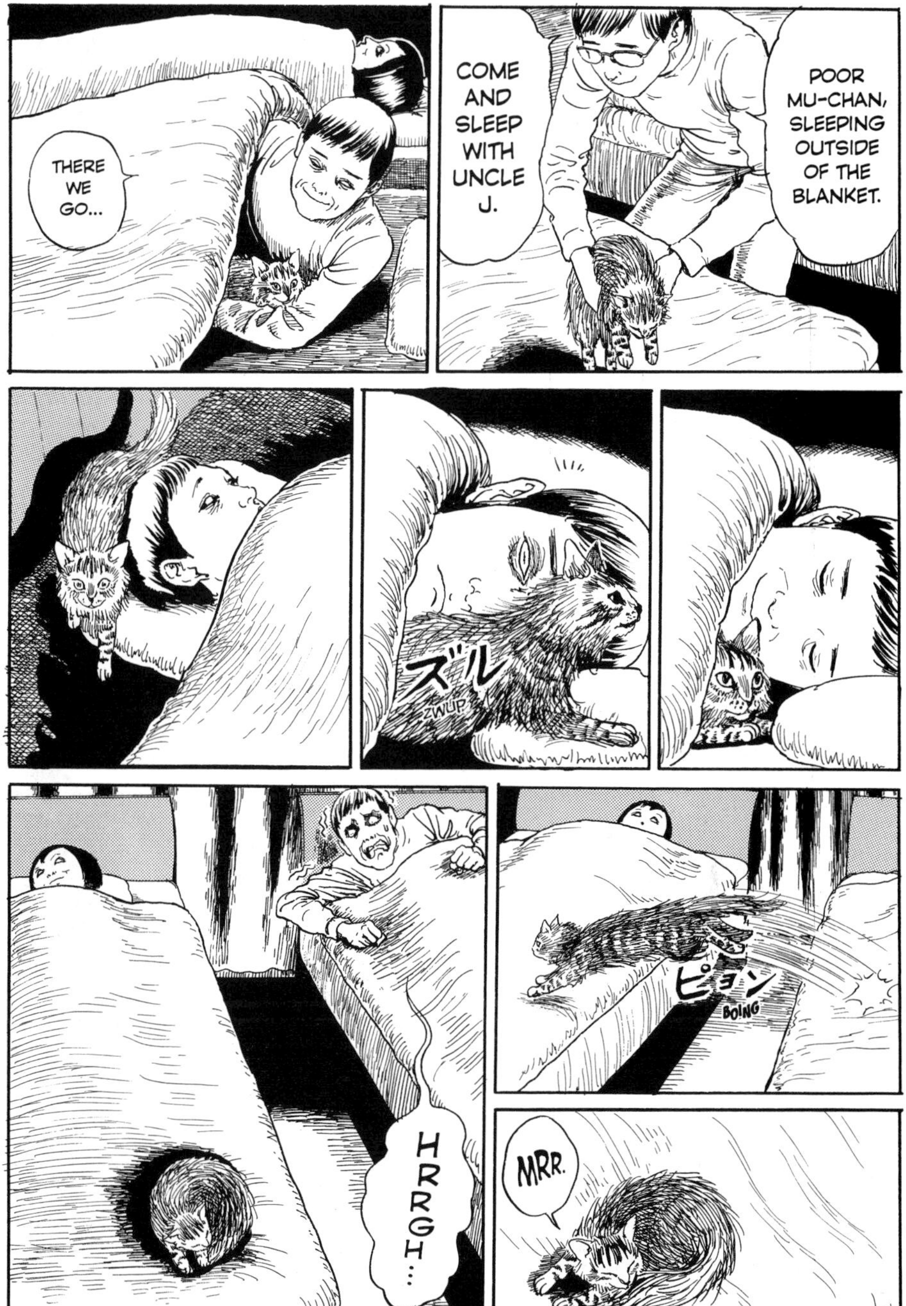
POOR MU-CHAN, SLEEPING OUTSIDE OF THE BLANKET.
COME AND SLEEP WITH UNCLE J.
THERE WE GO...
ズル
ZWUP
ピョン
BOING
MRR.
HRRGH...

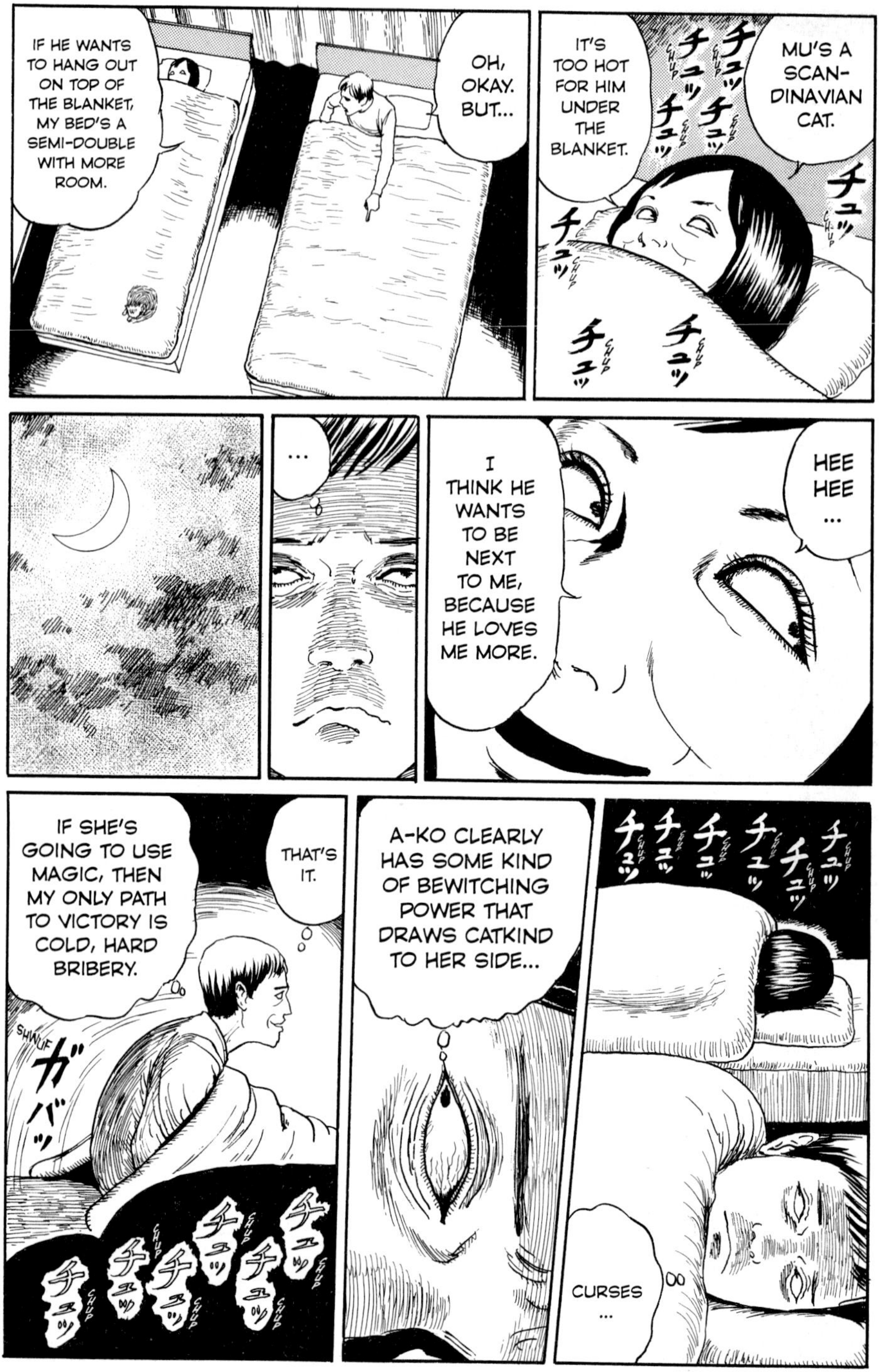
MU'S A SCAN-DINAVIAN CAT.
IT'S TOO HOT FOR HIM UNDER THE BLANKET.
チュッ CHUP
OH, OKAY. BUT...
IF HE WANTS TO HANG OUT ON TOP OF THE BLANKET, MY BED'S A SEMI-DOUBLE WITH MORE ROOM.
HEE HEE ...
I THINK HE WANTS TO BE NEXT TO ME, BECAUSE HE LOVES ME MORE.
...
チュッ CHUP
CURSES ...
A-KO CLEARLY HAS SOME KIND OF BEWITCHING POWER THAT DRAWS CATKIND TO HER SIDE...
THAT'S IT.
IF SHE'S GOING TO USE MAGIC, THEN MY ONLY PATH TO VICTORY IS COLD, HARD BRIBERY.
ガバッ SHWUF
チュッ CHUP

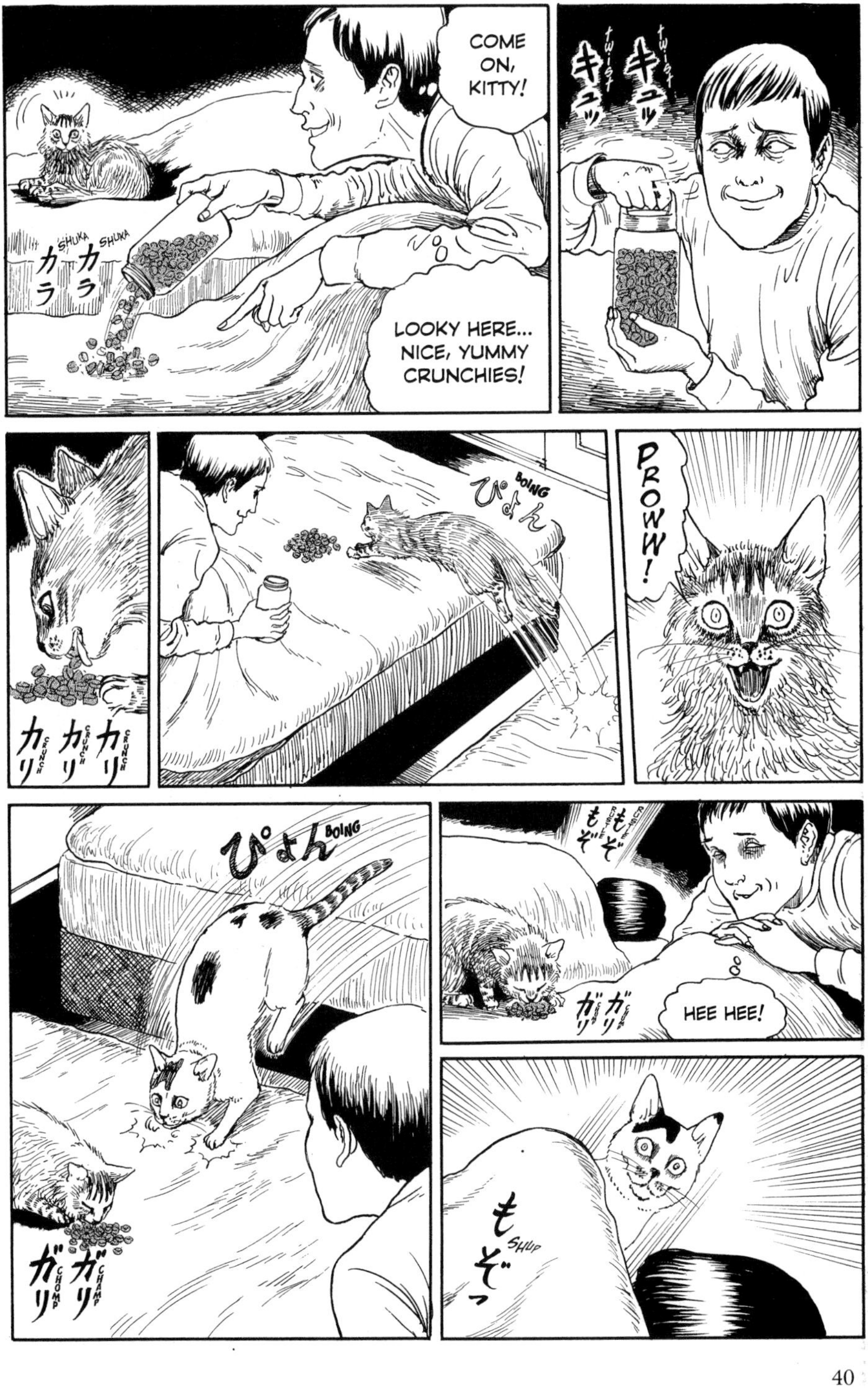
キュッ TWIST
キュッ TWIST
COME ON, KITTY!
カラ SHUKA
カラ SHUKA
LOOKY HERE... NICE, YUMMY CRUNCHIES!
PROWW!
ぴょん BOING
カリ CRUNCH
カリ CRUNCH
カリ CRUNCH
もぞ RUSTLE
もぞ RUSTLE
HEE HEE!
ガリ CHOMP
ガリ CHOMP
もぞっ SHUP
ぴょん BOING
ガリ CHOMP
ガリ CHOMP

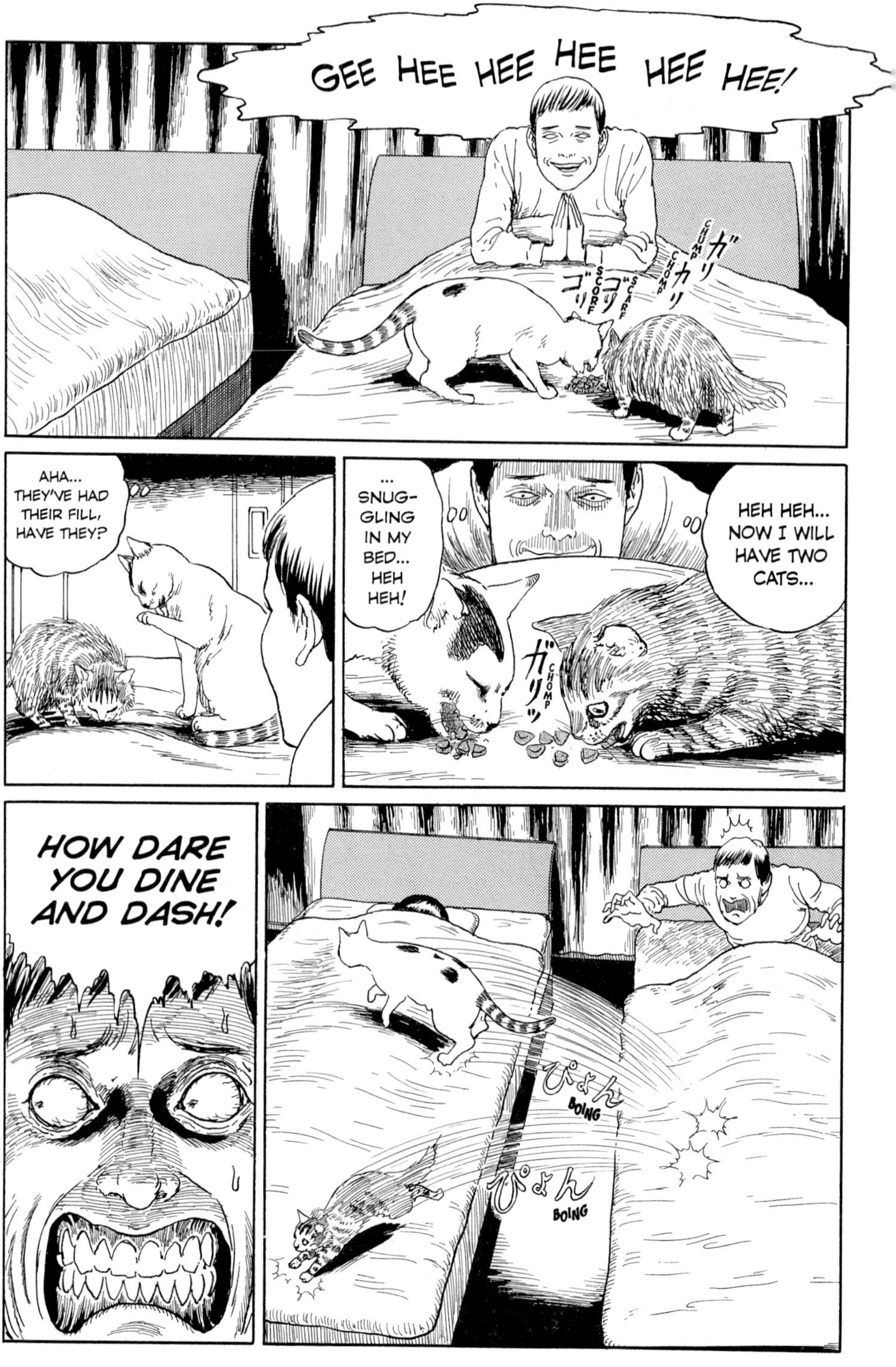
GEE HEE HEE HEE HEE HEE!
ガリ CHOMP
カリ CHOMP
ゴリ SCARF
ゴリ SCORF
HEH HEH... NOW I WILL HAVE TWO CATS...
... SNUG-GLING IN MY BED... HEH HEH!
ガリッ CHOMP
AHA... THEY'VE HAD THEIR FILL, HAVE THEY?
ぴょん BOING
ぴょん BOING
HOW DARE YOU DINE AND DASH!

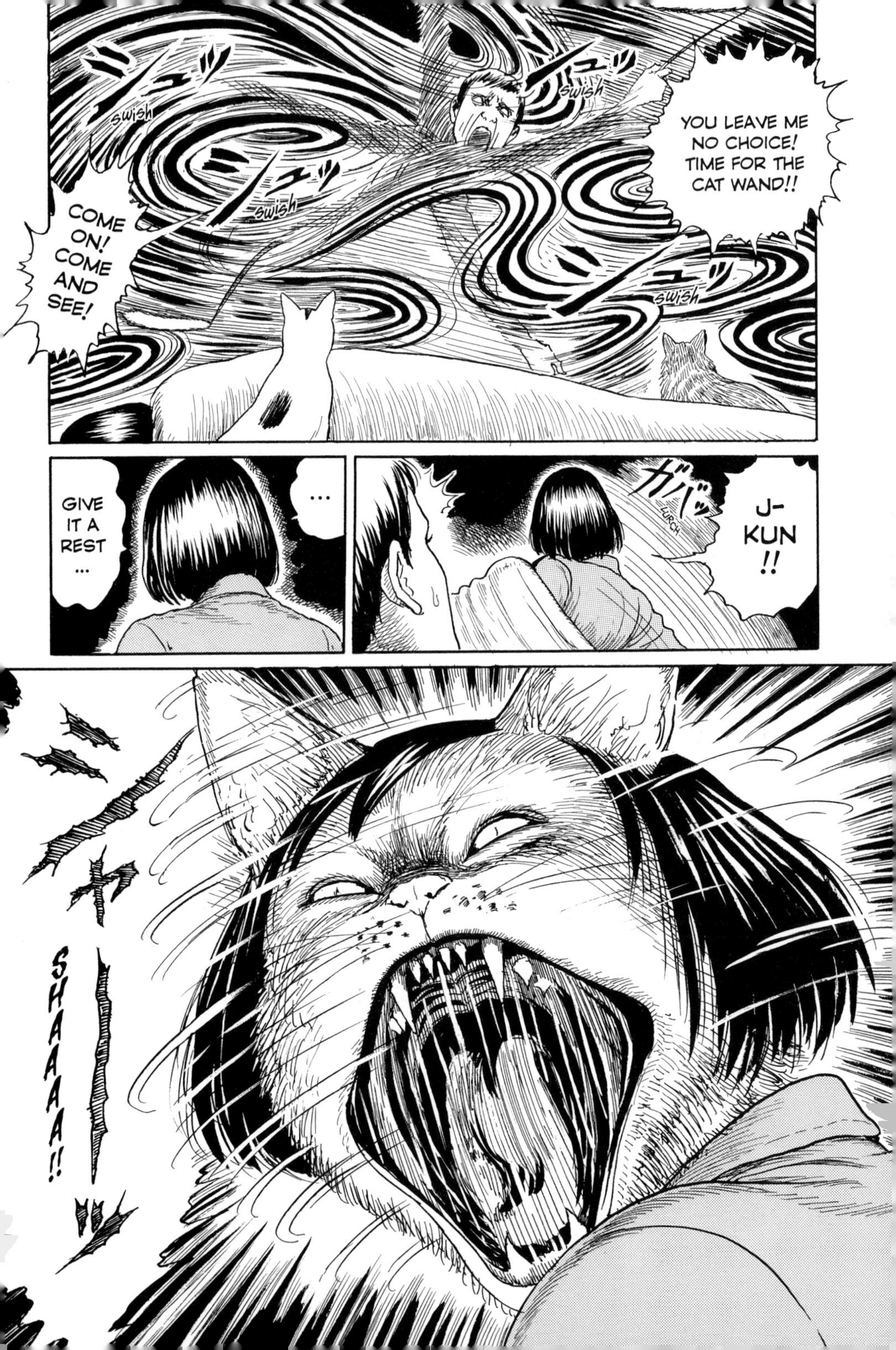
YOU LEAVE ME NO CHOICE! TIME FOR THE CAT WAND!!
swish
swish
swish
swish
COME ON! COME AND SEE!
J-KUN!!
LURCH
...
GIVE IT A REST ...
SHAAAAA!!

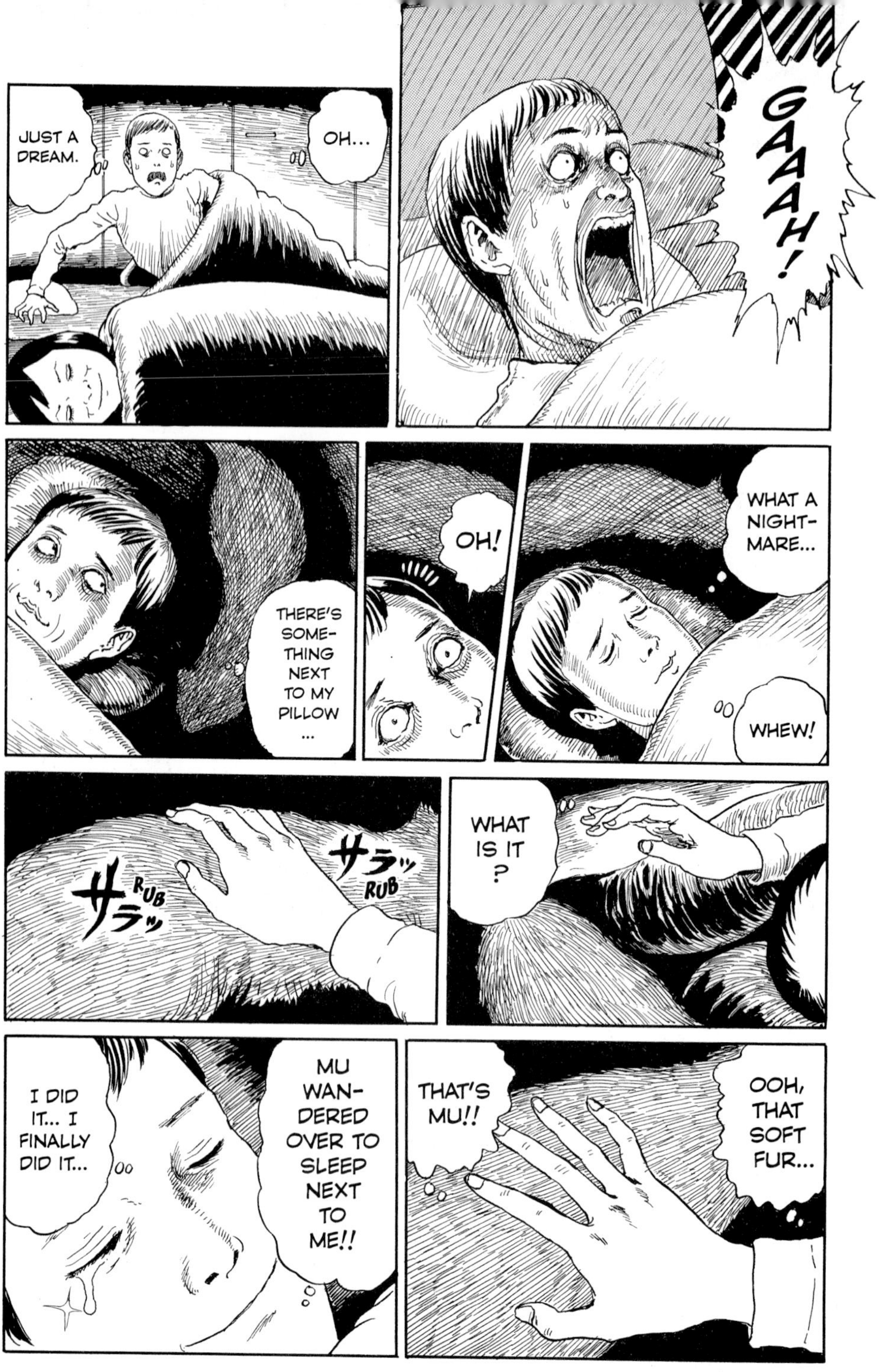
GAAAH!
OH...
JUST A DREAM.
WHAT A NIGHTMARE...
WHEW!
OH!
THERE'S SOMETHING NEXT TO MY PILLOW ...
WHAT IS IT ?
サラッ RUB
サラッ RUB
OOH, THAT SOFT FUR...
THAT'S MU!!
MU WANDERED OVER TO SLEEP NEXT TO ME!!
I DID IT... I FINALLY DID IT...

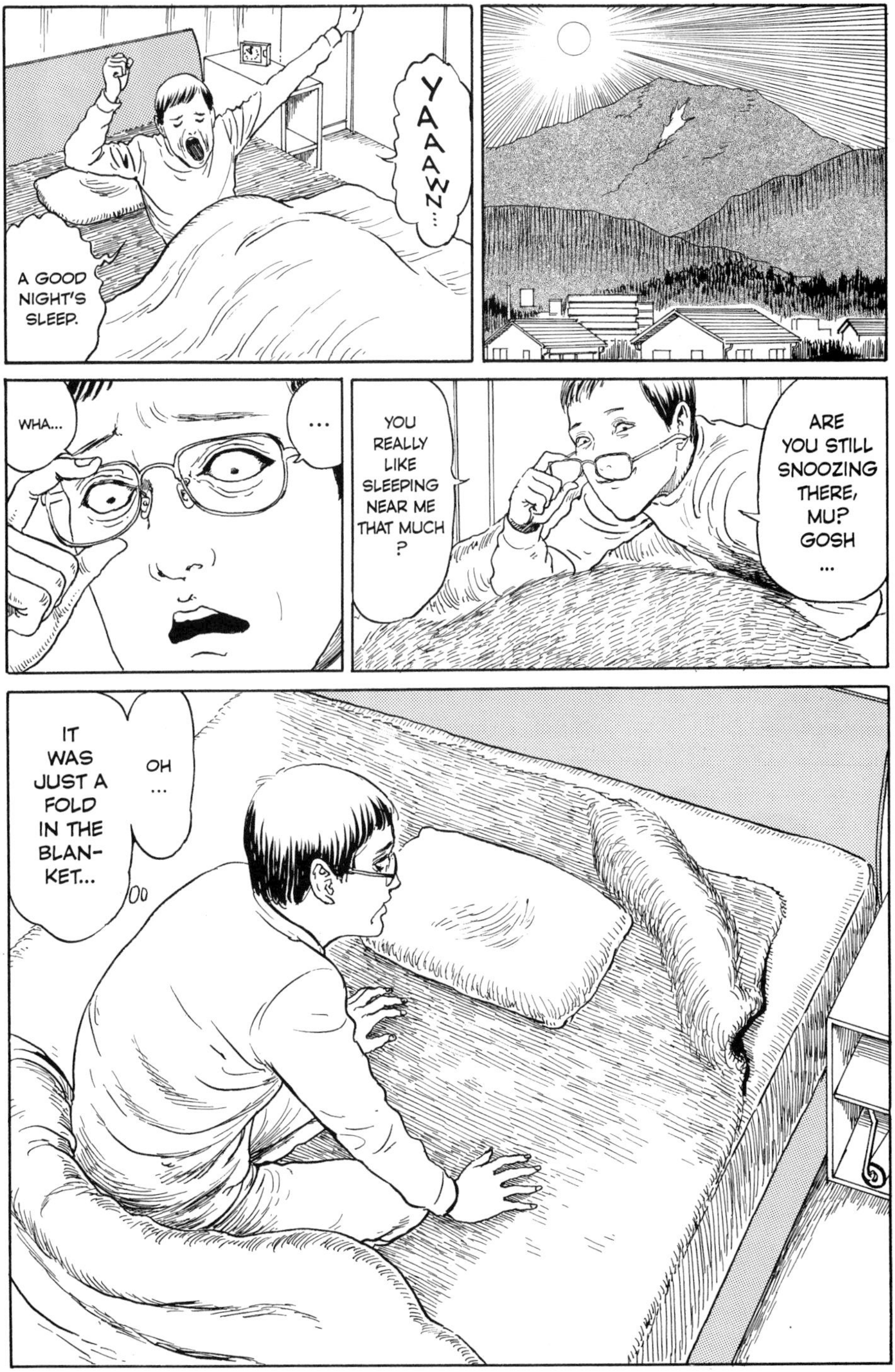
YAAAWN...
A GOOD NIGHT'S SLEEP.
ARE YOU STILL SNOOZING THERE, MU? GOSH ...
YOU REALLY LIKE SLEEPING NEAR ME THAT MUCH ?
...
WHA...
OH ...
IT WAS JUST A FOLD IN THE BLAN- KET...

Question for you, J-SENSEI!

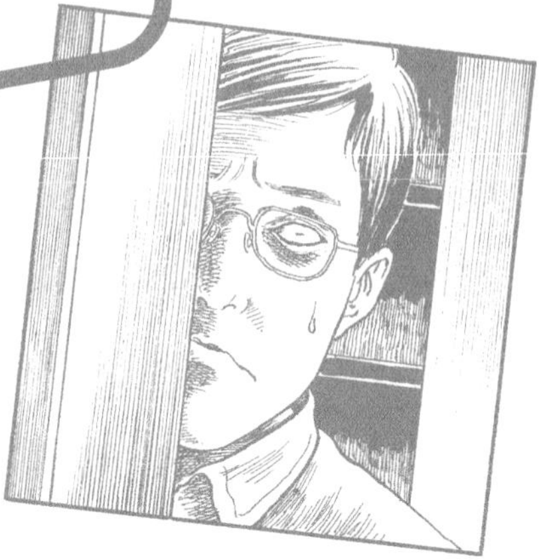

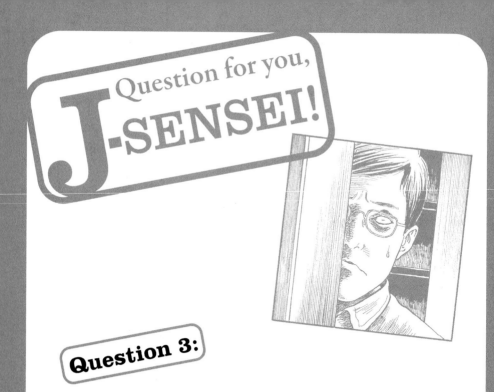

Question 3:

Have you ever used your prior experience as a dental technician in your manga work? I really got a sense of your skill from how well you make your plaster figures (for sketching human forms).

Answer:

The job of a dental technician is to create objects that will be placed in the patient's mouth. Therefore, dentures and the like must be made smooth as to not damage the mouth. When creating manga, I sometimes fashion tools by hand and put my skills as a technician to use. I make my tools very smooth.

Question for you, J-SENSEI!

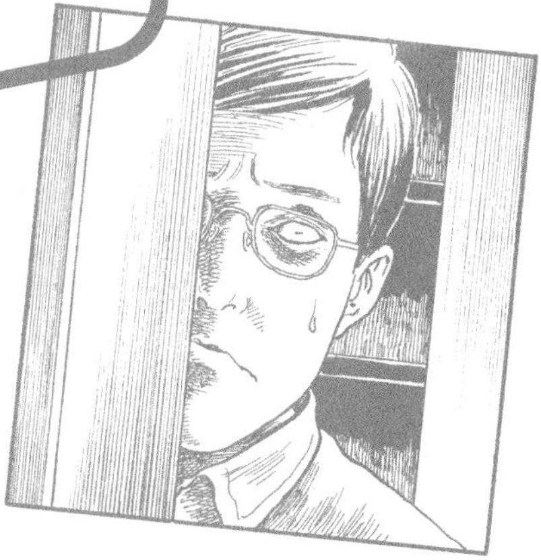

Question 4:

I hear that *Yon & Mu* has gotten quite a response from your family. What kind of feedback did you get?

Answer:

My wife gave me plenty of guidance about the personalities of the cats. She's also commented on my storyboards for me. My mother said, "It's quite a funny manga." My sister put in a request to include her longhair cat, Ran-chan (full name: Ran Purahachi Daruma Tsuchinoko Bandit Katsushin), into the manga, but there wasn't really space for it. Sorry.

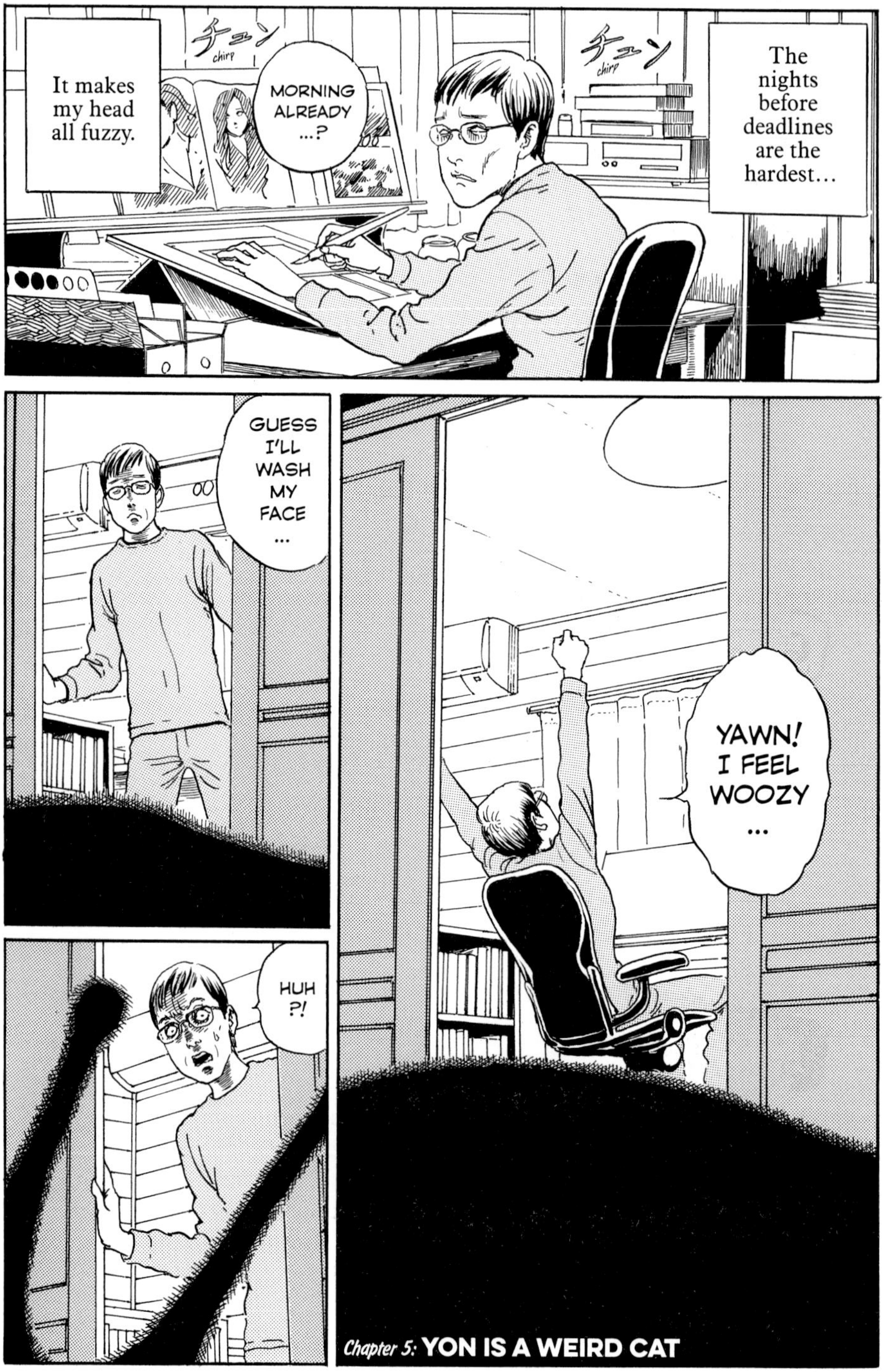
The nights before deadlines are the hardest…
チュン chirp
MORNING ALREADY ...?
チュン chirp
It makes my head all fuzzy.
YAWN! I FEEL WOOZY ...
Chapter 5: YON IS A WEIRD CAT
GUESS I'LL WASH MY FACE ...
HUH ?!

SLURRRM
HYOOOO!!
WHUH ?!

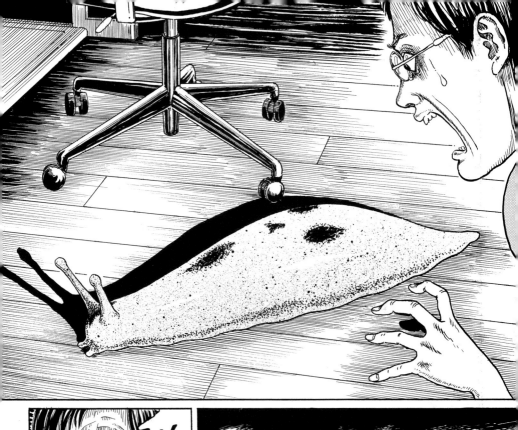

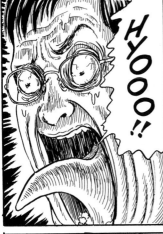

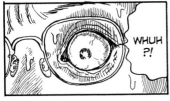

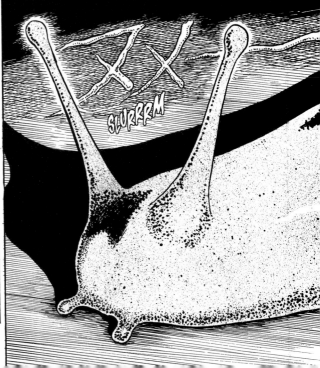

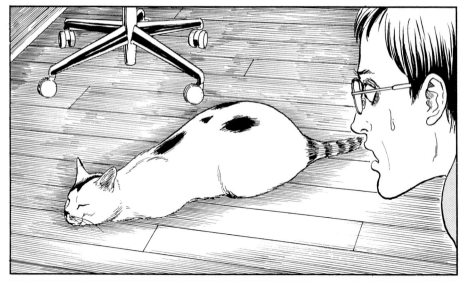

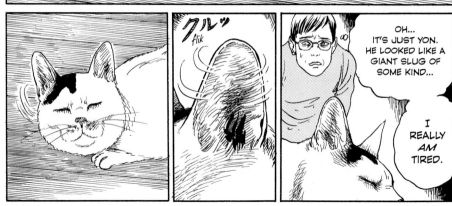

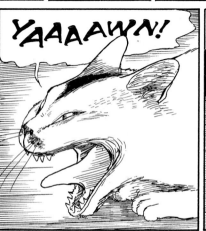

OH...
IT'S JUST YON.
HE LOOKED LIKE A
GIANT SLUG OF
SOME KIND...

I
REALLY
AM
TIRED.

クルッ
flik

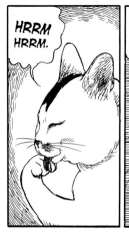

HRRM
HRRM.

YAAAAWN!

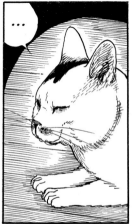

...

49

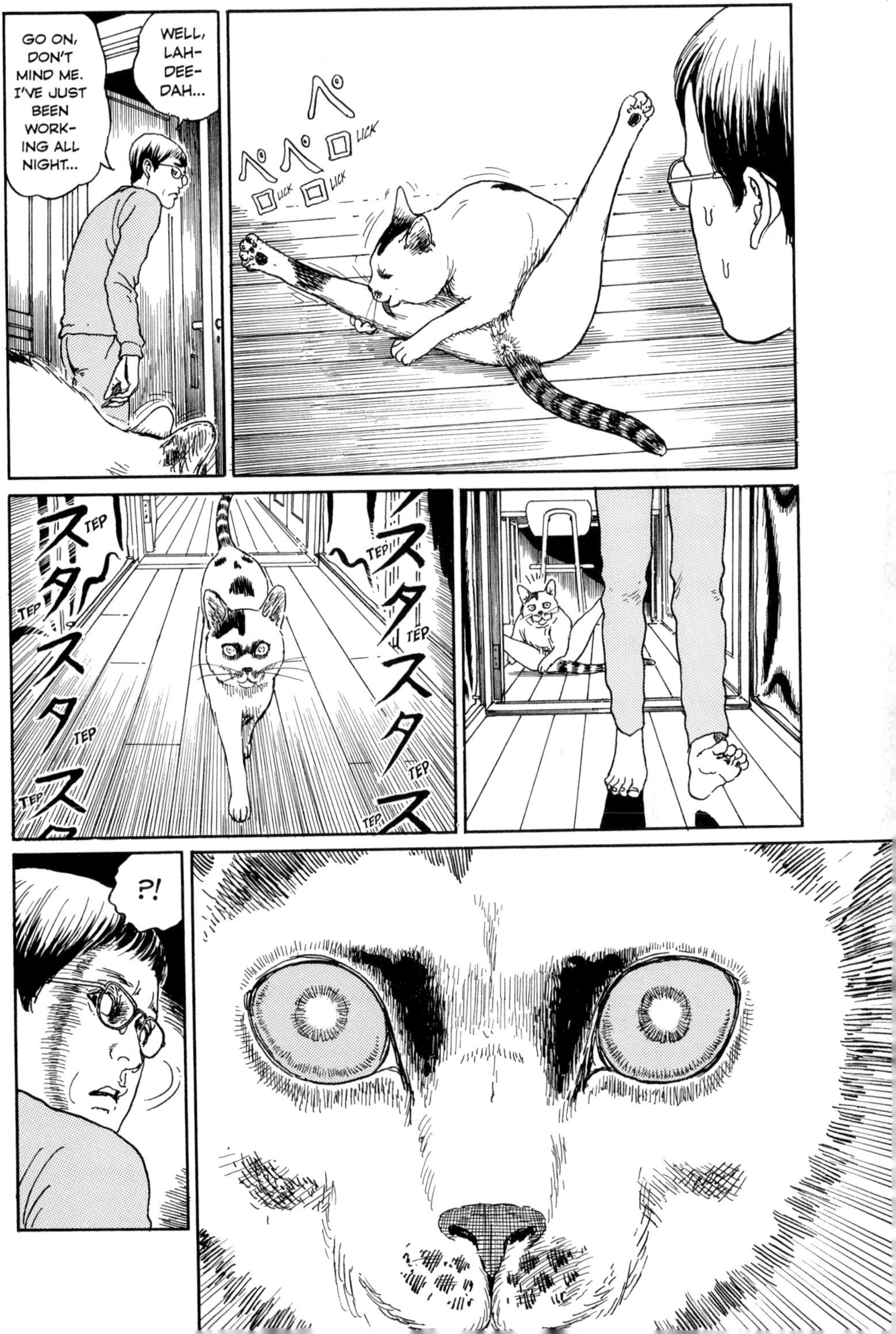

ペ
ペロ LICK
ペロ LICK
LICK
WELL, LAH-DEE-DAH...
GO ON, DON'T MIND ME. I'VE JUST BEEN WORKING ALL NIGHT...
スタスタスタ
TEP TEP TEP TEP
スタスタスタ
TEP TEP TEP TEP
?!

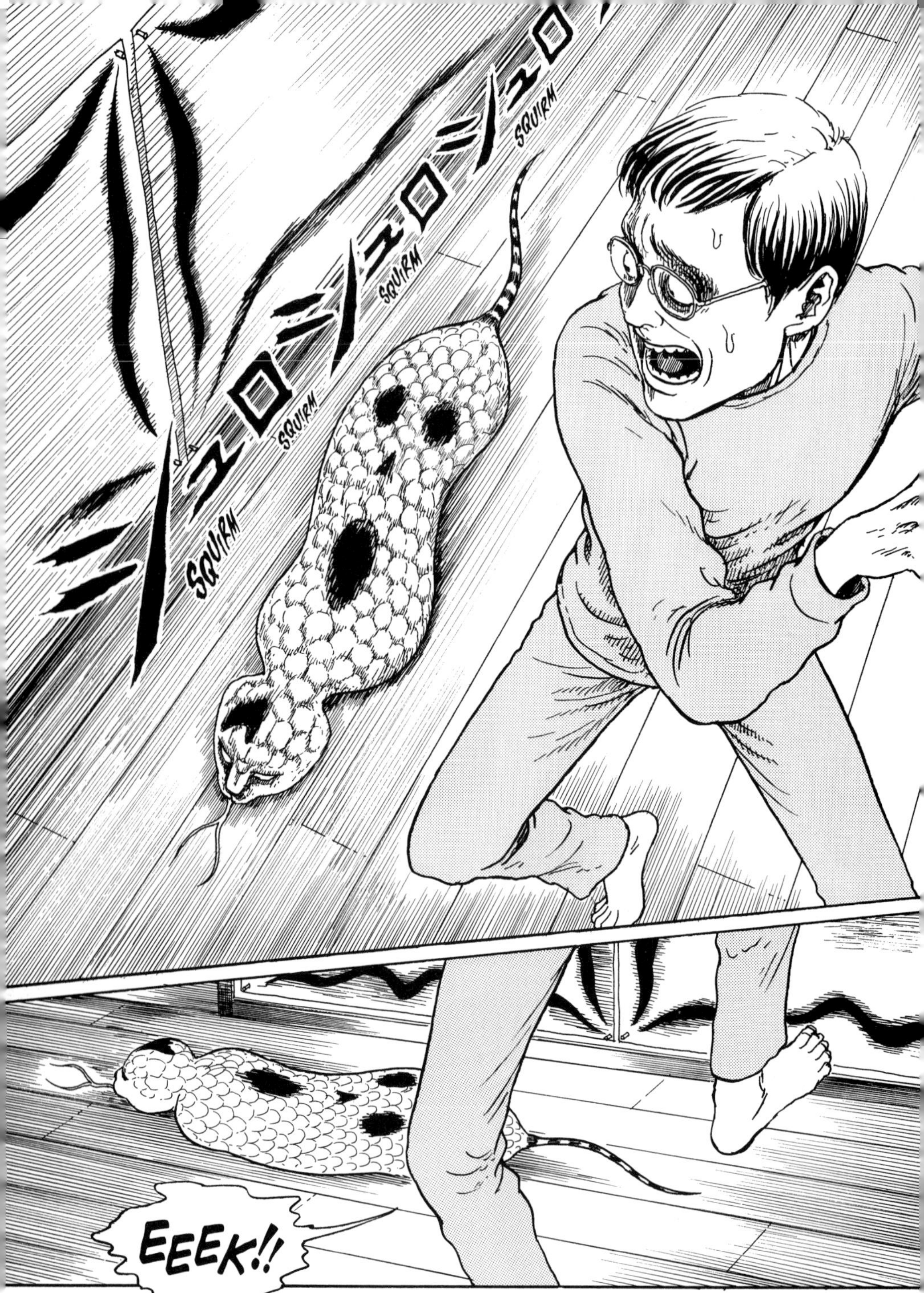
SQUIRM
SQUIRM
SQUIRM
SQUIRM
EEEK!!

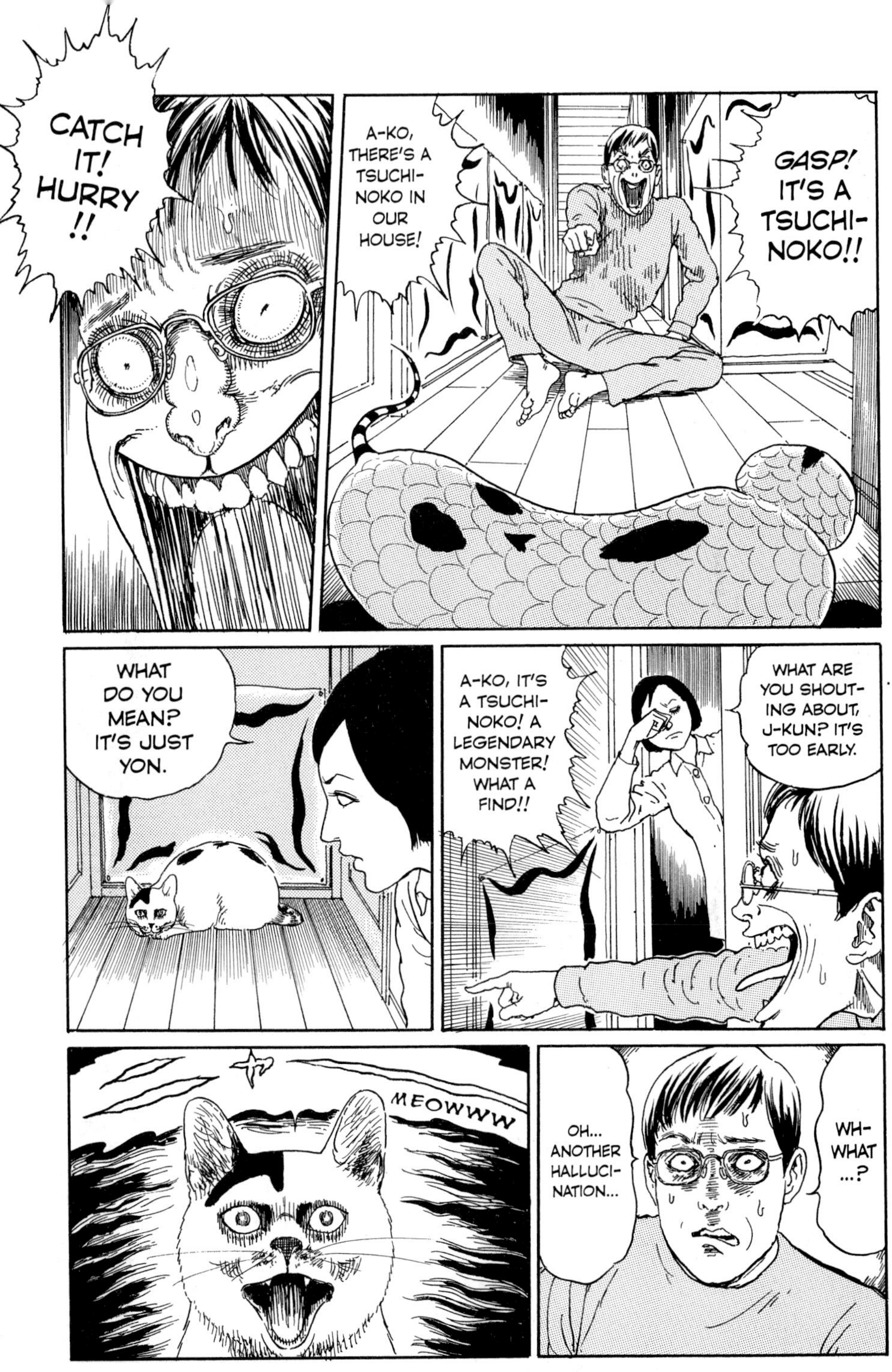
GASP! IT'S A TSUCHI-NOKO!!
A-KO, THERE'S A TSUCHI-NOKO IN OUR HOUSE!
CATCH IT! HURRY!!
WHAT ARE YOU SHOUT-ING ABOUT, J-KUN? IT'S TOO EARLY.
A-KO, IT'S A TSUCHI-NOKO! A LEGENDARY MONSTER! WHAT A FIND!!
WHAT DO YOU MEAN? IT'S JUST YON.
WH-WHAT ...?
OH... ANOTHER HALLUCI-NATION...
MEOWWW

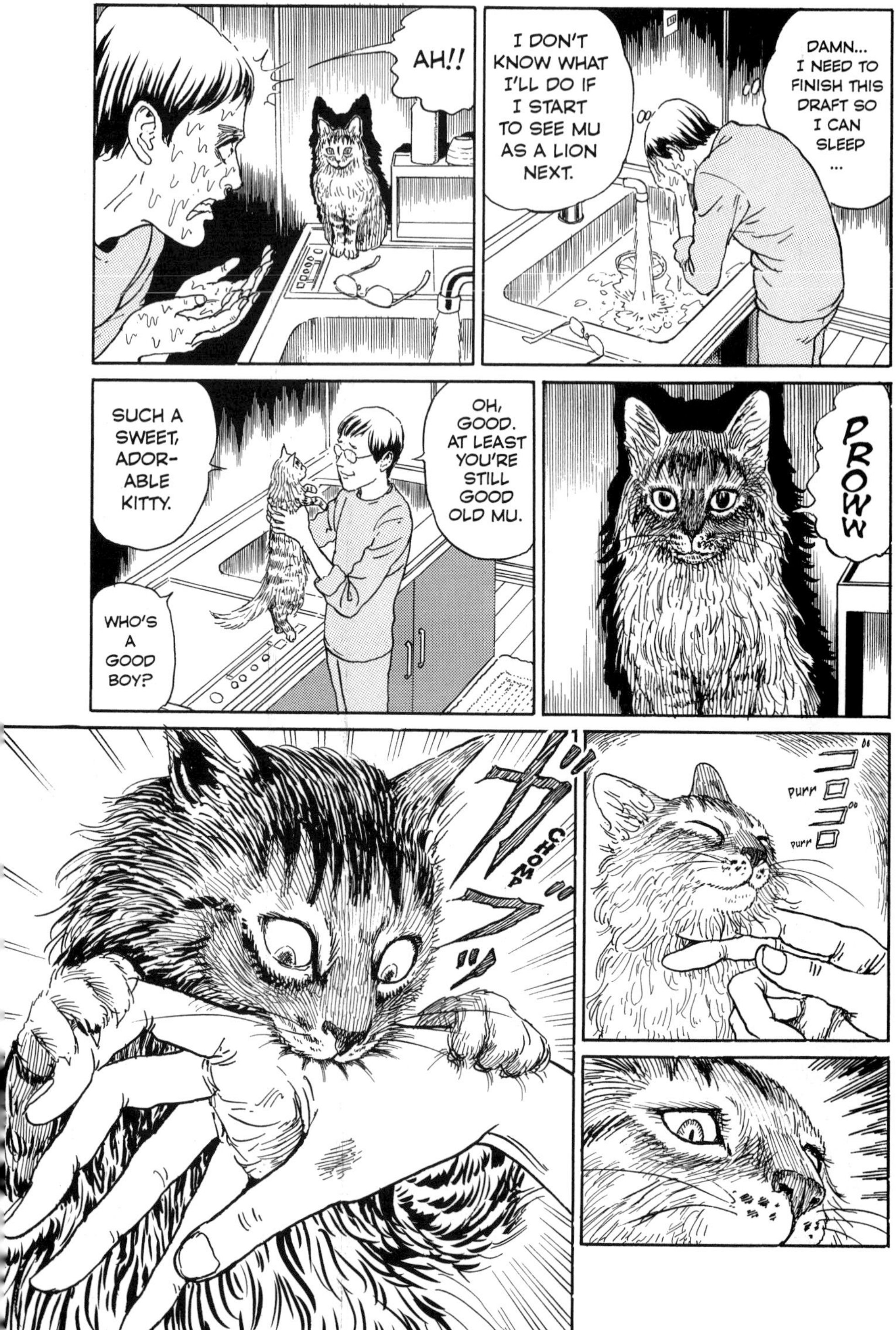
DAMN... I NEED TO FINISH THIS DRAFT SO I CAN SLEEP ...
I DON'T KNOW WHAT I'LL DO IF I START TO SEE MU AS A LION NEXT.
AH!!
PROWW
OH, GOOD. AT LEAST YOU'RE STILL GOOD OLD MU.
SUCH A SWEET, ADORABLE KITTY.
WHO'S A GOOD BOY?
purr
purr
CHOMP

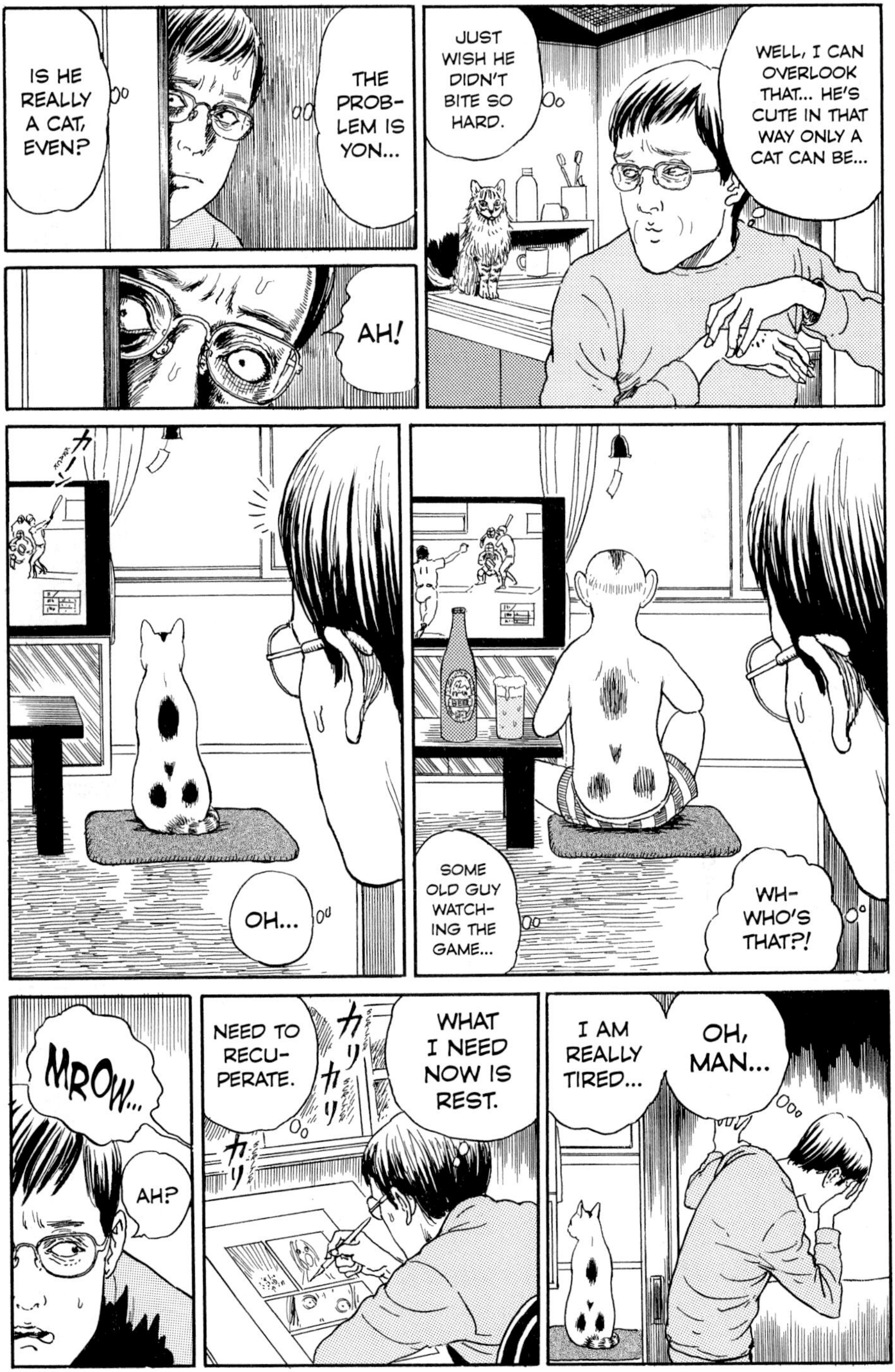
WELL, I CAN OVERLOOK THAT... HE'S CUTE IN THAT WAY ONLY A CAT CAN BE...
JUST WISH HE DIDN'T BITE SO HARD.
THE PROBLEM IS YON...
IS HE REALLY A CAT, EVEN?
AH!
WH-WHO'S THAT?!
SOME OLD GUY WATCHING THE GAME...
OH...
OH, MAN...
I AM REALLY TIRED...
WHAT I NEED NOW IS REST.
カリ
カリ
NEED TO RECUPERATE.
カリ
MROW...
AH?

MROWW...
YON...
ぴょん
BOING
クル
FLOP
WH-WHAT'S THIS...
WHAT'S ALL THIS ABOUT ...?
ブルン
PURR
ブルン
PURR
ブルン
PURR
ブルン
PURR
ブルン
PURR
ブルン
PURR
ブルン
PURR
ブルン
PURR

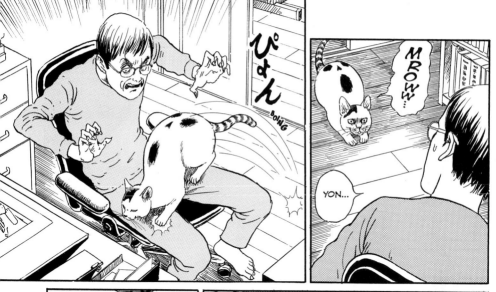

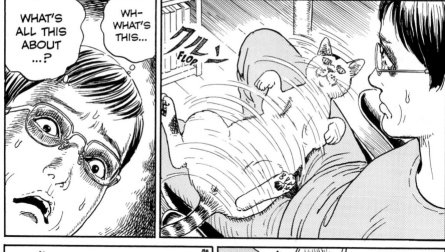

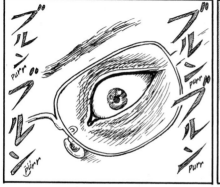

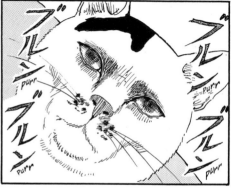

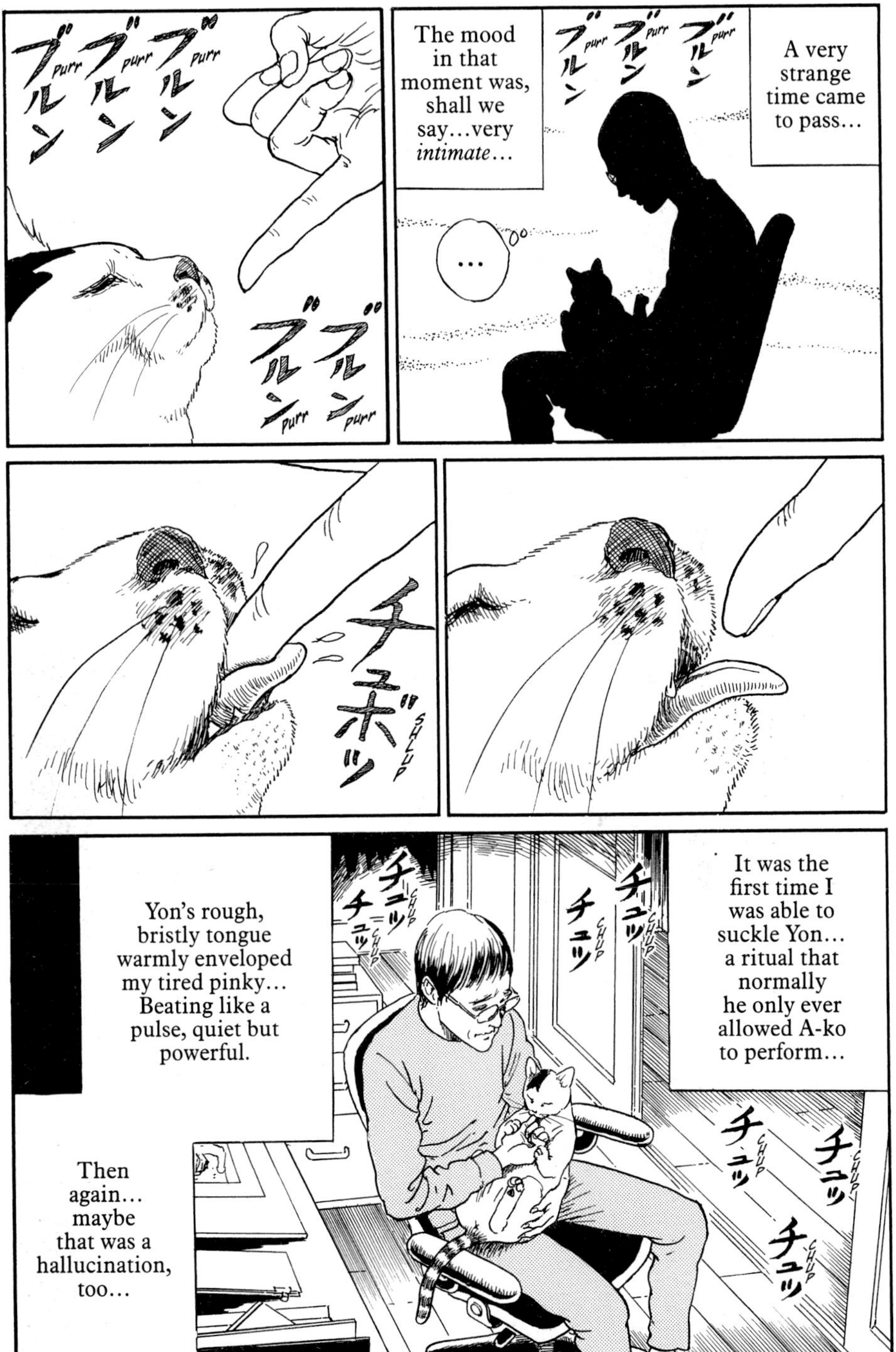
A very strange time came to pass…
The mood in that moment was, shall we say…very *intimate*…
ブルン purr
ブルン purr
ブルン purr
…
ブルン purr
ブルン purr
ブルン purr
ブルン purr
ブルン purr
チュポッ SHLUP
It was the first time I was able to suckle Yon… a ritual that normally he only ever allowed A-ko to perform…
チュッ CHUP
チュッ CHUP
チュッ CHUP
チュッ CHUP
チュッ CHUP
チュッ CHUP
チュッ CHUP
Yon's rough, bristly tongue warmly enveloped my tired pinky… Beating like a pulse, quiet but powerful.
Then again… maybe that was a hallucination, too…

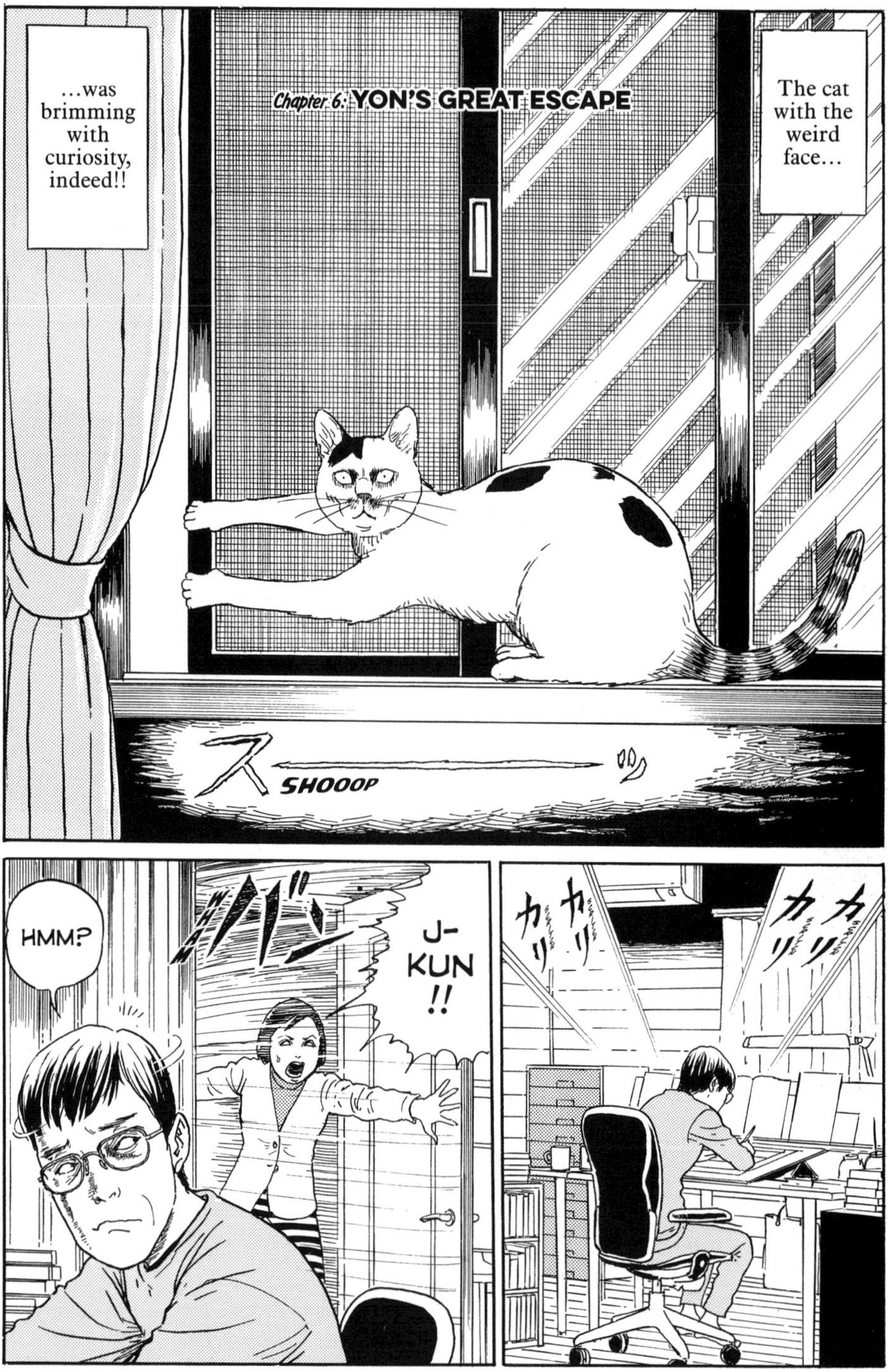
The cat with the weird face…
Chapter 6: YON'S GREAT ESCAPE
…was brimming with curiosity, indeed!!
SHOOOP
カリカリ
カリカリ
J-KUN!!
WHAM
HMM?

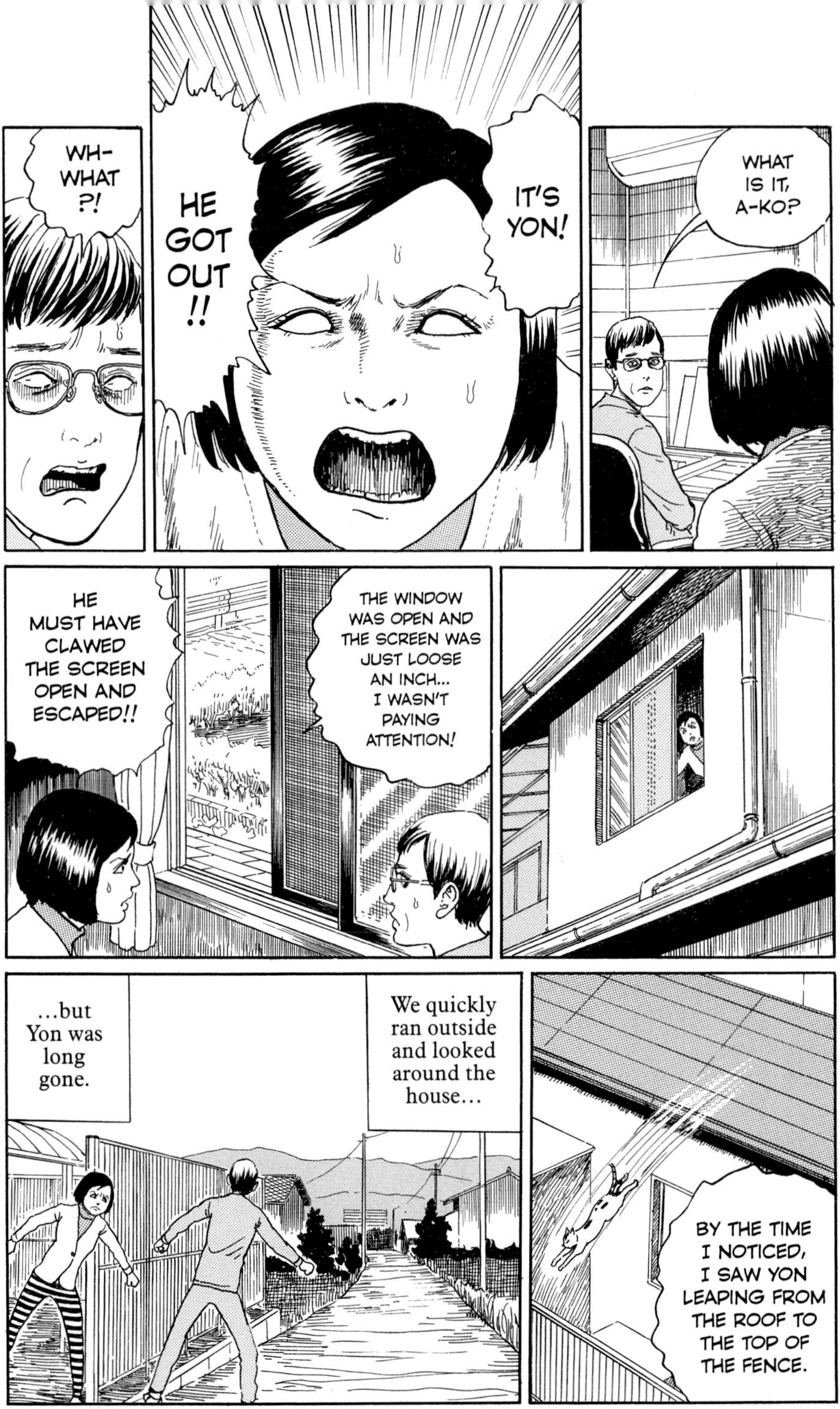
WHAT IS IT, A-KO?
IT'S YON!
HE GOT OUT!!
WH-WHAT?!
THE WINDOW WAS OPEN AND THE SCREEN WAS JUST LOOSE AN INCH... I WASN'T PAYING ATTENTION!
HE MUST HAVE CLAWED THE SCREEN OPEN AND ESCAPED!!
BY THE TIME I NOTICED, I SAW YON LEAPING FROM THE ROOF TO THE TOP OF THE FENCE.
We quickly ran outside and looked around the house…
…but Yon was long gone.

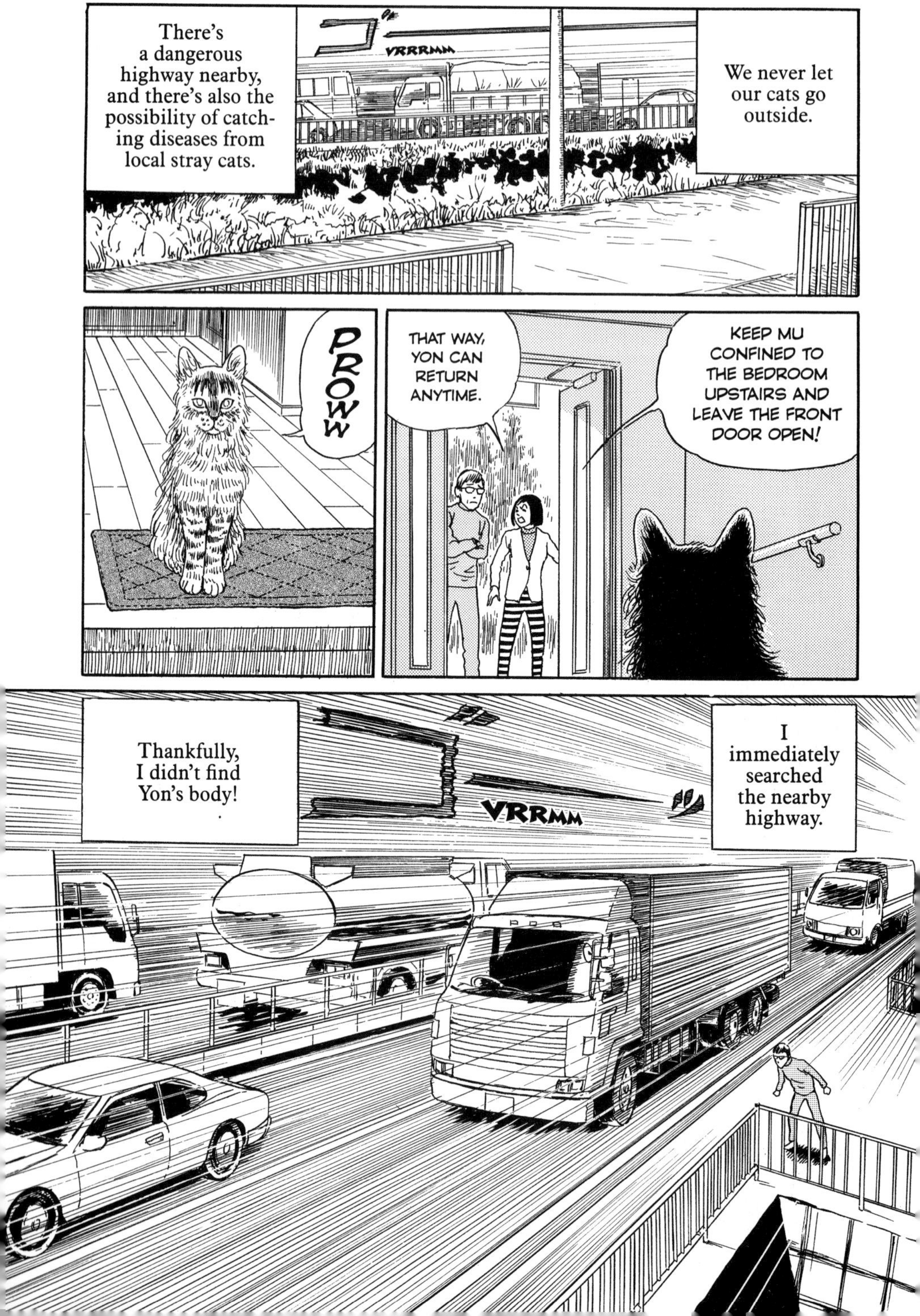
We never let our cats go outside.
There's a dangerous highway nearby, and there's also the possibility of catching diseases from local stray cats.
VRRRMM
KEEP MU CONFINED TO THE BEDROOM UPSTAIRS AND LEAVE THE FRONT DOOR OPEN!
THAT WAY, YON CAN RETURN ANYTIME.
PROWW
I immediately searched the nearby highway.
VRRMM
Thankfully, I didn't find Yon's body!

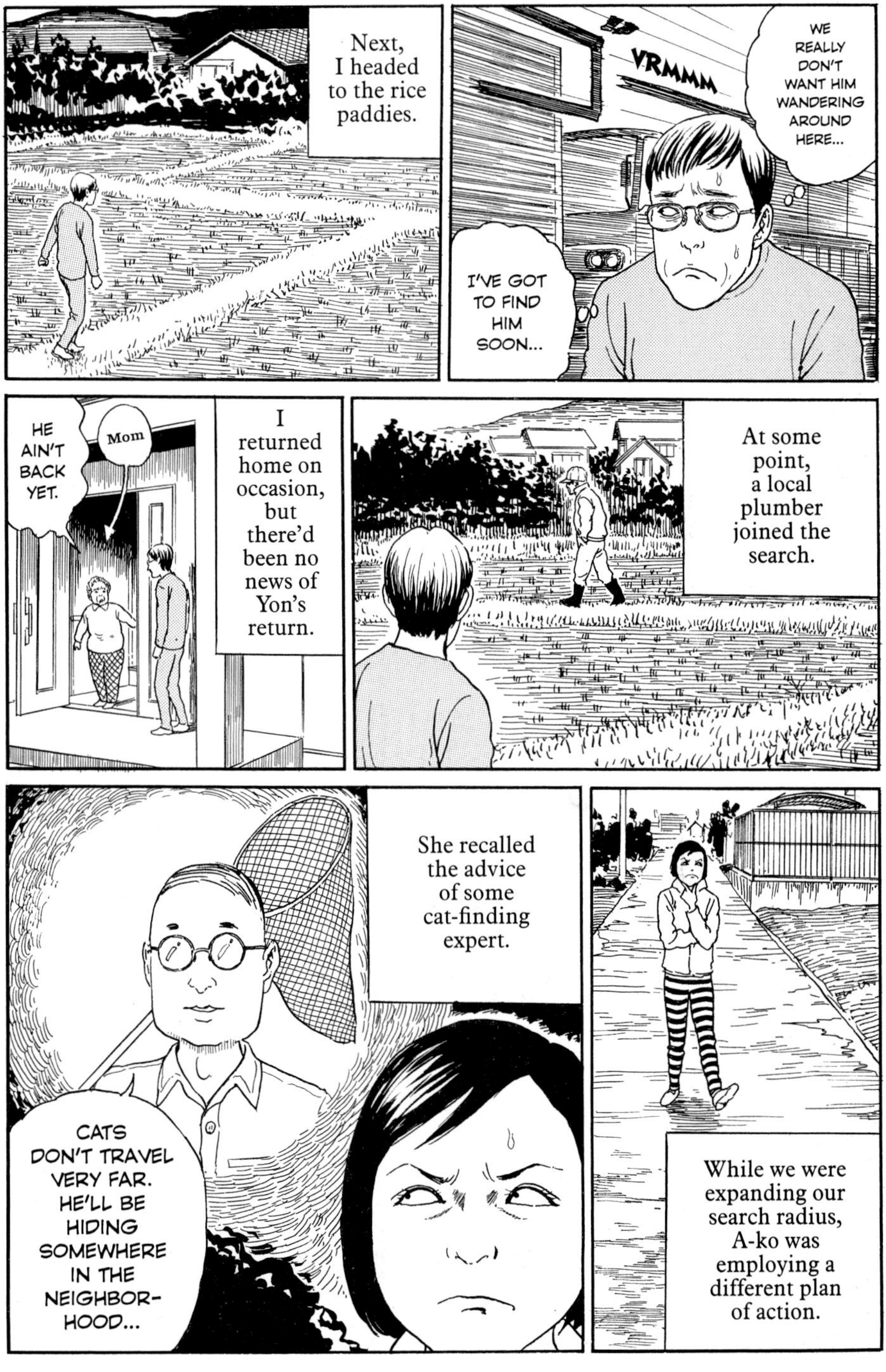
WE REALLY DON'T WANT HIM WANDERING AROUND HERE...
VRMMM
I'VE GOT TO FIND HIM SOON...
Next, I headed to the rice paddies.
At some point, a local plumber joined the search.
I returned home on occasion, but there'd been no news of Yon's return.
Mom
HE AIN'T BACK YET.
While we were expanding our search radius, A-ko was employing a different plan of action.
She recalled the advice of some cat-finding expert.
CATS DON'T TRAVEL VERY FAR. HE'LL BE HIDING SOMEWHERE IN THE NEIGHBOR-HOOD...

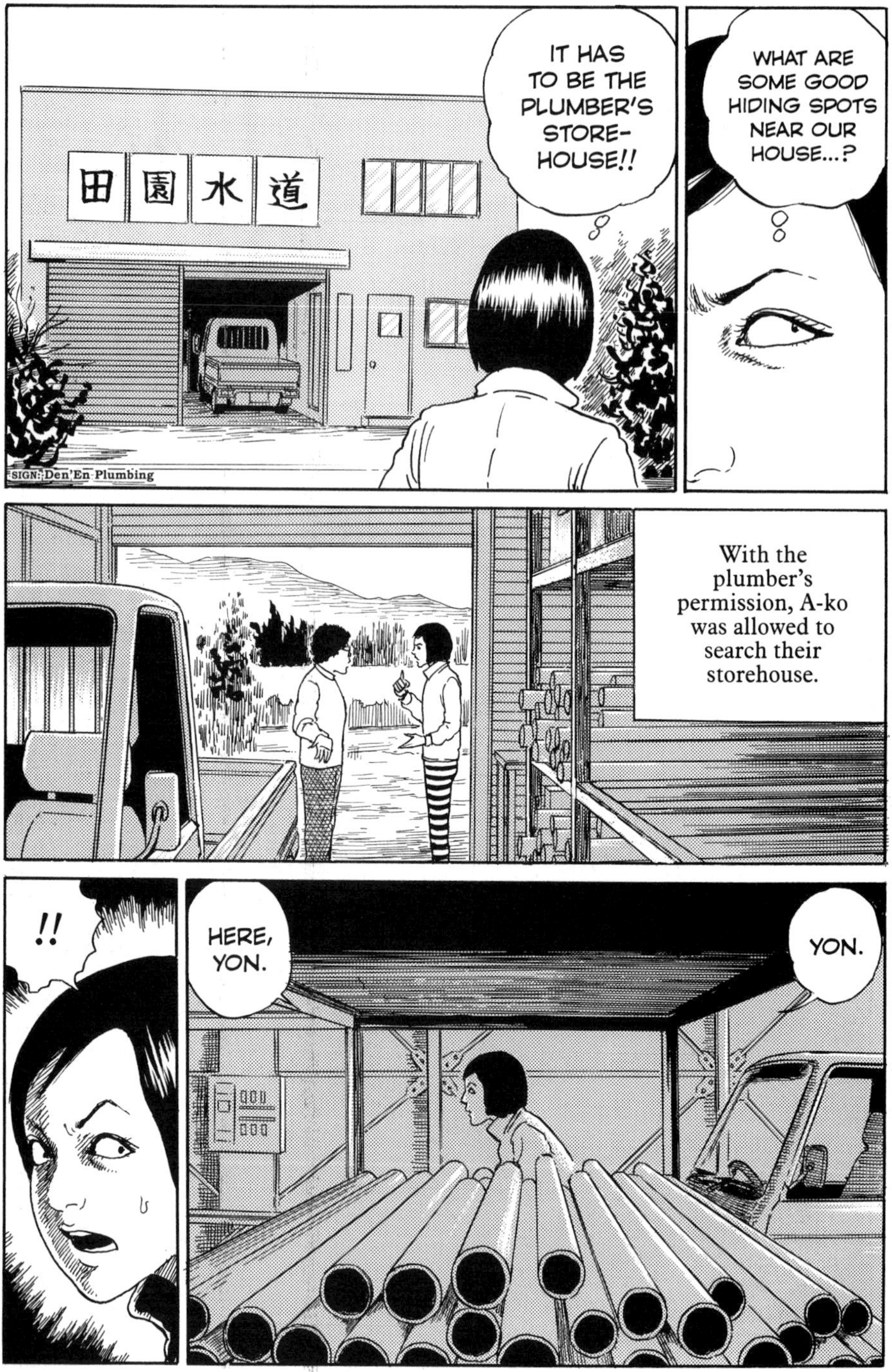
WHAT ARE SOME GOOD HIDING SPOTS NEAR OUR HOUSE...?
IT HAS TO BE THE PLUMBER'S STORE-HOUSE!!
田園水道
SIGN: Den'En Plumbing
With the plumber's permission, A-ko was allowed to search their storehouse.
YON.
HERE, YON.
!!

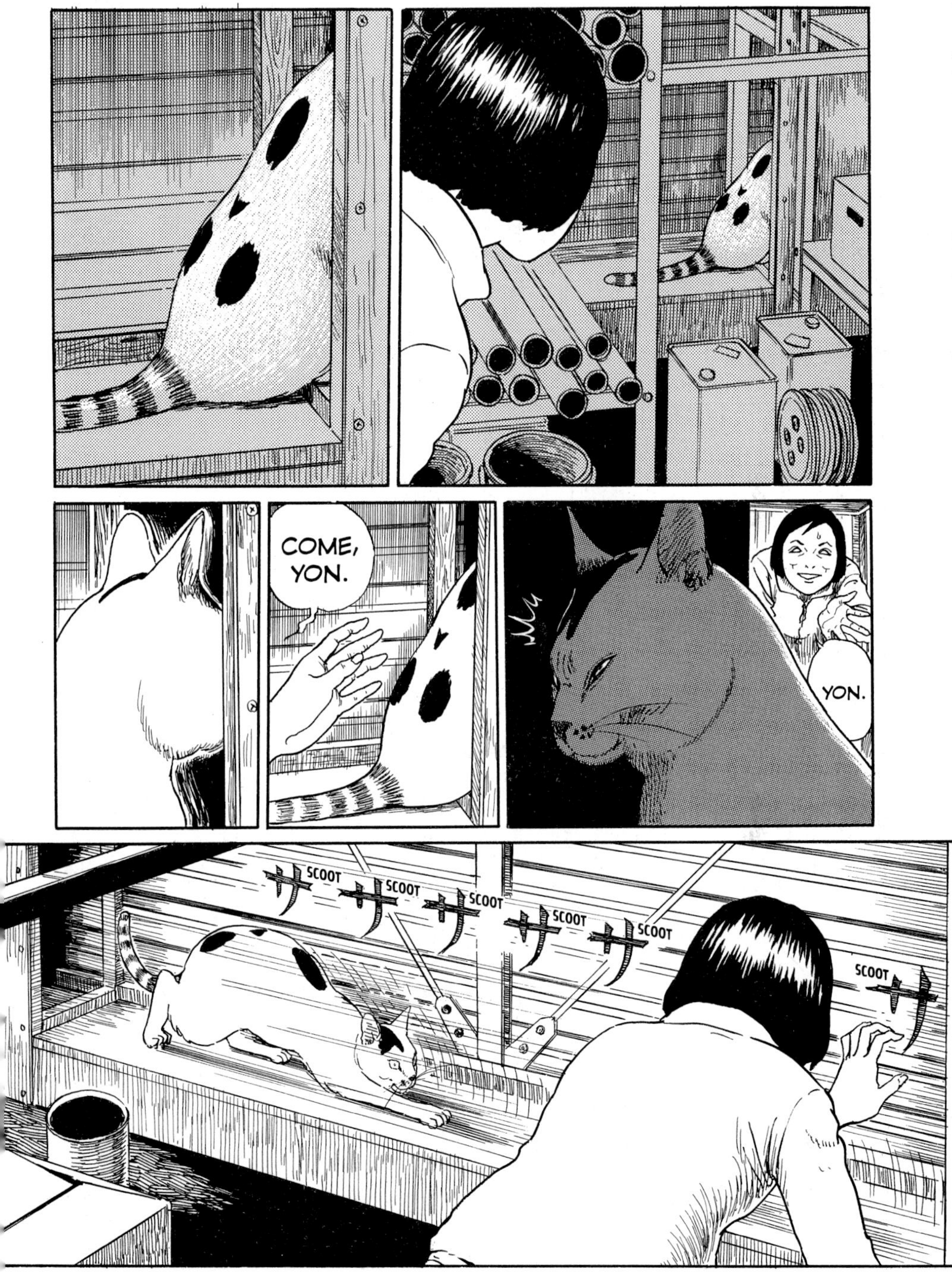
YON.
COME, YON.
SCOOT
SCOOT
SCOOT
SCOOT
SCOOT
SCOOT

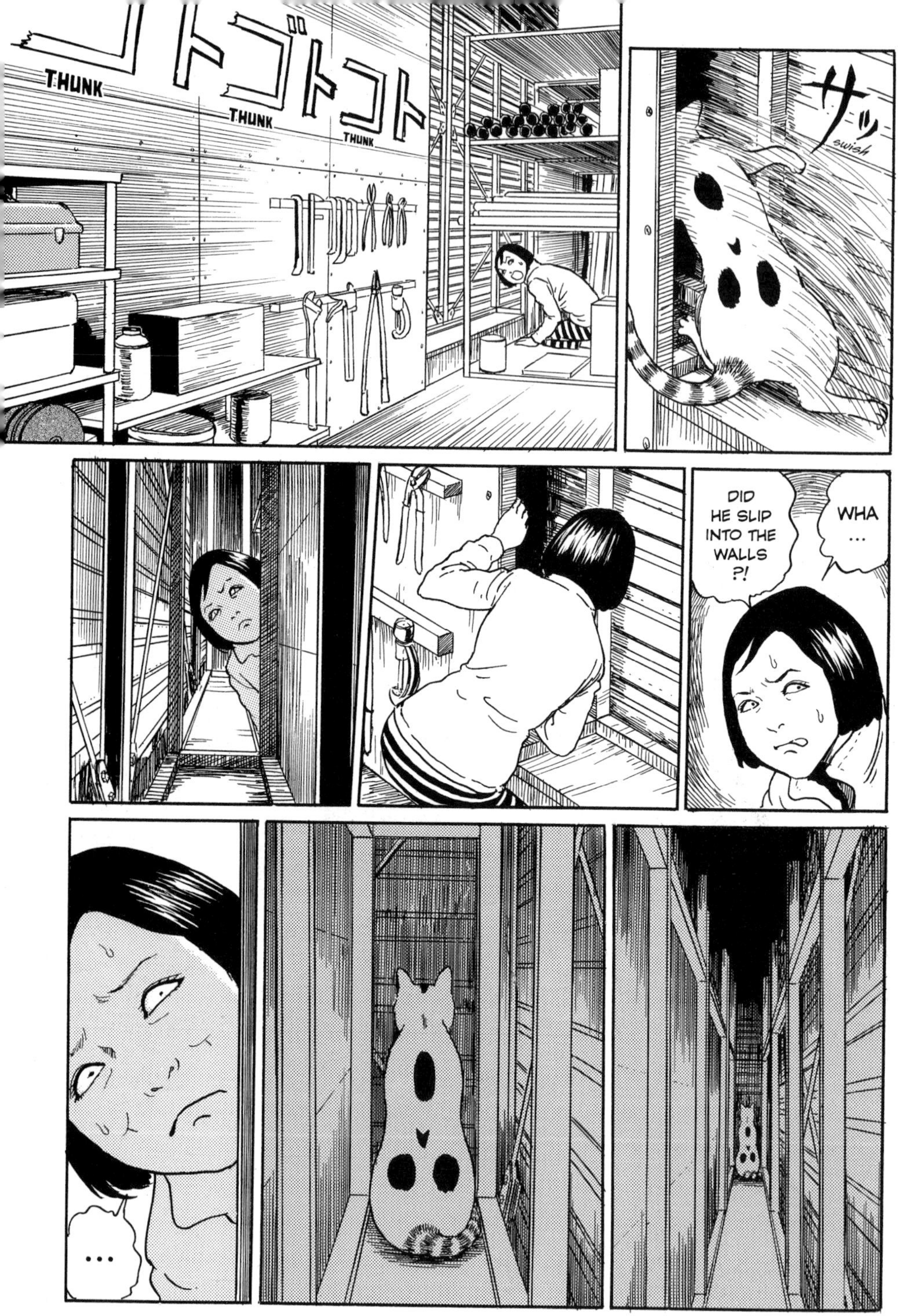
サッ
swish
コトゴトコト
THUNK
THUNK
THUNK
WHA ...
DID HE SLIP INTO THE WALLS ?!
...

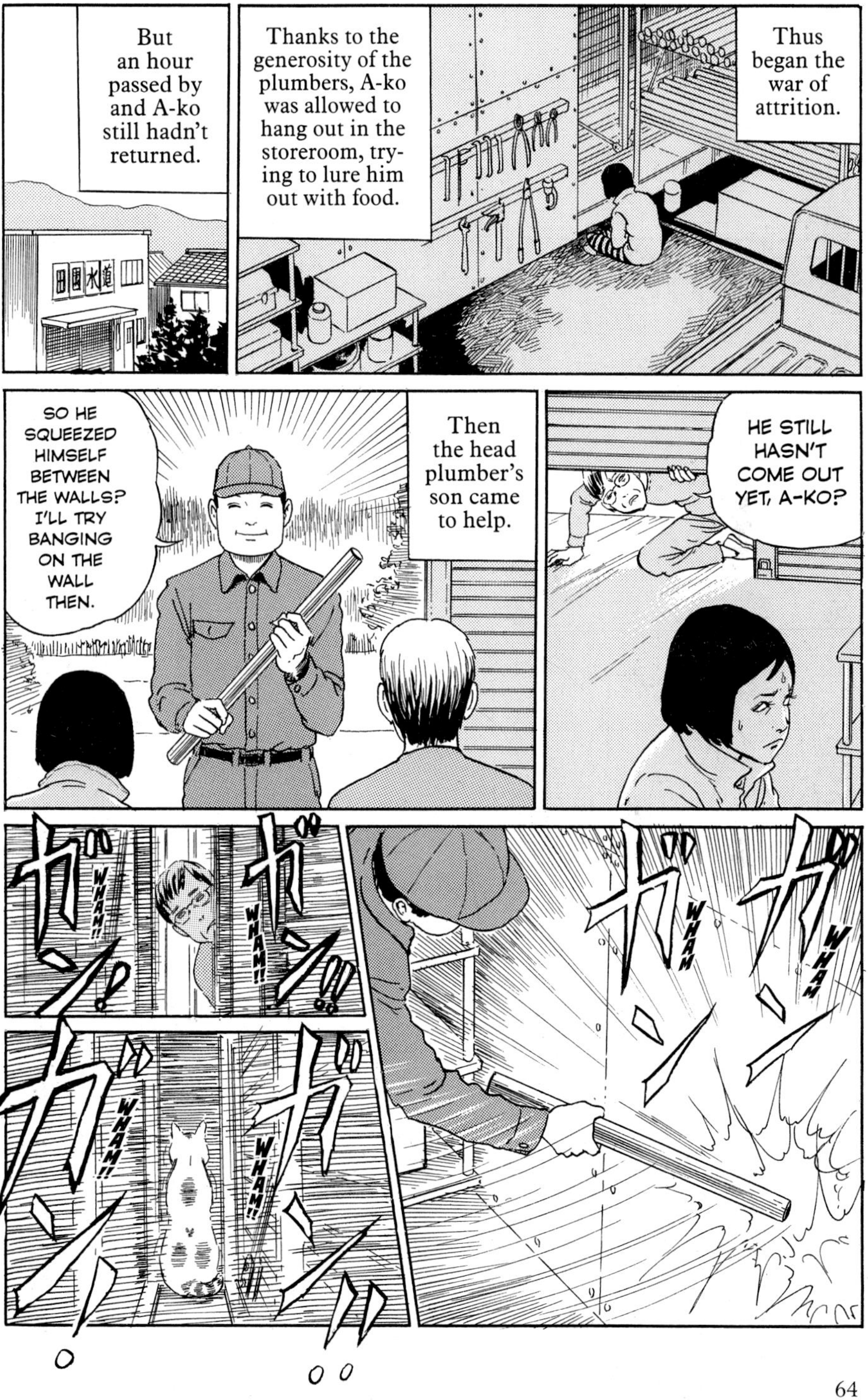
Thus began the war of attrition.
Thanks to the generosity of the plumbers, A-ko was allowed to hang out in the storeroom, trying to lure him out with food.
But an hour passed by and A-ko still hadn't returned.
田園水道
HE STILL HASN'T COME OUT YET, A-KO?
Then the head plumber's son came to help.
SO HE SQUEEZED HIMSELF BETWEEN THE WALLS? I'LL TRY BANGING ON THE WALL THEN.
ガン
WHAM
ガン
WHAM
ガン!!
WHAM!!
ガン!
WHAM!!
ガン
WHAM!!
ガン
WHAM!!

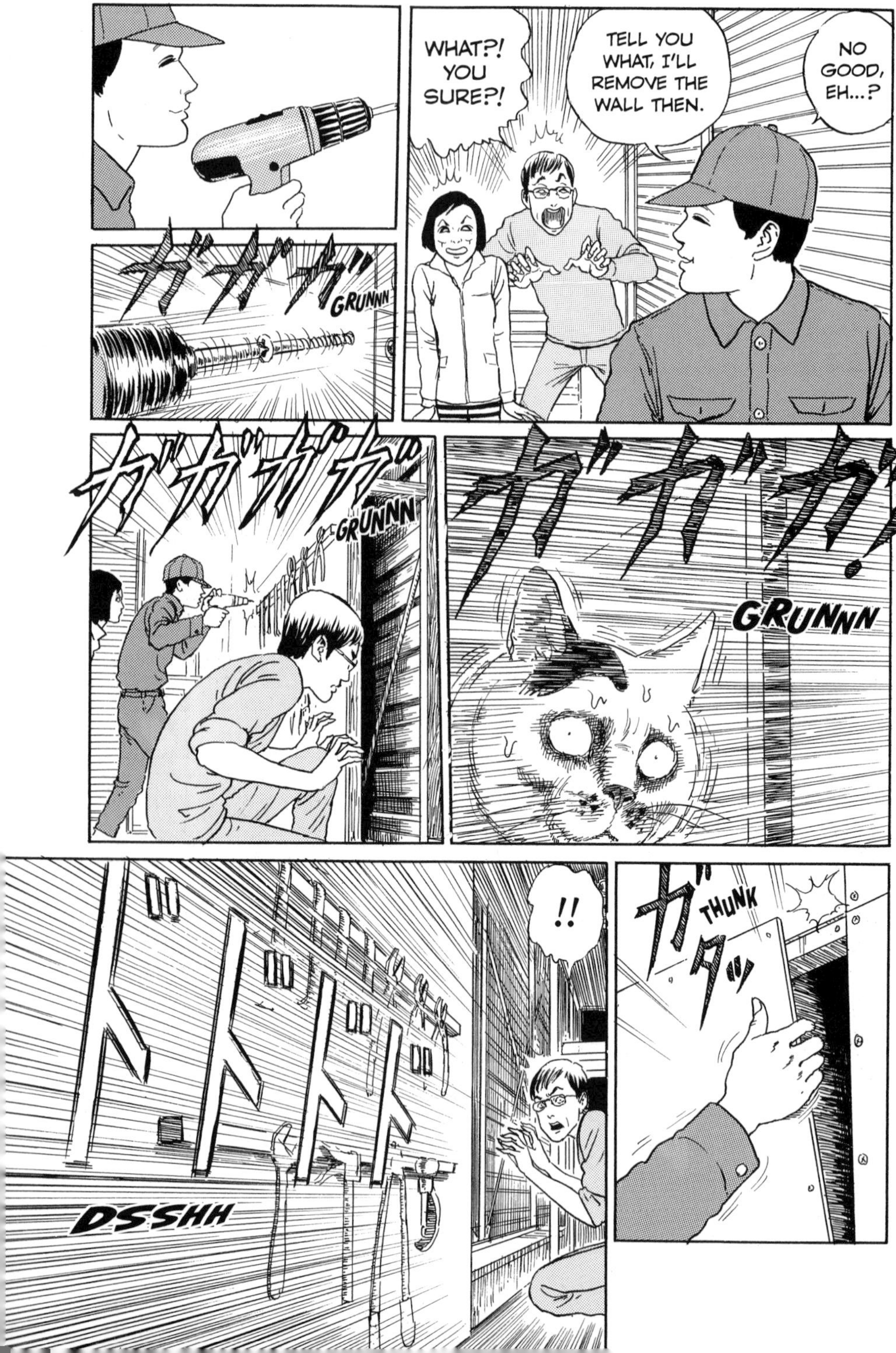
NO GOOD, EH...?
TELL YOU WHAT, I'LL REMOVE THE WALL THEN.
WHAT?! YOU SURE?!
ガガガ
GRUNNN
ガガガ!!
GRUNNN
ガガガガ
GRUNNN
ガタッ
THUNK
!!
ドドドド
DSSHH

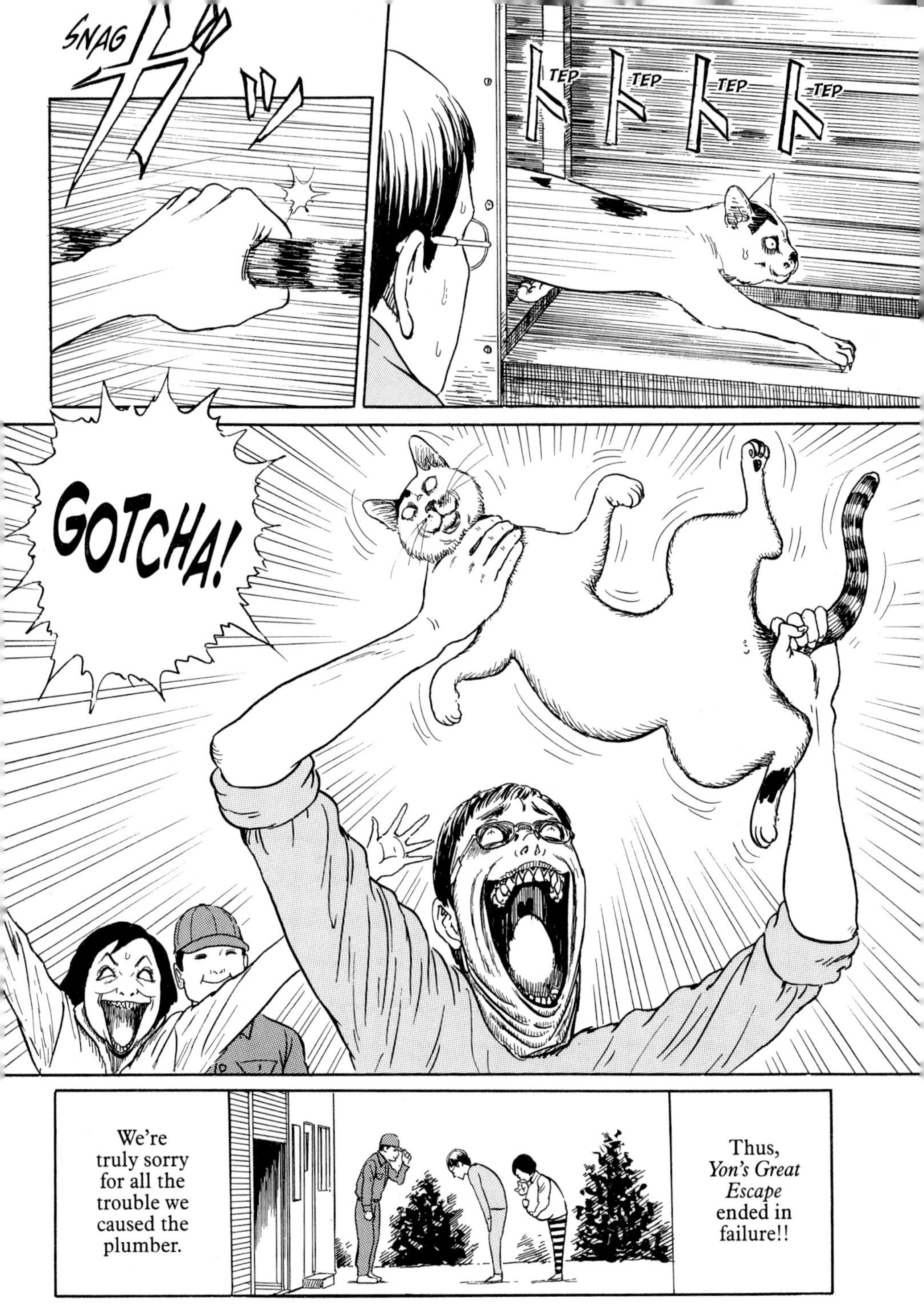
TEP TEP TEP TEP
SNAG
GOTCHA!
Thus, *Yon's Great Escape* ended in failure!!
We're truly sorry for all the trouble we caused the plumber.

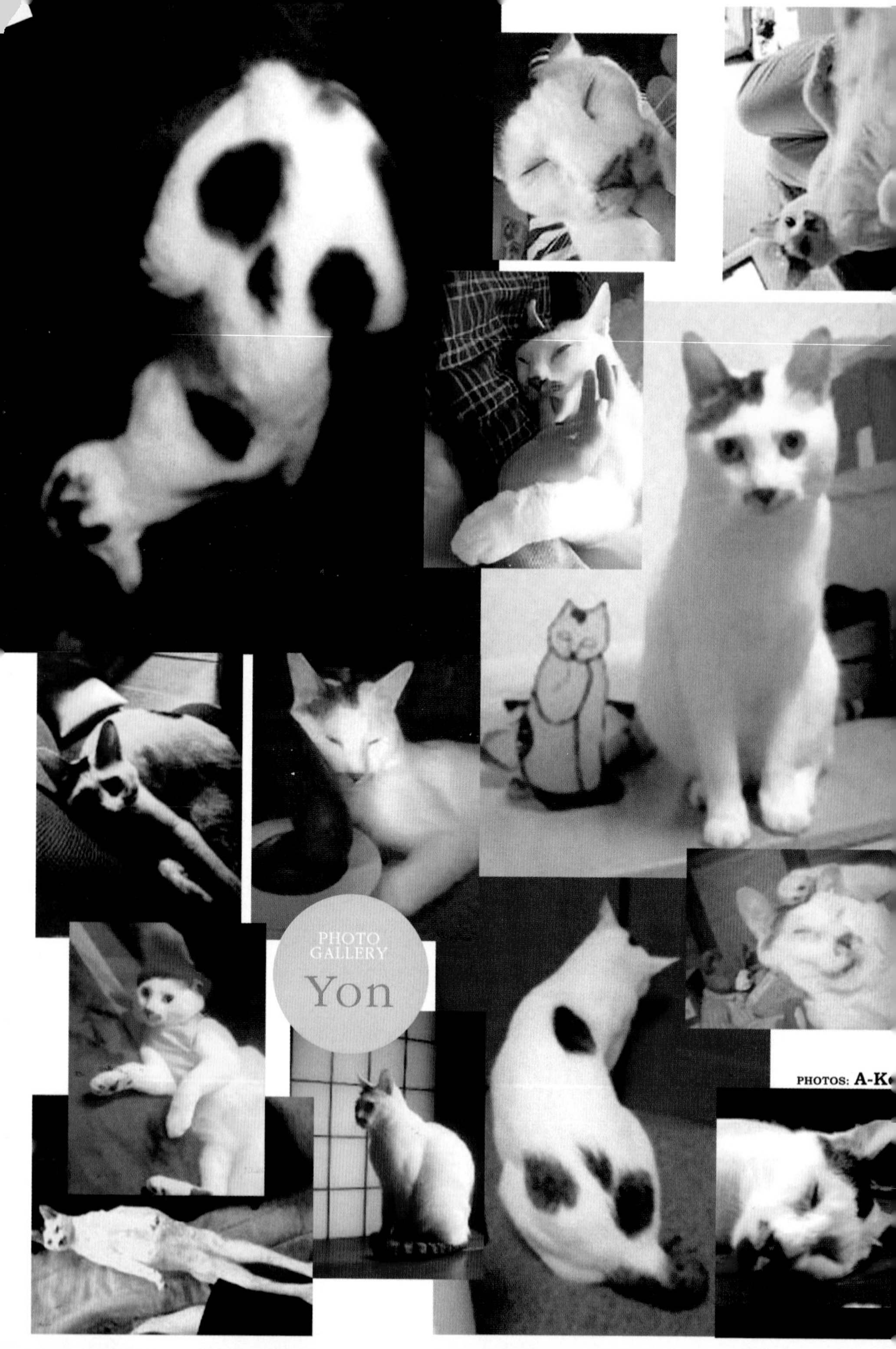

PHOTO GALLERY

Yon

PHOTOS: A-K

PHOTO GALLERY

Mû

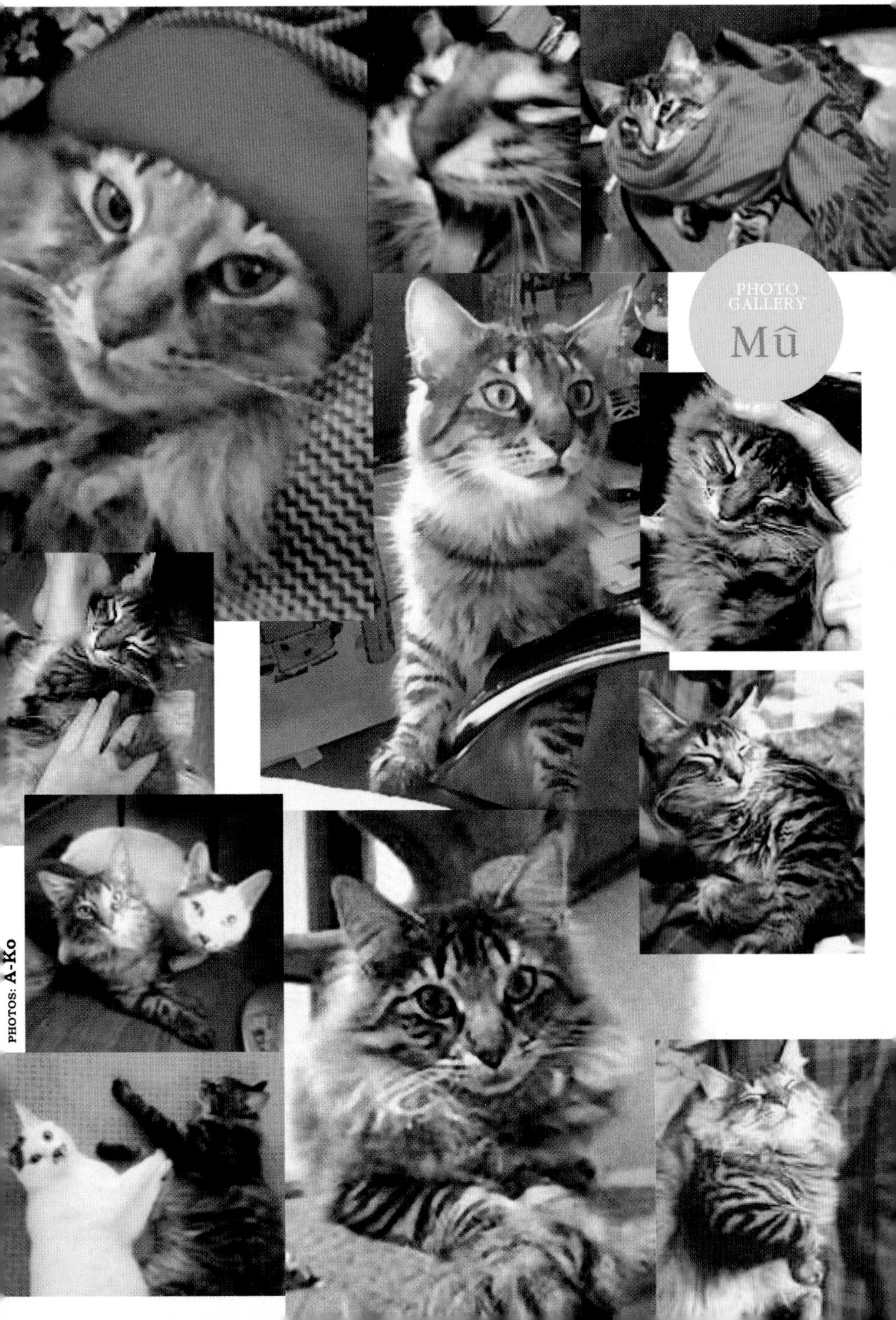

PHOTOS: A-Ko

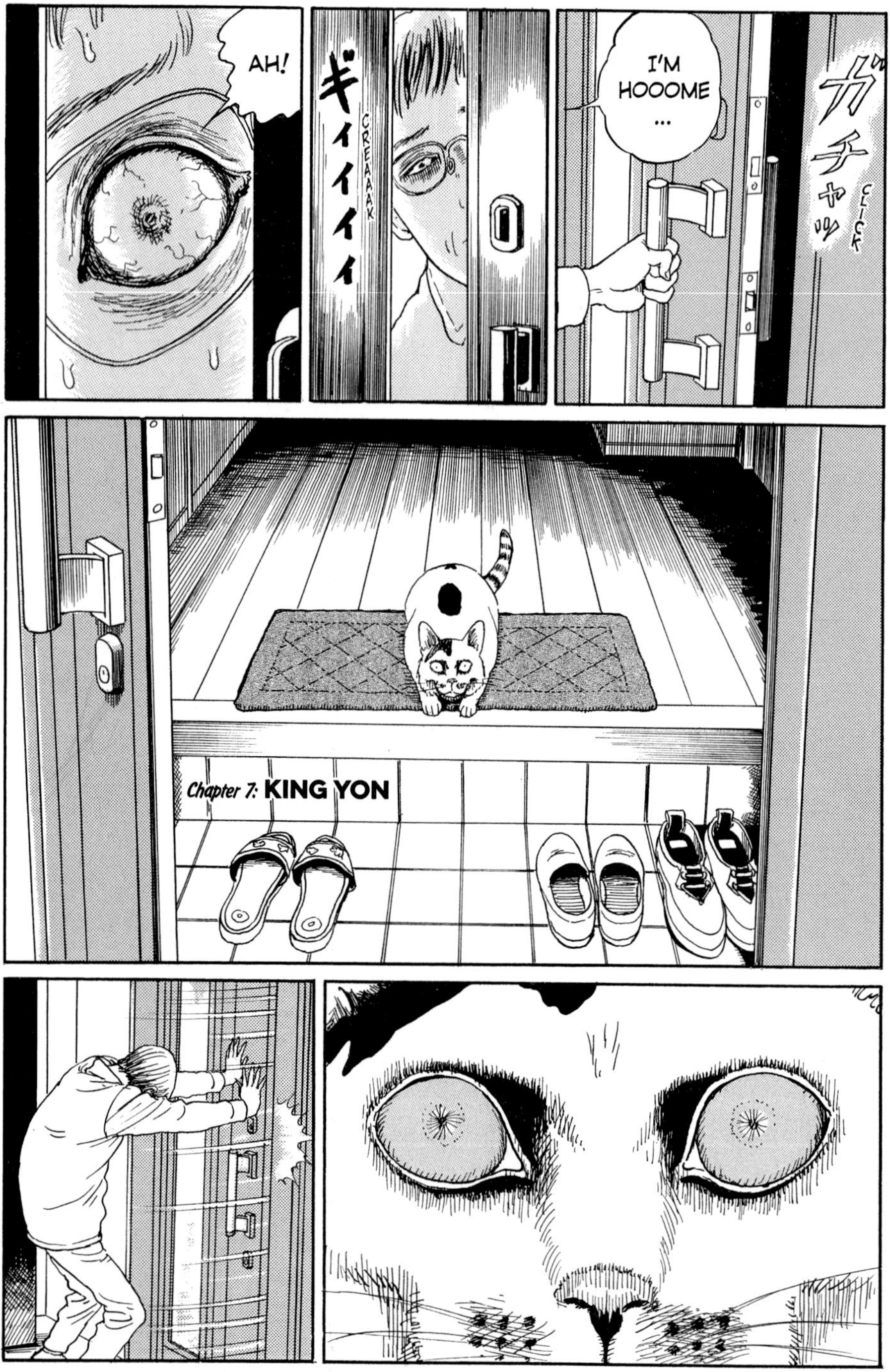
ガチャッ
CLICK
I'M HOOOME ...
ギイイイイ
CREAAAK
AH!
Chapter 7: KING YON

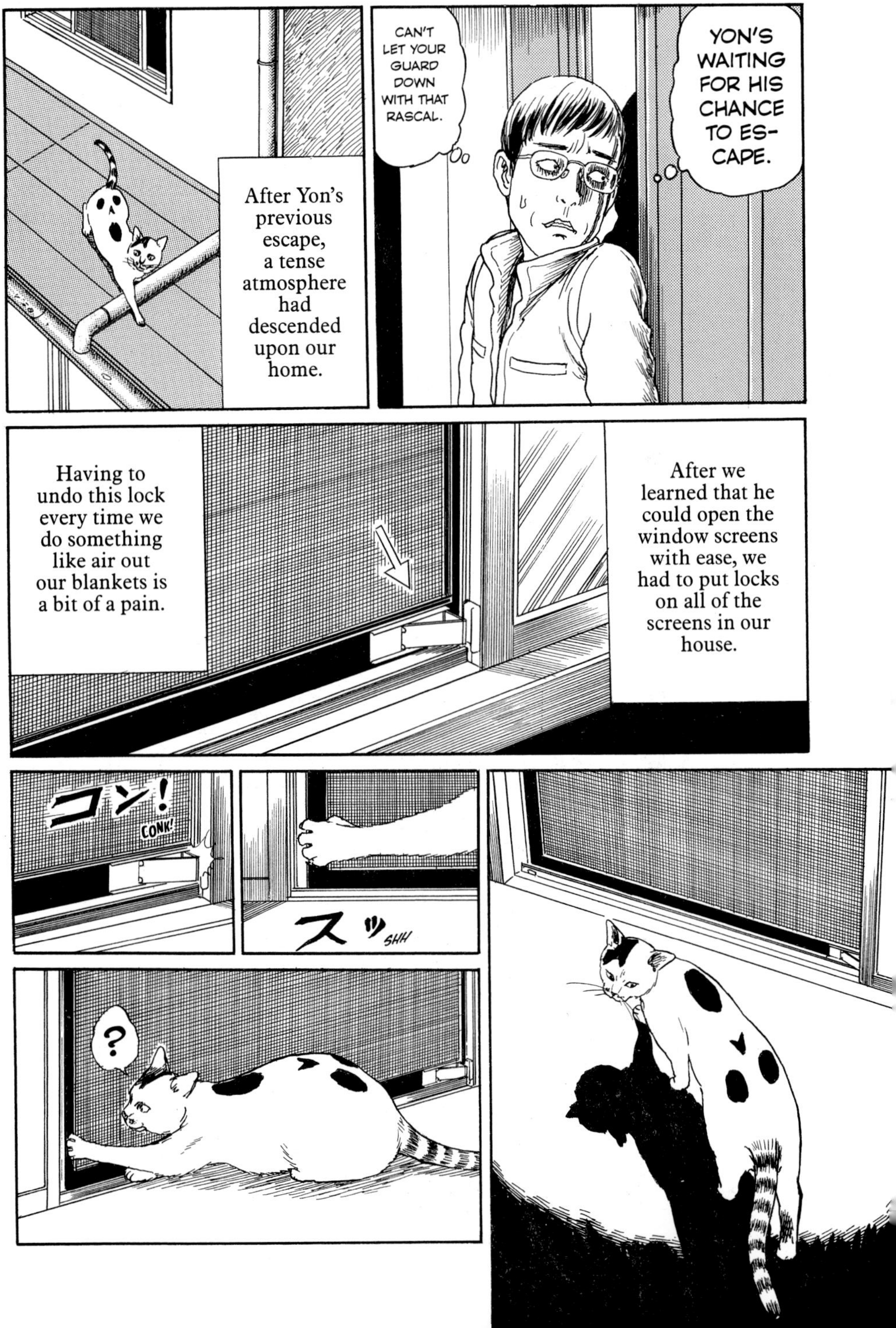
YON'S WAITING FOR HIS CHANCE TO ES-CAPE.
CAN'T LET YOUR GUARD DOWN WITH THAT RASCAL.
After Yon's previous escape, a tense atmosphere had descended upon our home.
After we learned that he could open the window screens with ease, we had to put locks on all of the screens in our house.
Having to undo this lock every time we do something like air out our blankets is a bit of a pain.
スッ
SHH
コン!
CONK!
?

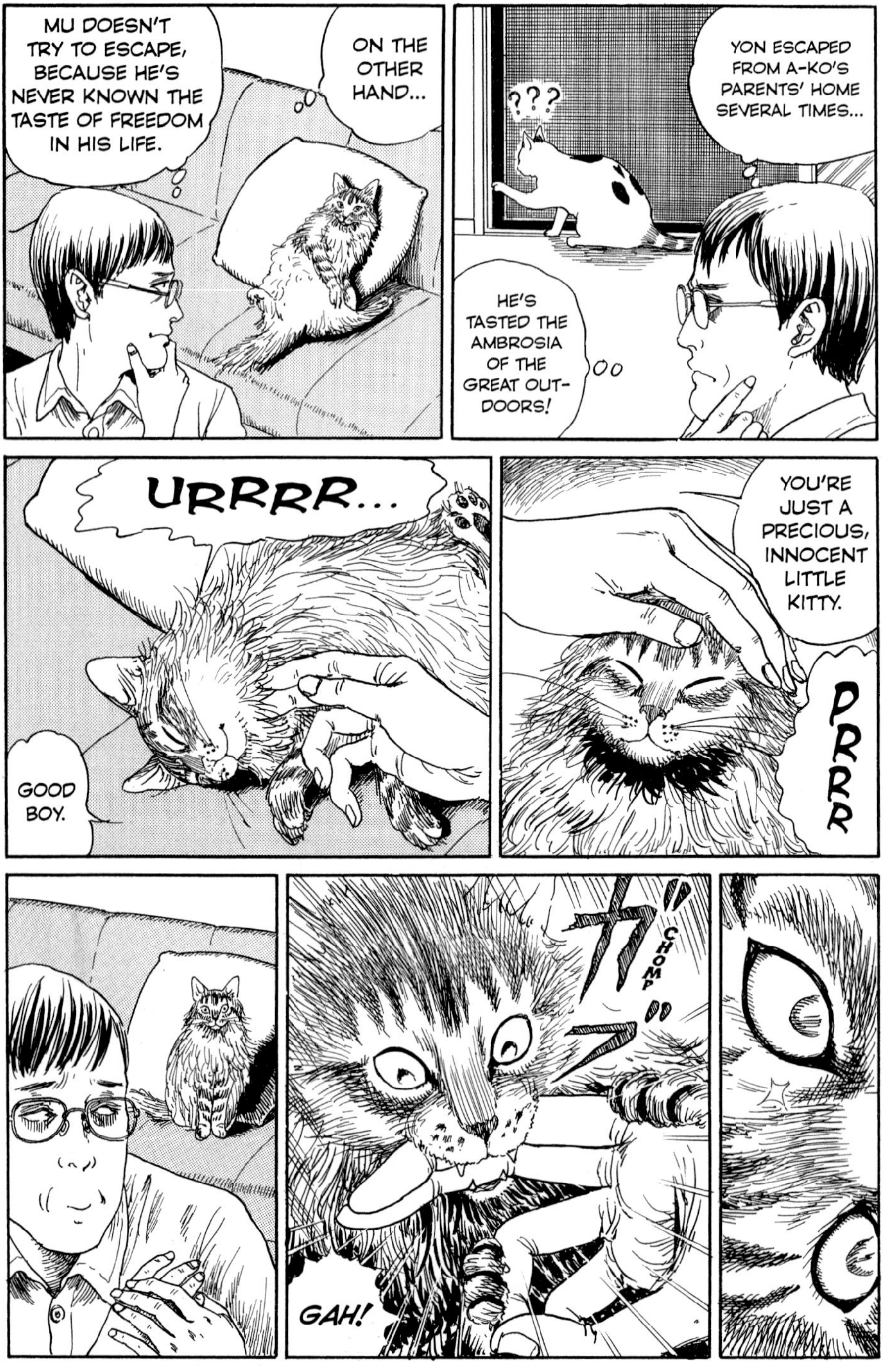
MU DOESN'T TRY TO ESCAPE, BECAUSE HE'S NEVER KNOWN THE TASTE OF FREEDOM IN HIS LIFE.
ON THE OTHER HAND...
???
YON ESCAPED FROM A-KO'S PARENTS' HOME SEVERAL TIMES...
HE'S TASTED THE AMBROSIA OF THE GREAT OUT-DOORS!
URRRR...
GOOD BOY.
YOU'RE JUST A PRECIOUS, INNOCENT LITTLE KITTY.
PRRR
CHOMP
GAH!

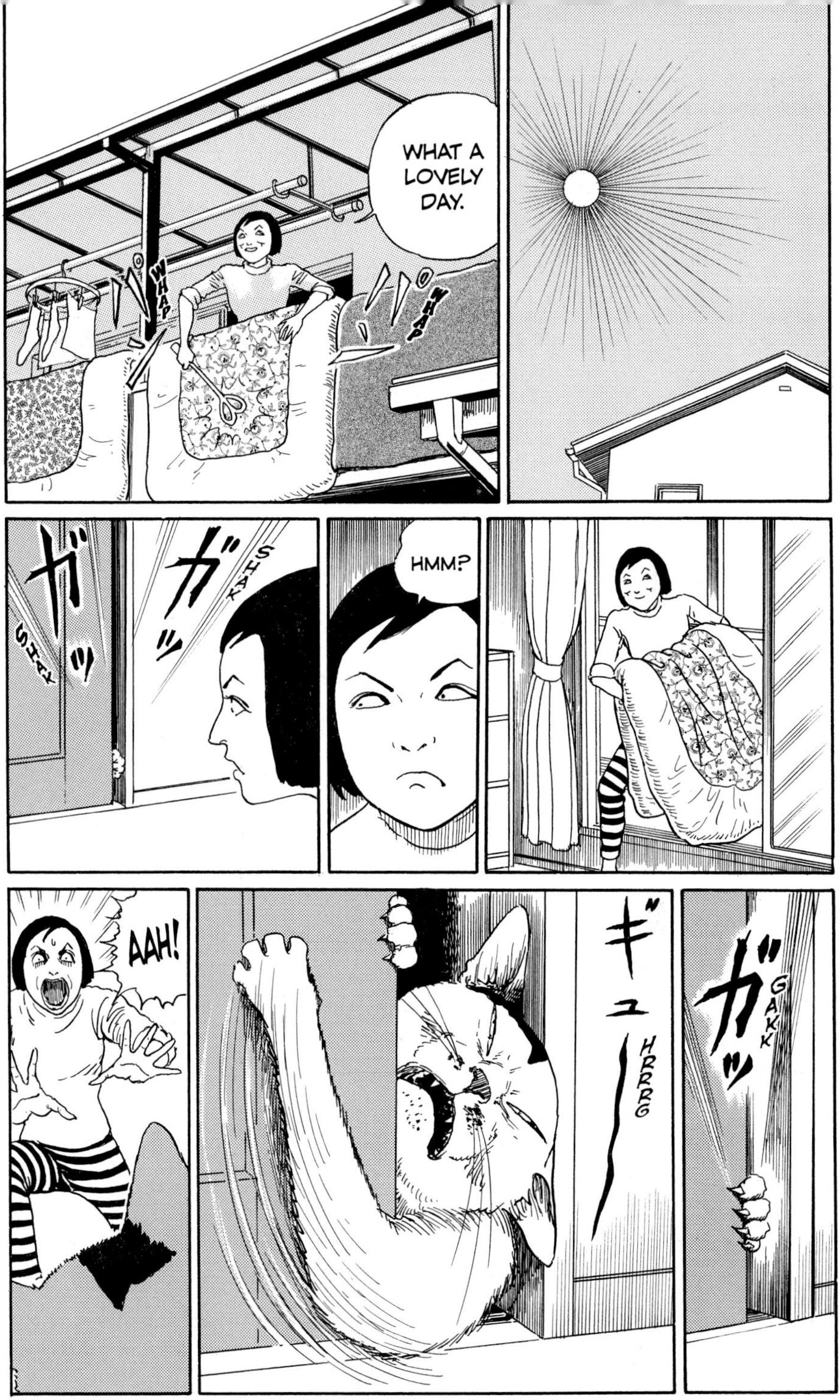
WHAT A LOVELY DAY.
WHAP
WHAP
HMM?
ガッ
SHAK
ガッ
SHAK
ガッ
GAKK
ギュー
HRRRG
AAH!

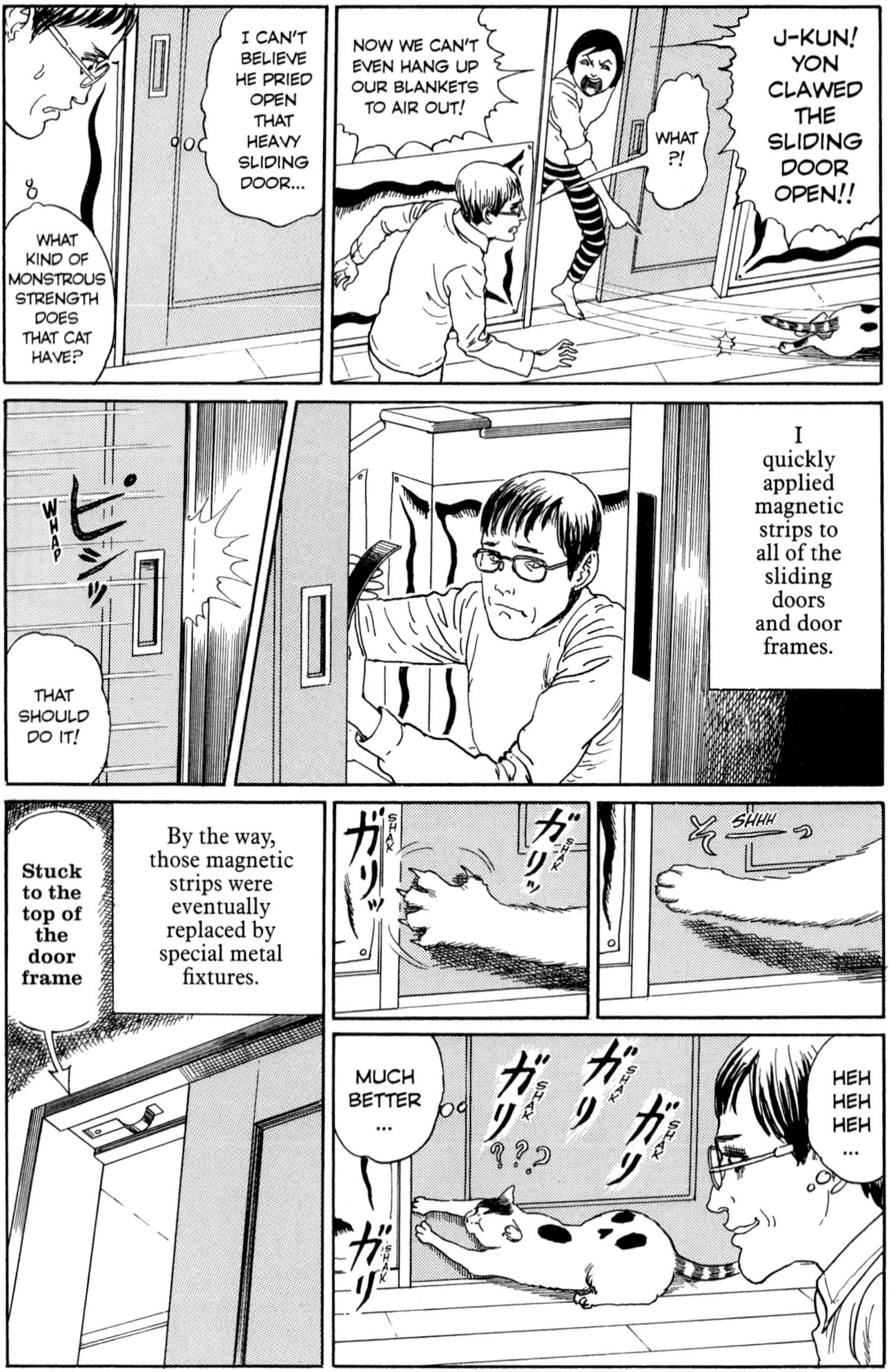
J-KUN! YON CLAWED THE SLIDING DOOR OPEN!!
WHAT?!
NOW WE CAN'T EVEN HANG UP OUR BLANKETS TO AIR OUT!
I CAN'T BELIEVE HE PRIED OPEN THAT HEAVY SLIDING DOOR...
WHAT KIND OF MONSTROUS STRENGTH DOES THAT CAT HAVE?
I quickly applied magnetic strips to all of the sliding doors and door frames.
ピシッ
WHAP
THAT SHOULD DO IT!
そー
SHHH
ガリッ
SHAK
ガリッ
SHAK
HEH HEH HEH ...
ガリ
SHAK
ガリ
SHAK
ガリ
SHAK
???
MUCH BETTER ...
ガリ
SHAK
By the way, those magnetic strips were eventually replaced by special metal fixtures.
Stuck to the top of the door frame

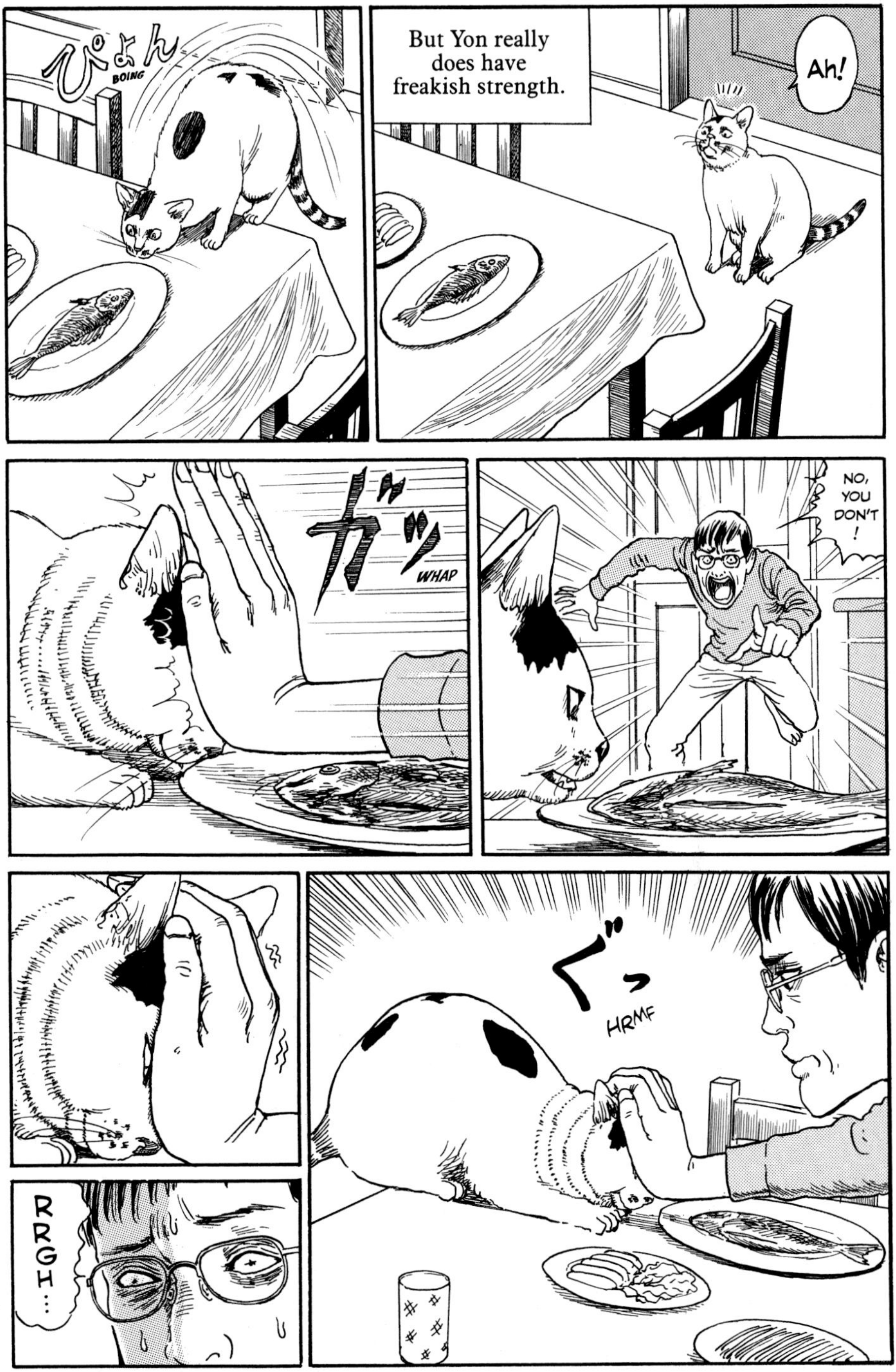
But Yon really does have freakish strength.
Ah!
ぴょん
BOING
NO, YOU DON'T!
ガッ
WHAP
ぐっ
HRMF
RRGH...

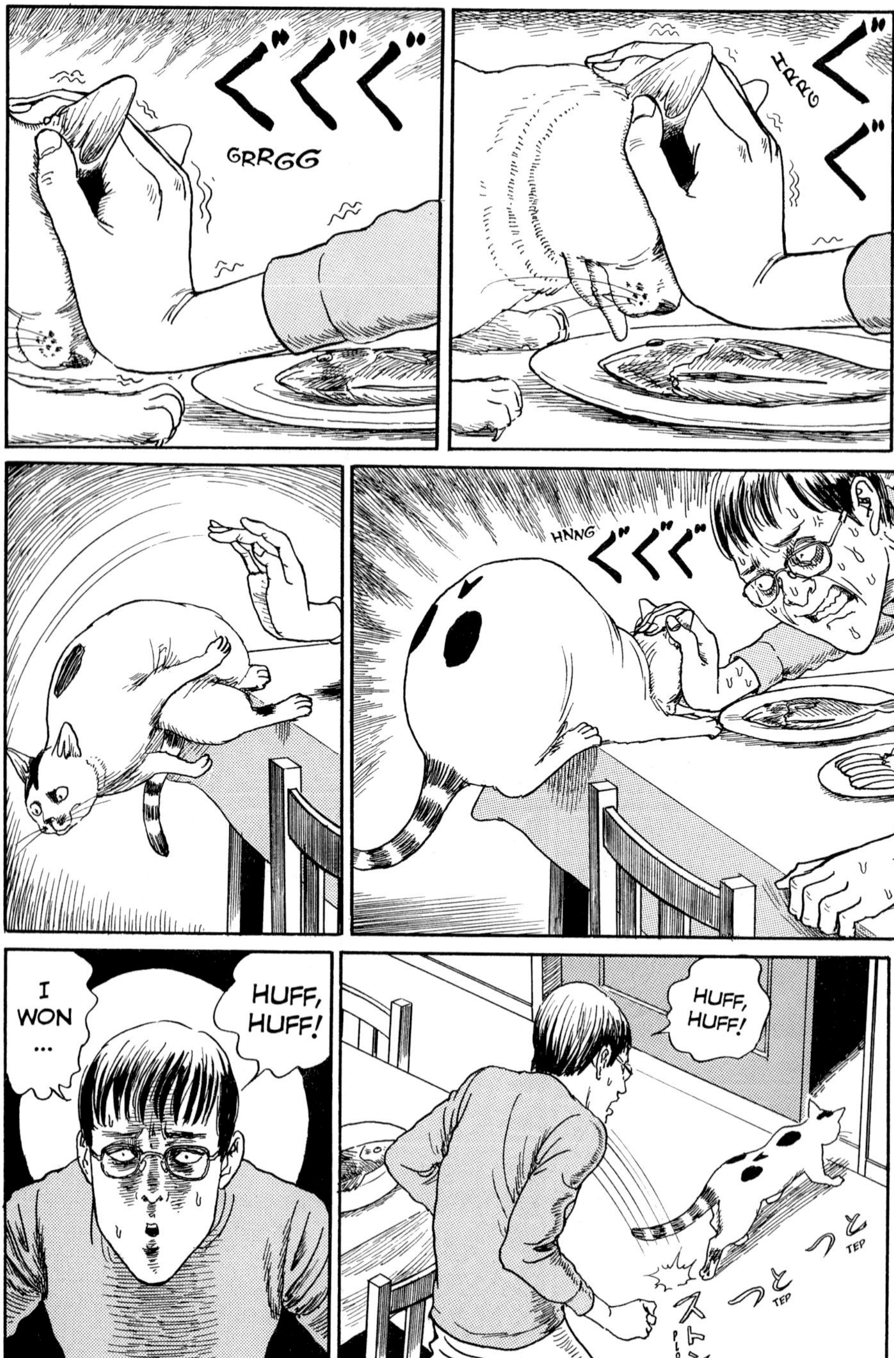
ぐぐ
HRRG
ぐぐぐ
GRRGG
HNNG
ぐぐぐ
HUFF, HUFF!
つと
TEP
つと
TEP
ストン
PLOP
HUFF, HUFF!
I WON ...

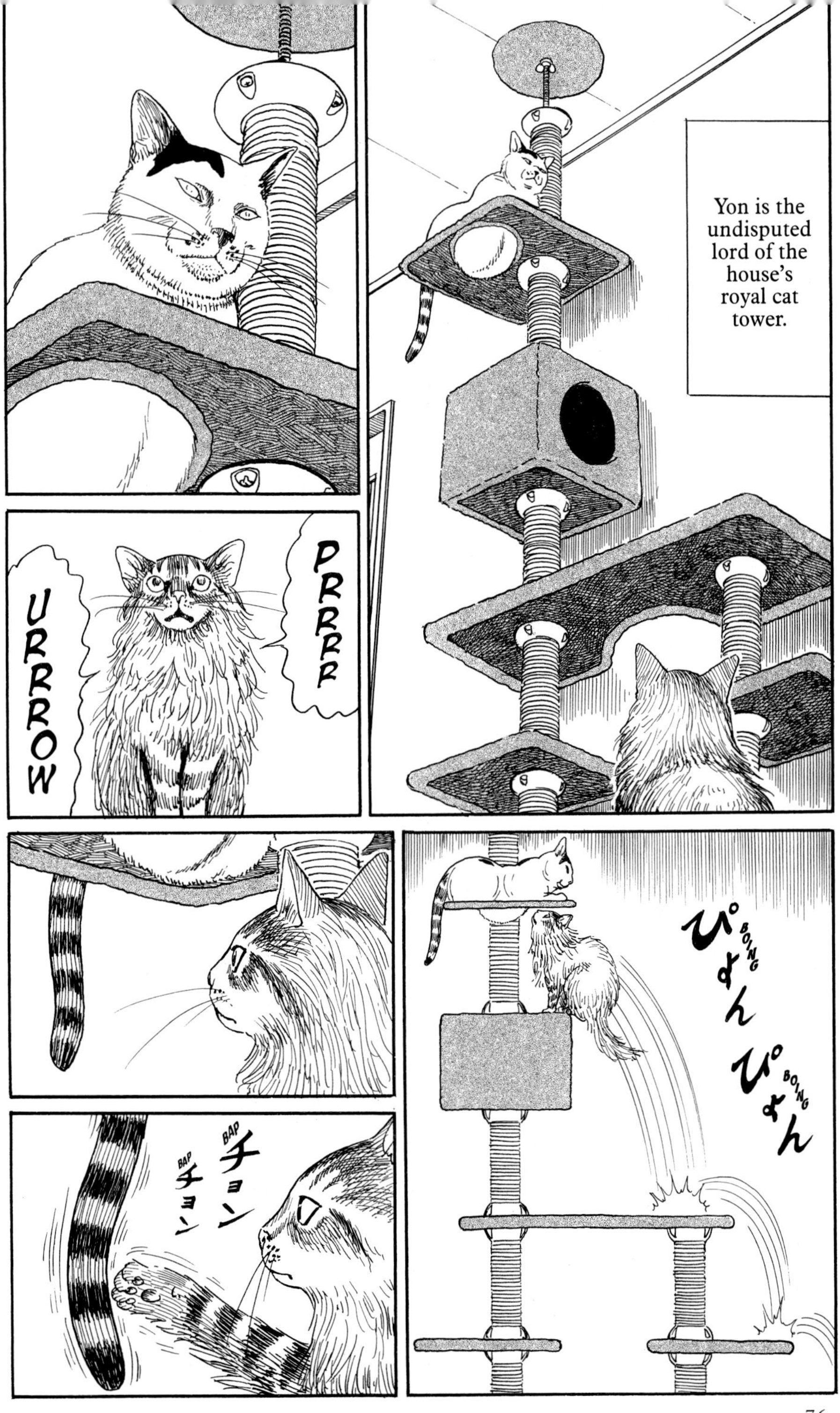
Yon is the undisputed lord of the house's royal cat tower.
PRRRR
URRROW
ぴょん BOING
ぴょん BOING
チョン BAP
チョン BAP

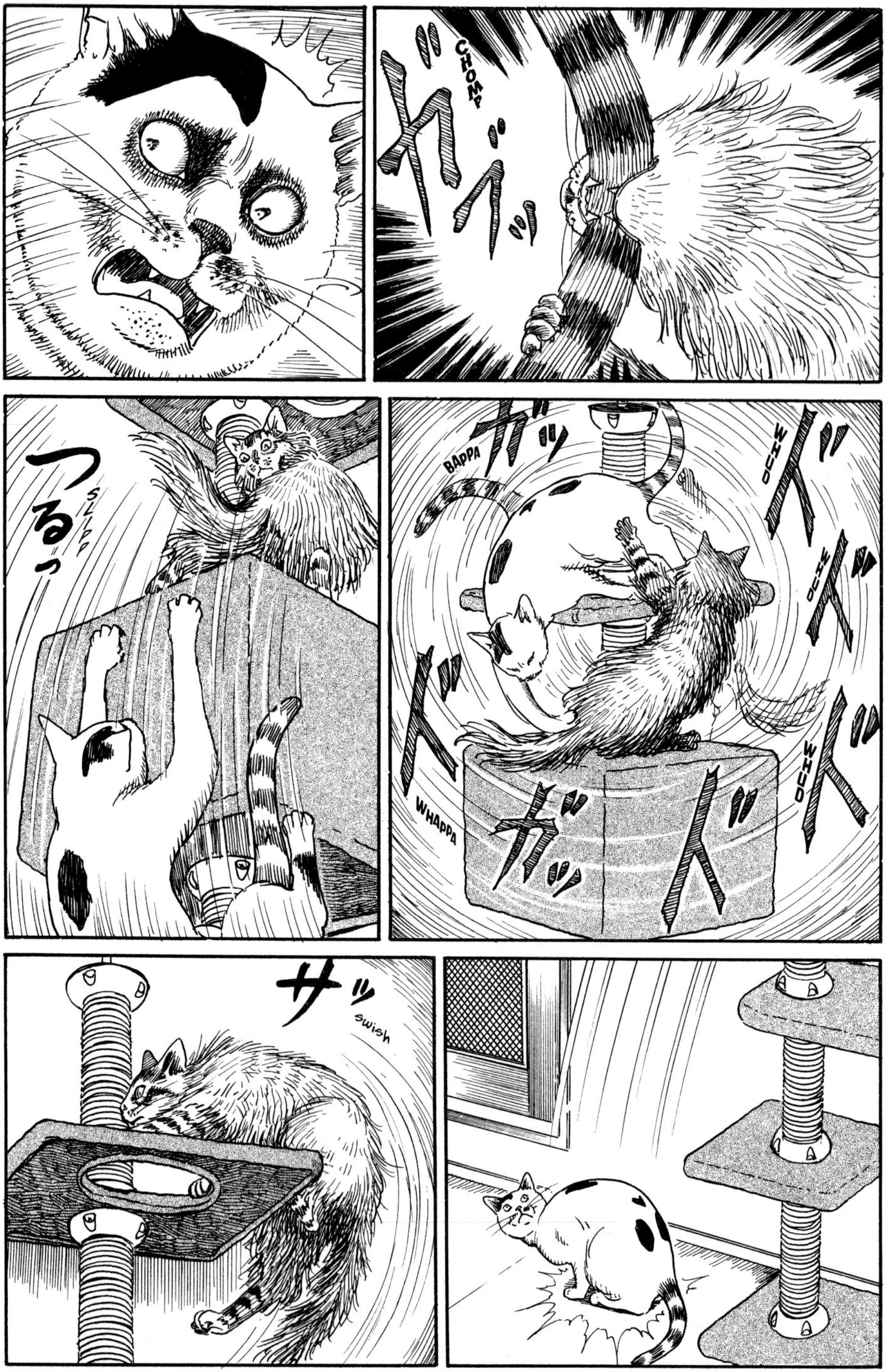
ガブッ
CHOMP
ガッ
BAPPA
WHUD
WHUD
WHAPPA
つるっ
SLIPP
サッ
swish

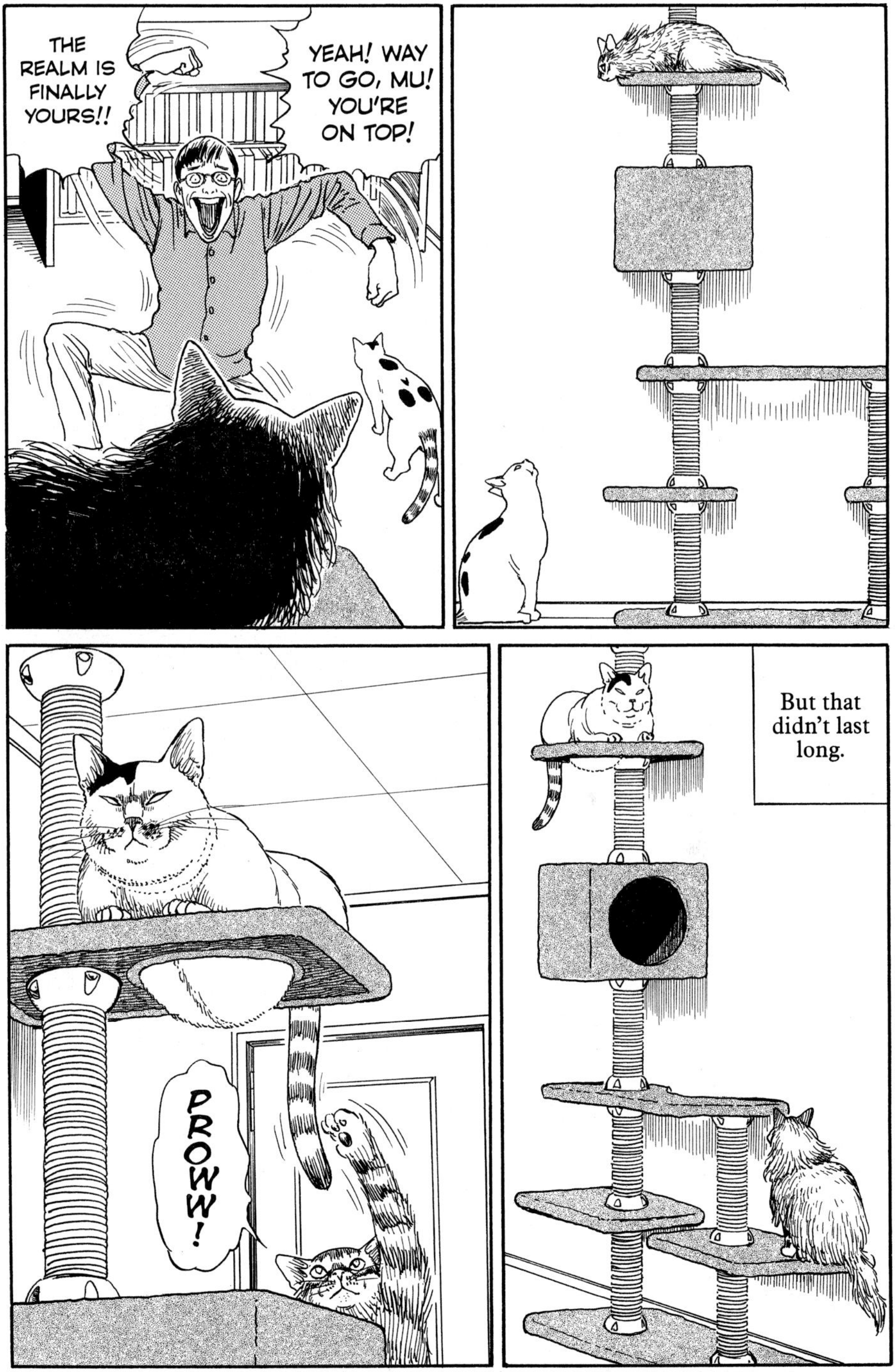
YEAH! WAY TO GO, MU! YOU'RE ON TOP!
THE REALM IS FINALLY YOURS!!
But that didn't last long.
PROWW!

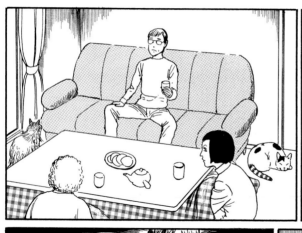

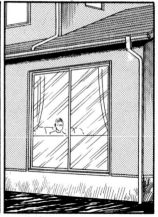

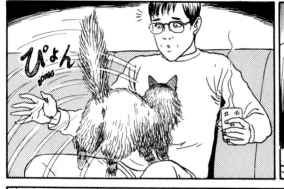

PRRRR.

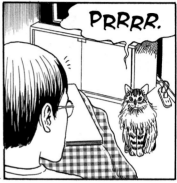

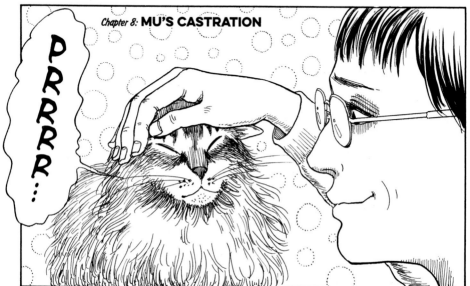

Chapter 8: **MU'S CASTRATION**

P R R R R...

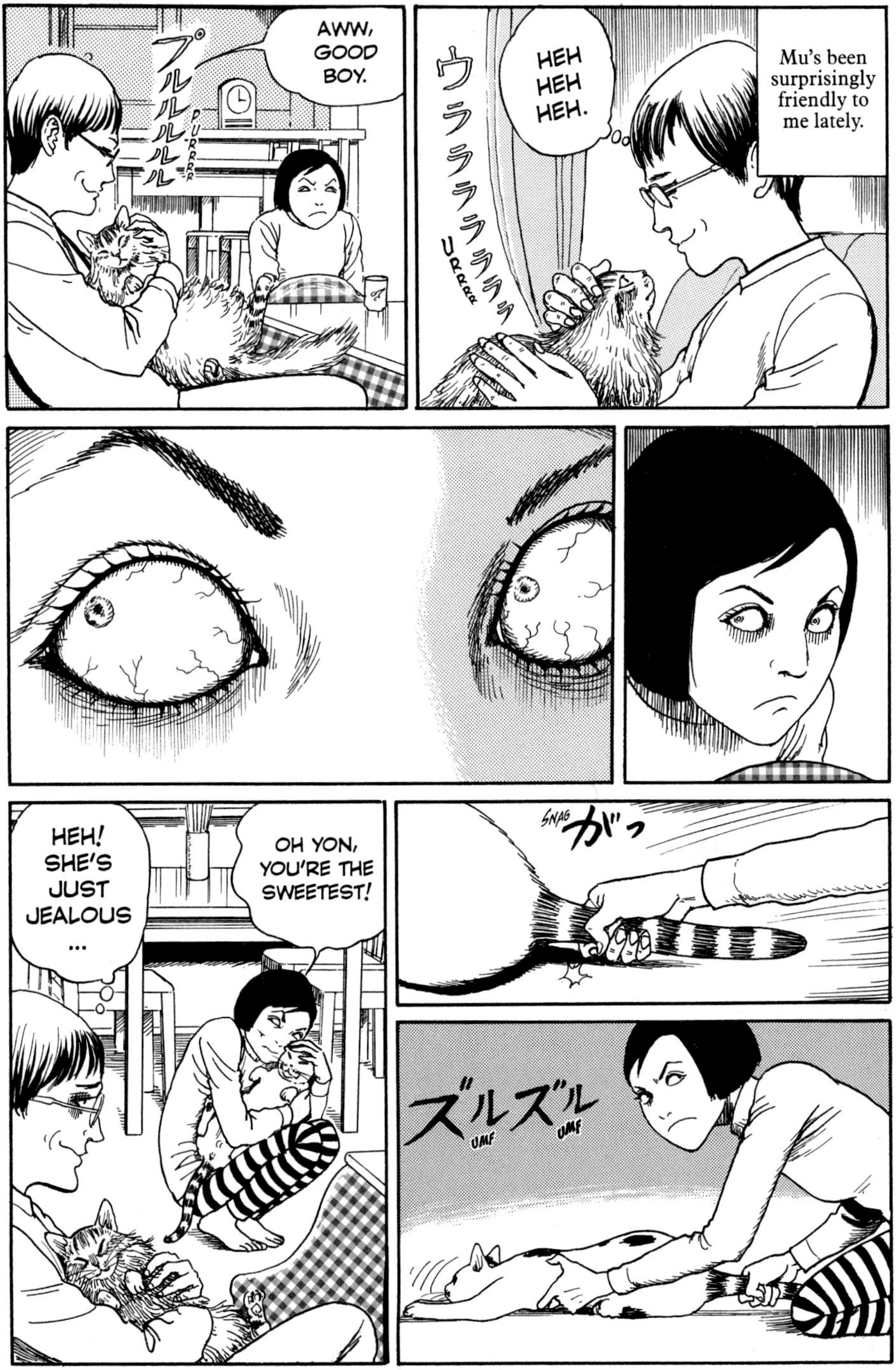
Mu's been surprisingly friendly to me lately.
HEH HEH HEH.
ウララララララララ
URRRR
AWW, GOOD BOY.
プルルルルル
PURRRR
SNAG
がっ
ズルズル
UMF UMF
OH YON, YOU'RE THE SWEETEST!
HEH! SHE'S JUST JEALOUS ...

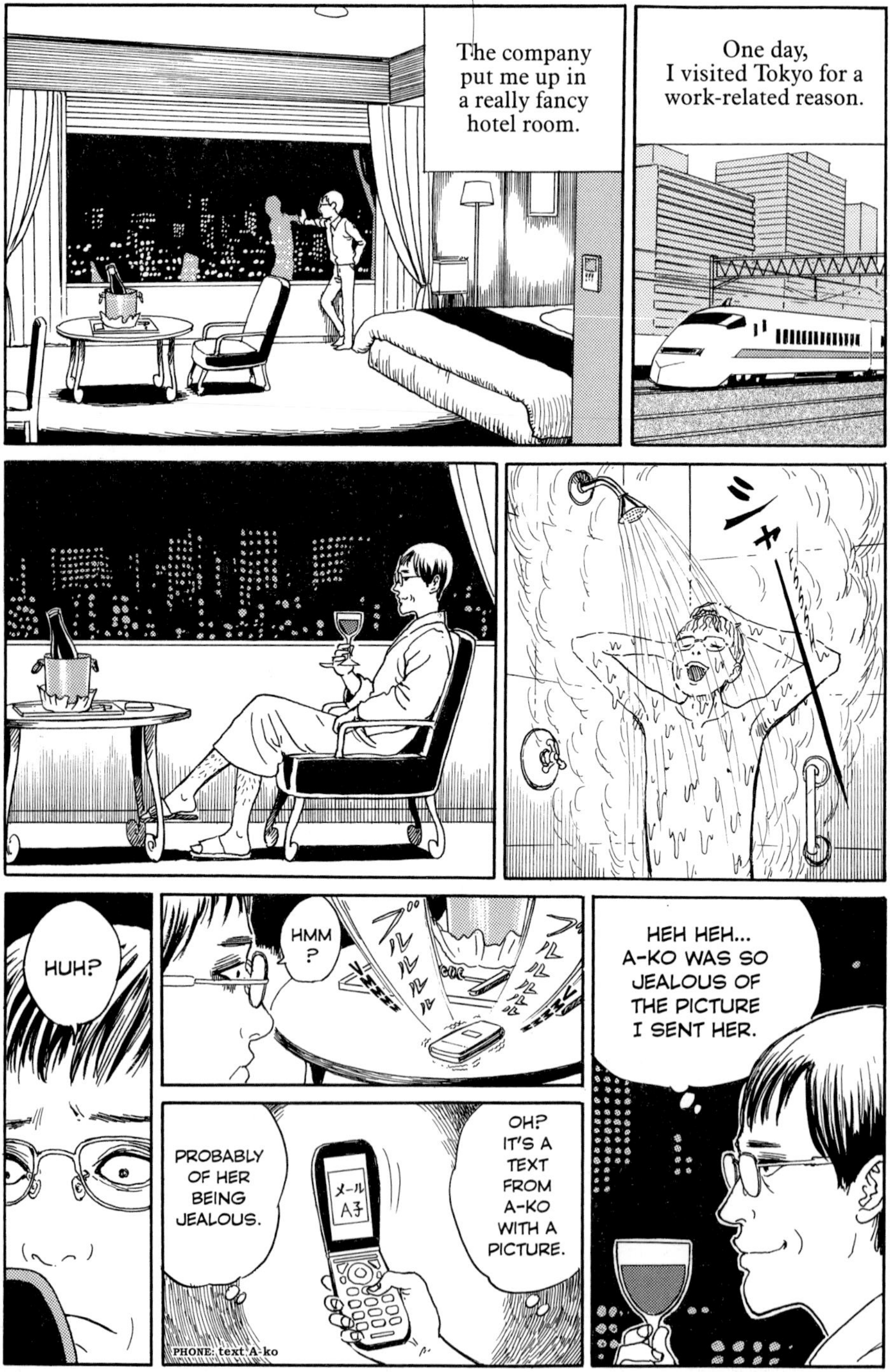
One day, I visited Tokyo for a work-related reason.
The company put me up in a really fancy hotel room.
シャ
HEH HEH... A-KO WAS SO JEALOUS OF THE PICTURE I SENT HER.
HMM ?
OH? IT'S A TEXT FROM A-KO WITH A PICTURE.
PROBABLY OF HER BEING JEALOUS.
メール A子
PHONE: text A-ko
HUH?

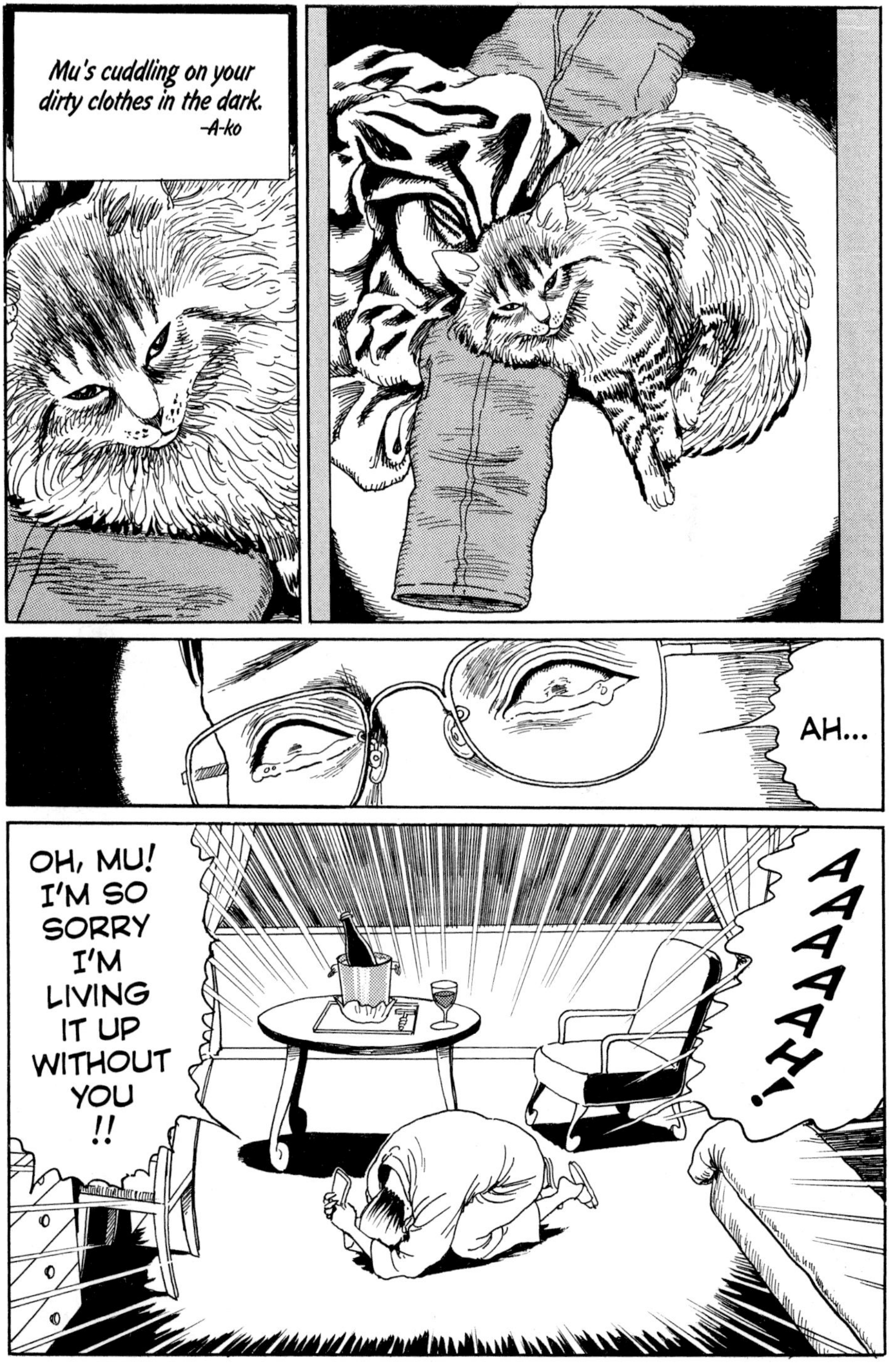
Mu's cuddling on your dirty clothes in the dark. -A-ko
AH...
AAAAAAH!
OH, MU! I'M SO SORRY I'M LIVING IT UP WITHOUT YOU!!

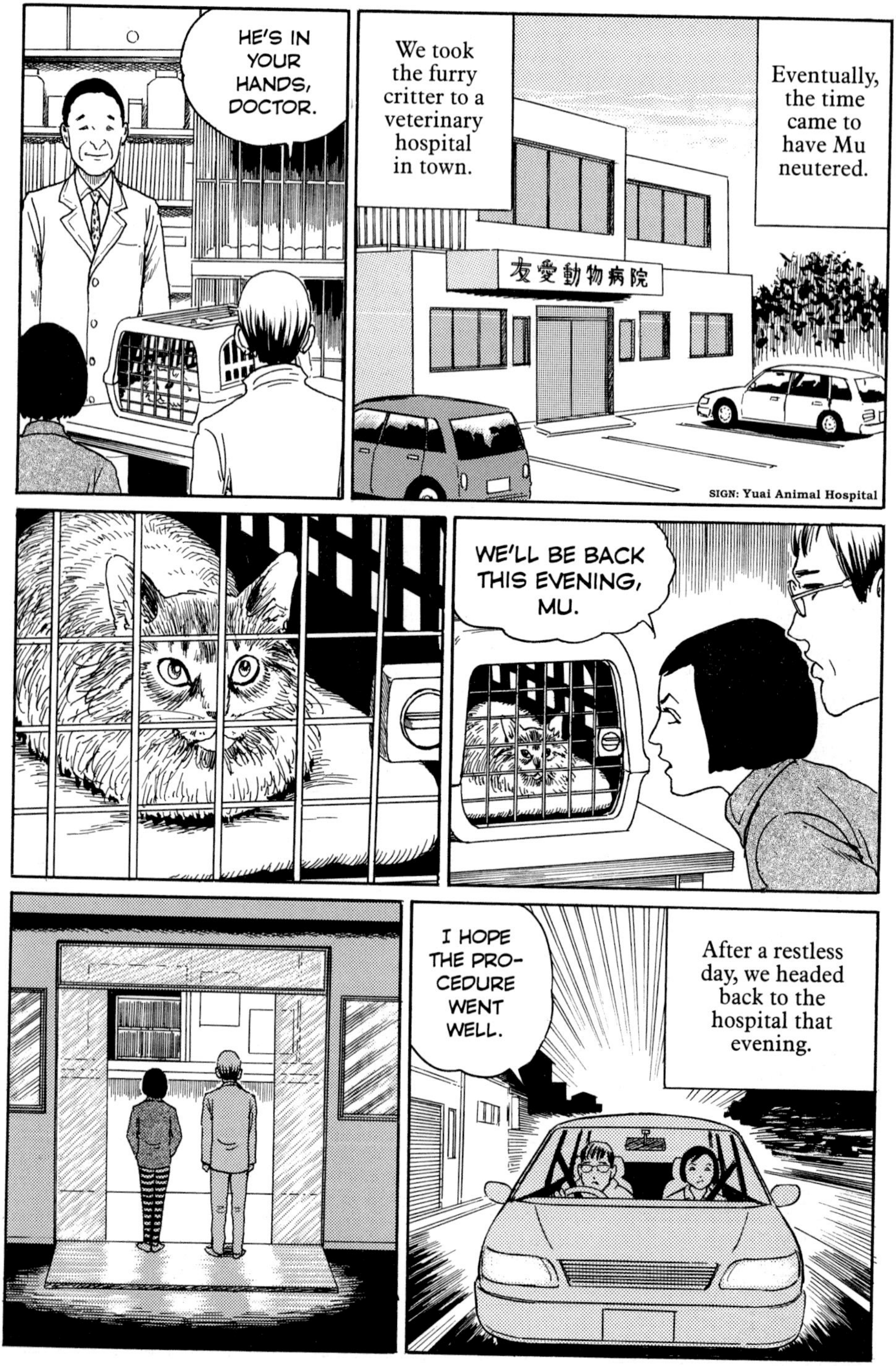

Eventually, the time came to have Mu neutered.
We took the furry critter to a veterinary hospital in town.
友愛動物病院
SIGN: Yuai Animal Hospital
HE'S IN YOUR HANDS, DOCTOR.
WE'LL BE BACK THIS EVENING, MU.
After a restless day, we headed back to the hospital that evening.
I HOPE THE PRO-CEDURE WENT WELL.

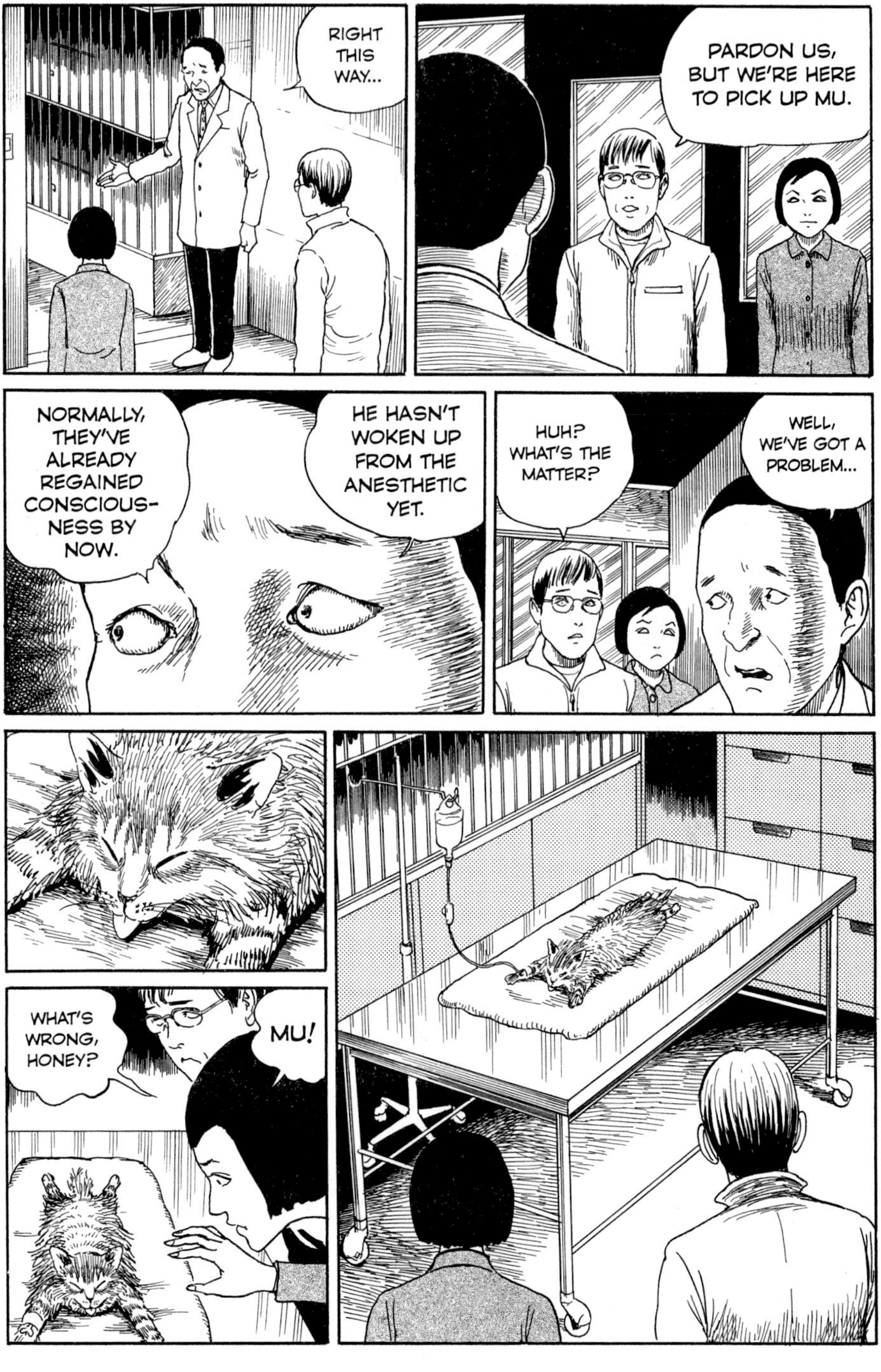
PARDON US, BUT WE'RE HERE TO PICK UP MU.
RIGHT THIS WAY...
WELL, WE'VE GOT A PROBLEM...
HUH? WHAT'S THE MATTER?
HE HASN'T WOKEN UP FROM THE ANESTHETIC YET.
NORMALLY, THEY'VE ALREADY REGAINED CONSCIOUS-NESS BY NOW.
MU!
WHAT'S WRONG, HONEY?

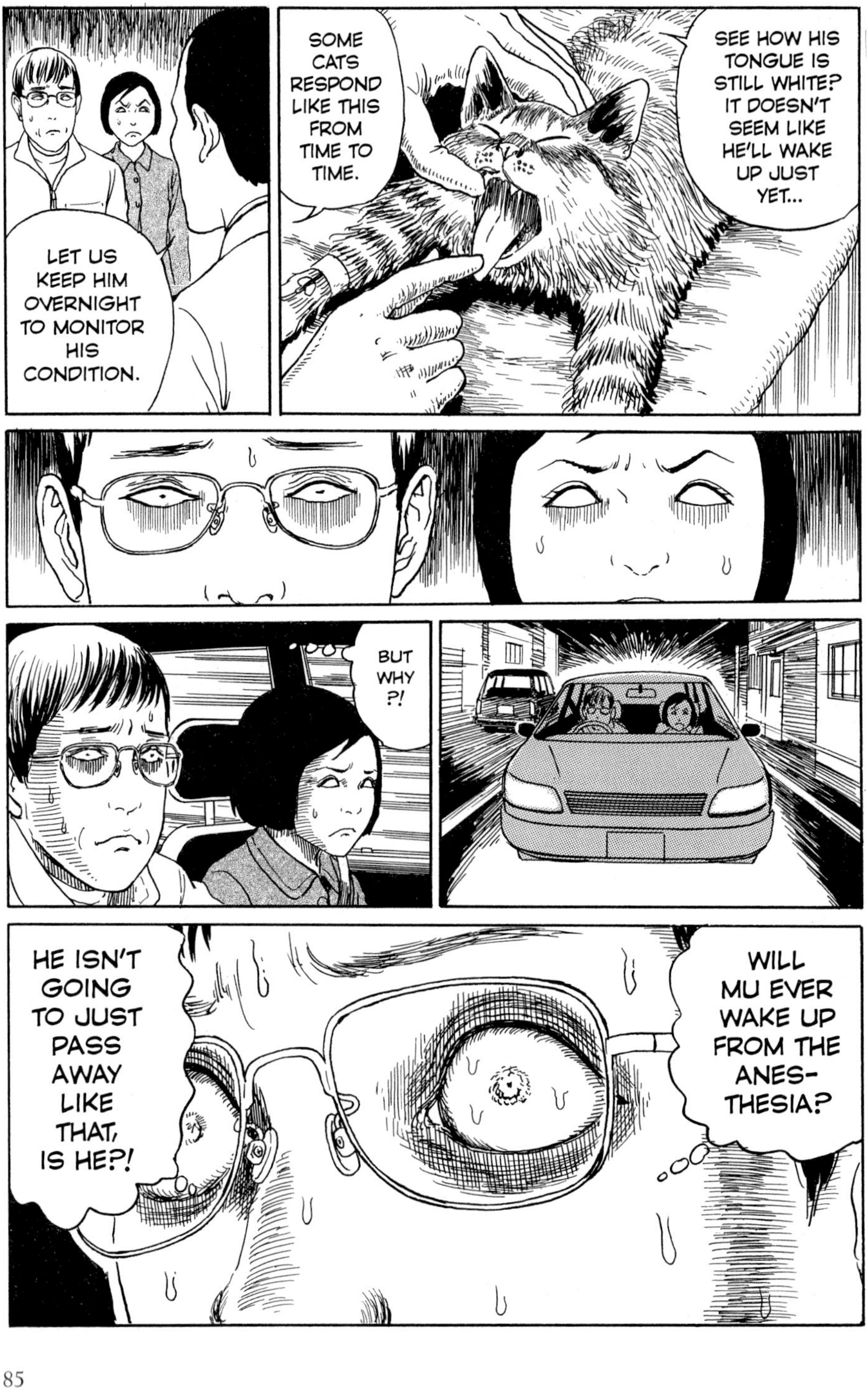
SEE HOW HIS TONGUE IS STILL WHITE? IT DOESN'T SEEM LIKE HE'LL WAKE UP JUST YET...
SOME CATS RESPOND LIKE THIS FROM TIME TO TIME.
LET US KEEP HIM OVERNIGHT TO MONITOR HIS CONDITION.
BUT WHY ?!
WILL MU EVER WAKE UP FROM THE ANES-THESIA?
HE ISN'T GOING TO JUST PASS AWAY LIKE THAT, IS HE?!

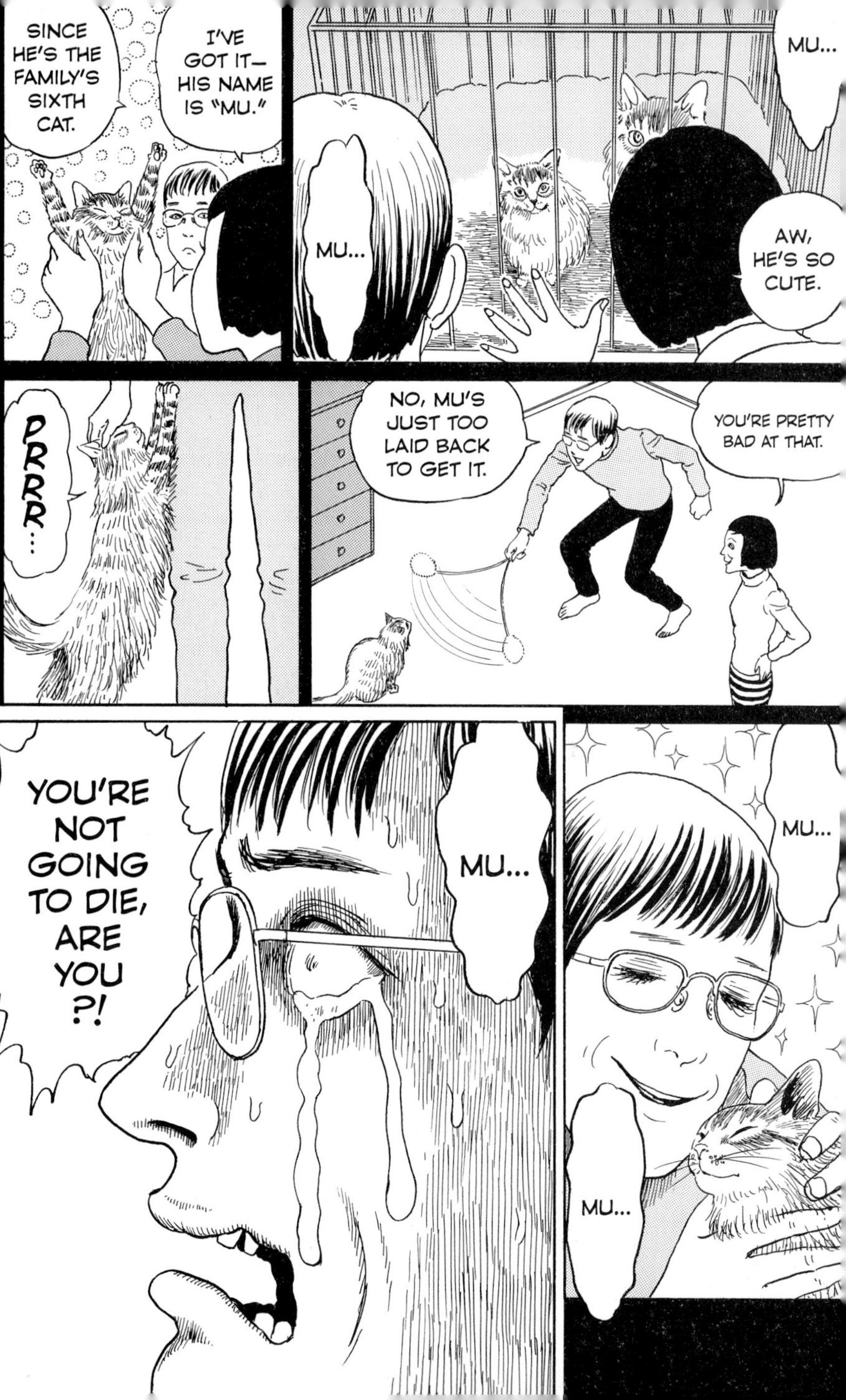
MU...
AW, HE'S SO CUTE.
MU...
I'VE GOT IT— HIS NAME IS "MU."
SINCE HE'S THE FAMILY'S SIXTH CAT.
YOU'RE PRETTY BAD AT THAT.
NO, MU'S JUST TOO LAID BACK TO GET IT.
PRRRR...
MU...
MU...
MU...
YOU'RE NOT GOING TO DIE, ARE YOU?!

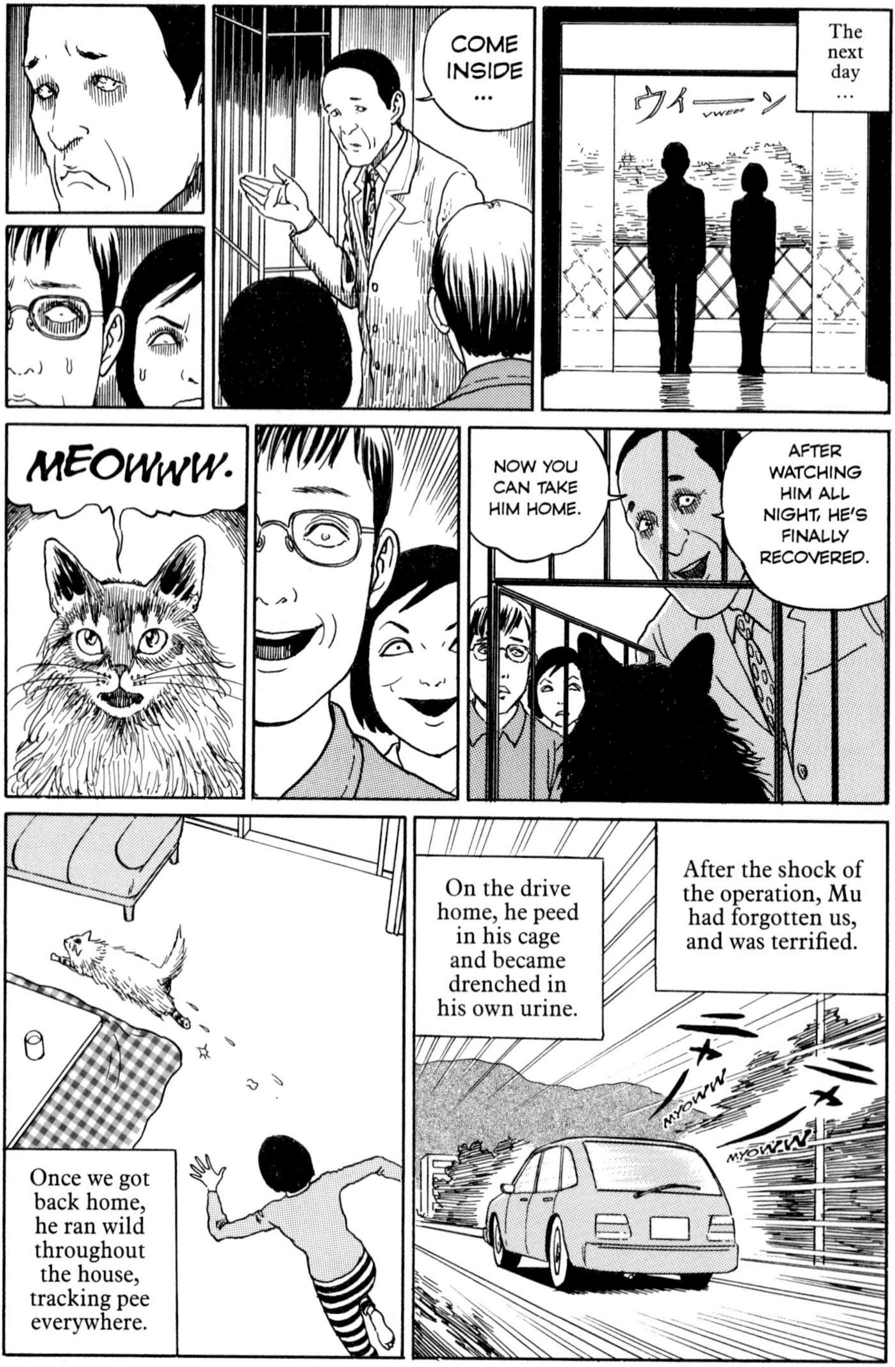
The next day …
ウィーン
VWEEP
COME INSIDE …
AFTER WATCHING HIM ALL NIGHT, HE'S FINALLY RECOVERED.
NOW YOU CAN TAKE HIM HOME.
MEOWWW.
After the shock of the operation, Mu had forgotten us, and was terrified.
On the drive home, he peed in his cage and became drenched in his own urine.
MYOWW
MYOWW
Once we got back home, he ran wild throughout the house, tracking pee everywhere.

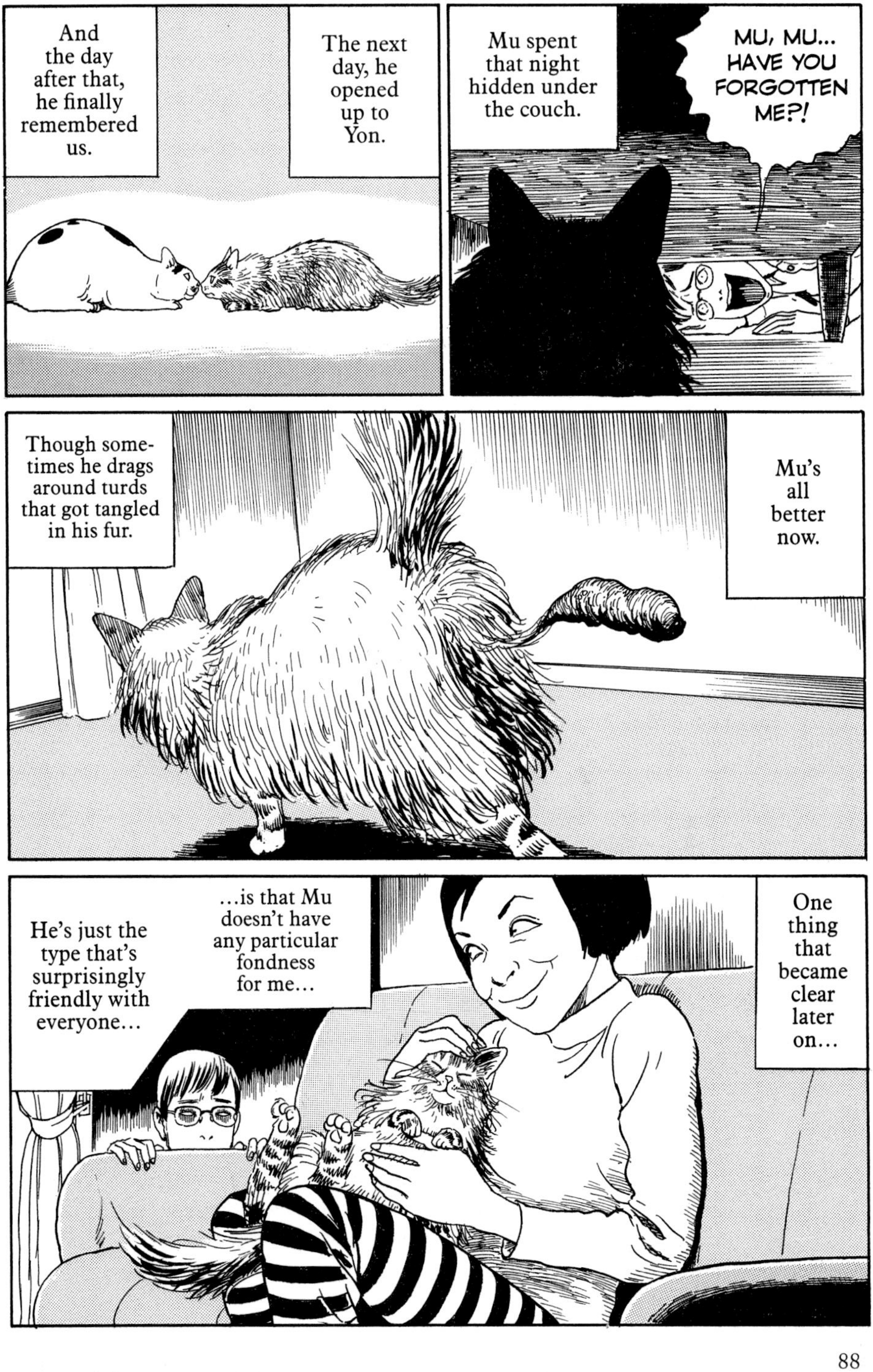
Mu spent that night hidden under the couch.
MU, MU... HAVE YOU FORGOTTEN ME?!
The next day, he opened up to Yon.
And the day after that, he finally remembered us.
Mu's all better now.
Though sometimes he drags around turds that got tangled in his fur.
One thing that became clear later on...
...is that Mu doesn't have any particular fondness for me...
He's just the type that's surprisingly friendly with everyone...

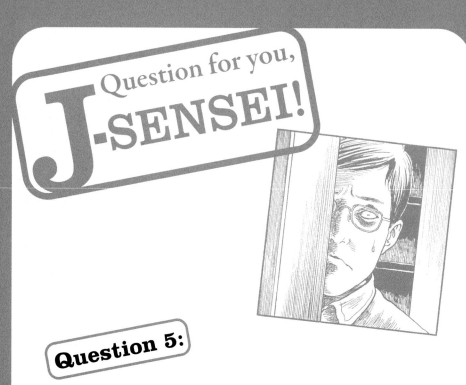

Question for you, J-SENSEI!

Question 5:

You draw A-ko's eyes almost entirely without pupils.
What does your wife think of this?

Answer:

She got mad at me. It seems that she doesn't like the haircut,
either. I've also been instructed to remove unnecessary lines
from her cheeks in a number of panels. Additionally, she
pointed out that A-ko's trademark striped pants are nowhere
to be found in her personal wardrobe. Aside from these minor
issues, my wife does not seem particularly displeased with this
manga.

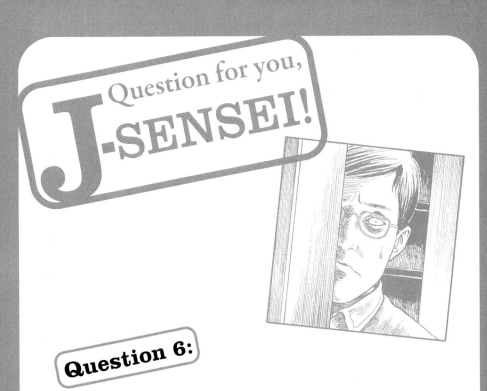

Question for you, J-SENSEI!

Question 6:

When you drew cats in your older works, they were quite scary. But in one of your manga, you drew a cat in a very cute way, and it seemed to catch the essence of a cat very well, so your cat-loving editor thought, "Aha! He's got a pet cat now," and forced you to draw a cat-centric manga. Have you been converted from a dog person to a cat person?

Answer:

Yes, I might be a cat person now. When I was a kid, the stray cats on the street corners looked mean and creepy to me, but when you actually live with one, the look in their eyes becomes familiar and adorable. Just as I was realizing that living with cats gives you lots of funny anecdotes and might be worth turning into a manga, my editor brought me this opportunity. I was in awe at my editor's keen insight.

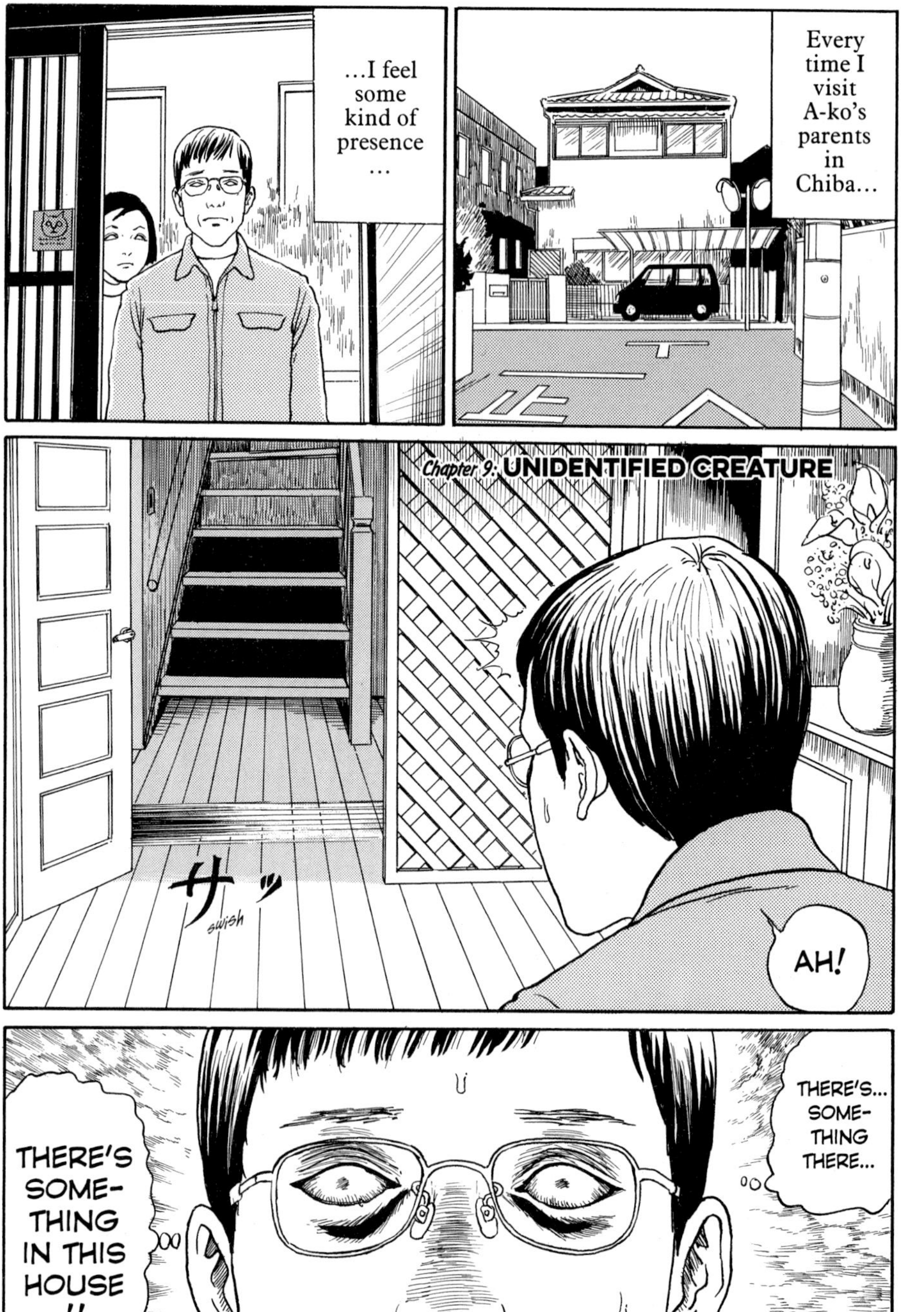
Every time I visit A-ko's parents in Chiba…
…I feel some kind of presence …
Chapter 9: UNIDENTIFIED CREATURE
AH!
サッ
swish
THERE'S... SOME-THING THERE...
THERE'S SOME-THING IN THIS HOUSE!!

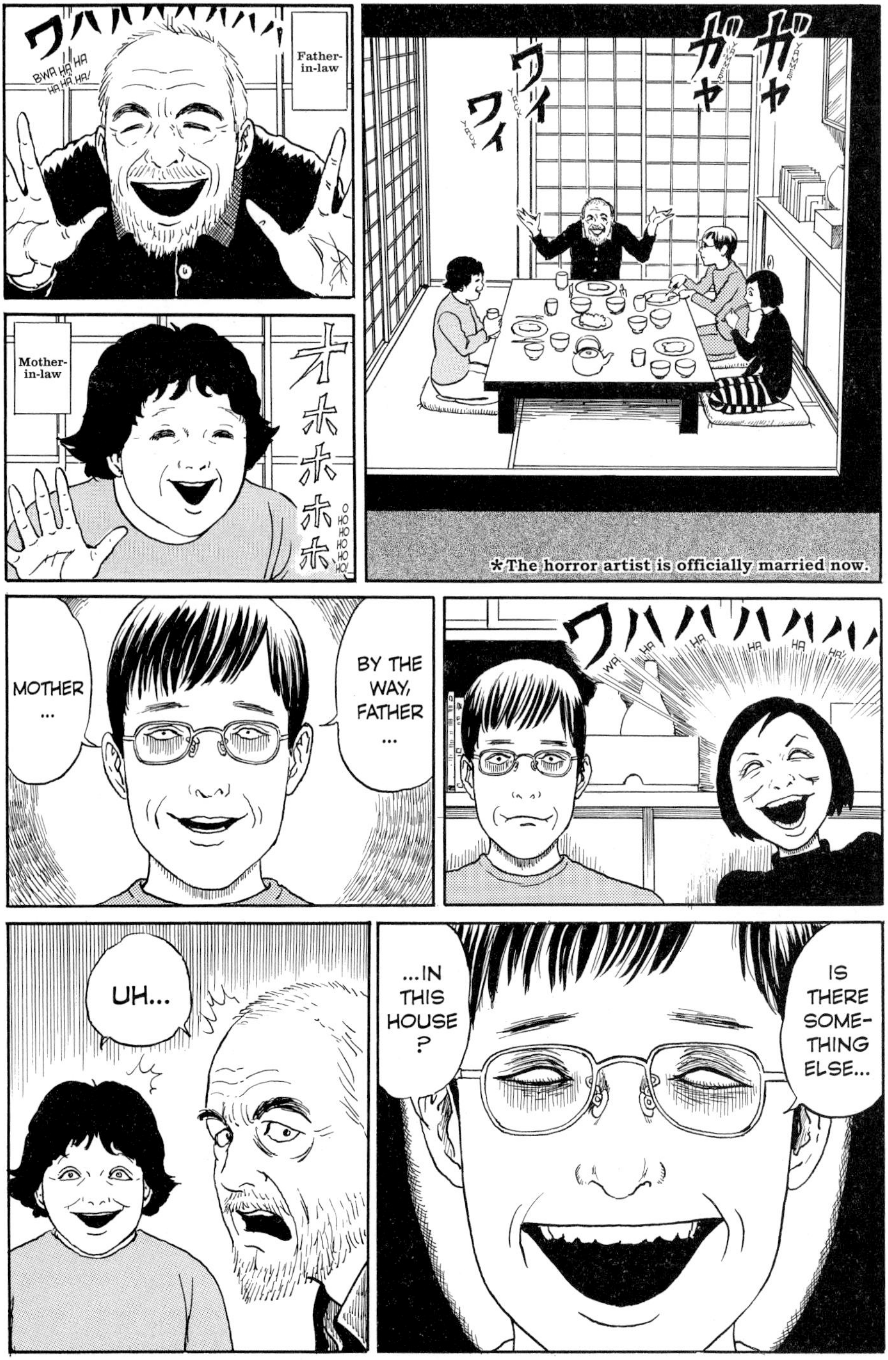
ガヤ
YAMMER
ガヤ
YAMMER
ワイ
YACK
ワイ
YACK
*The horror artist is officially married now.
Father-in-law
ワハハハハハハ
BWA HA HA HA HA HA!
Mother-in-law
オホホホホ
O HO HO HO HO HO!
ワハハハハハハ
WA HA HA HA HA HA!
BY THE WAY, FATHER ...
MOTHER ...
IS THERE SOMETHING ELSE...
...IN THIS HOUSE?
UH...

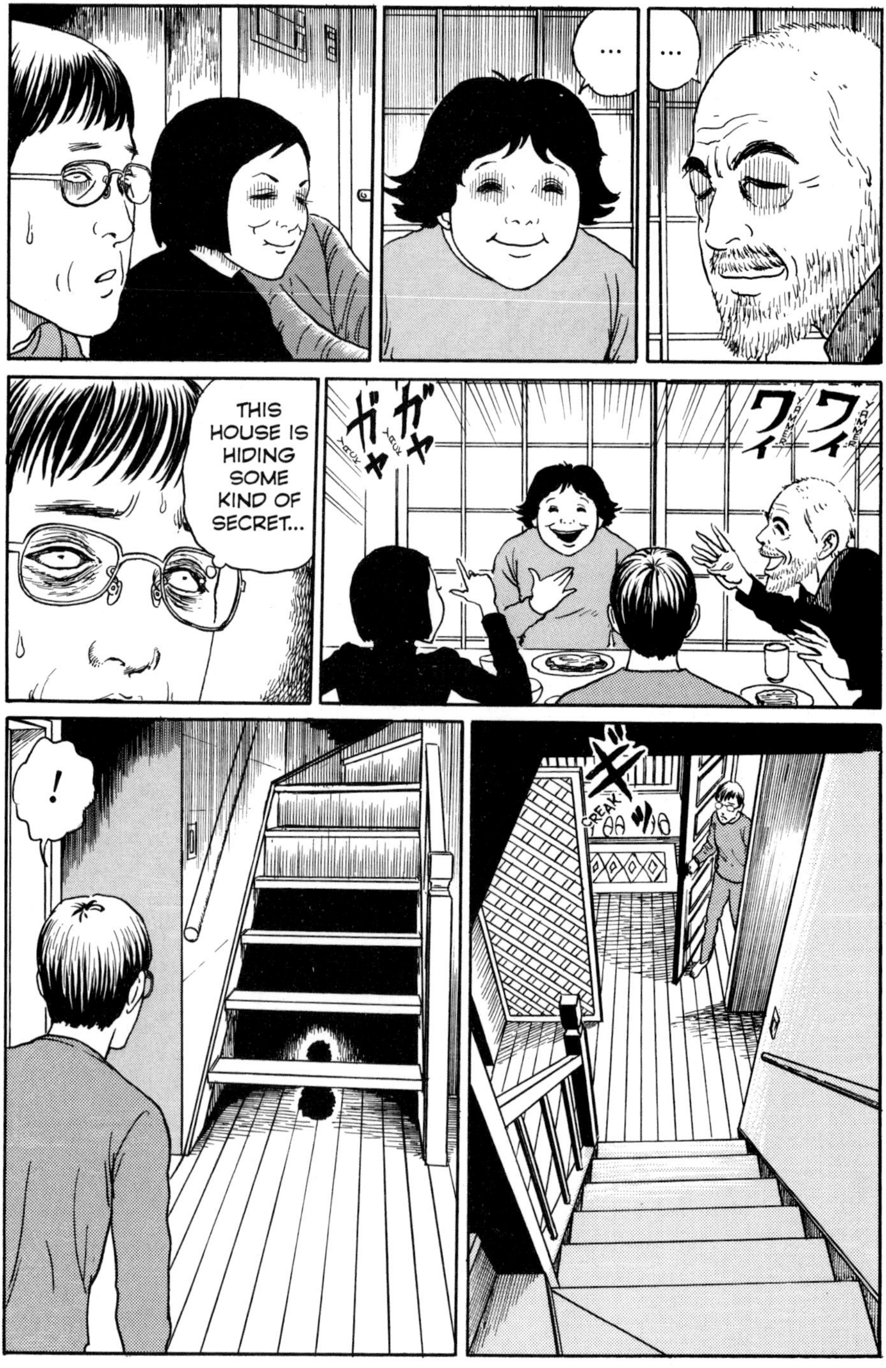
...
...
THIS HOUSE IS HIDING SOME KIND OF SECRET...
ワイ ワイ
YAMMER YAMMER
ガヤ ガヤ
YACK YACK
ギッ
CREAK
!

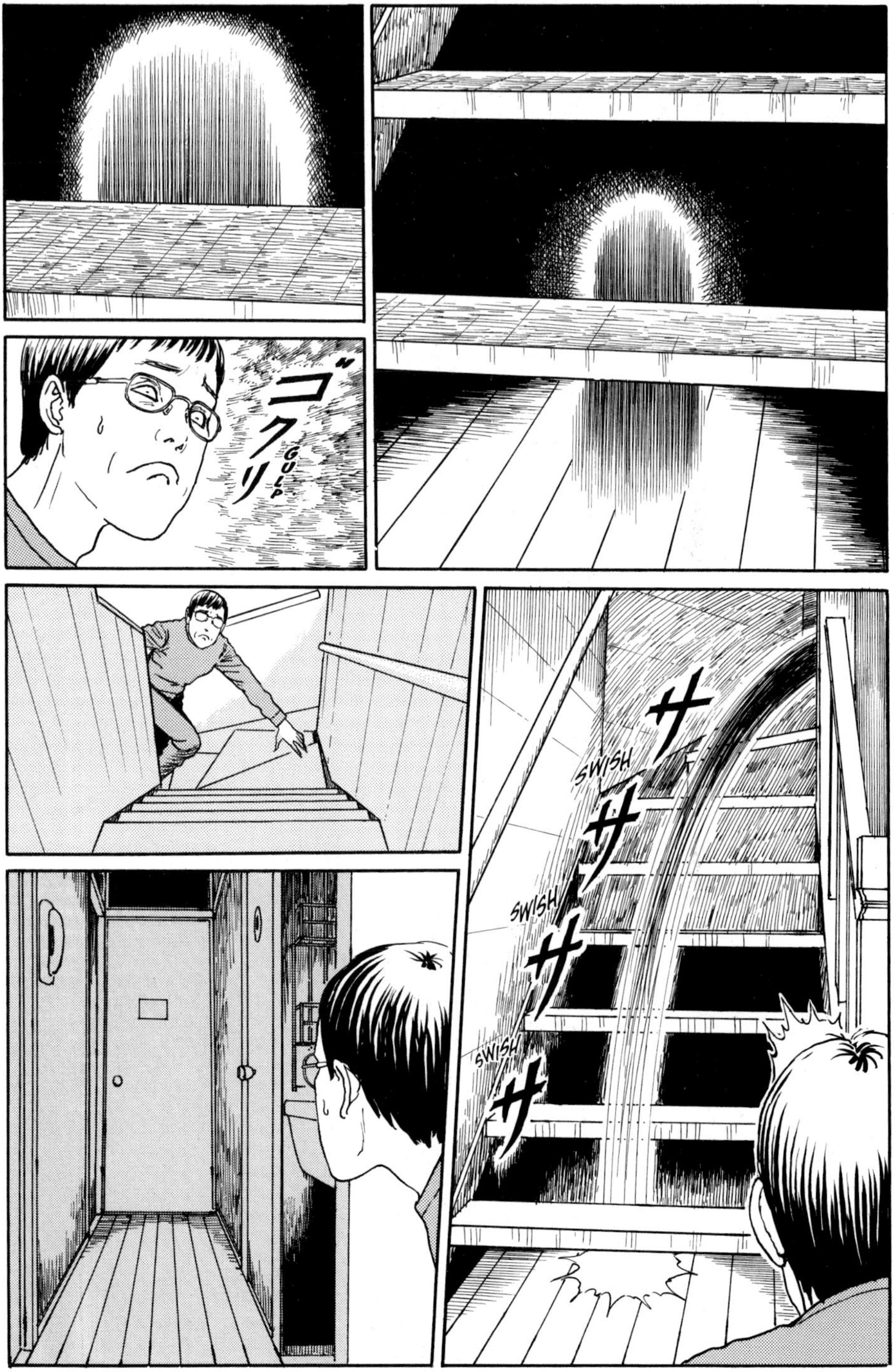
ゴクリ
GULP
サ
SWISH
サ
SWISH
サ
SWISH
サ

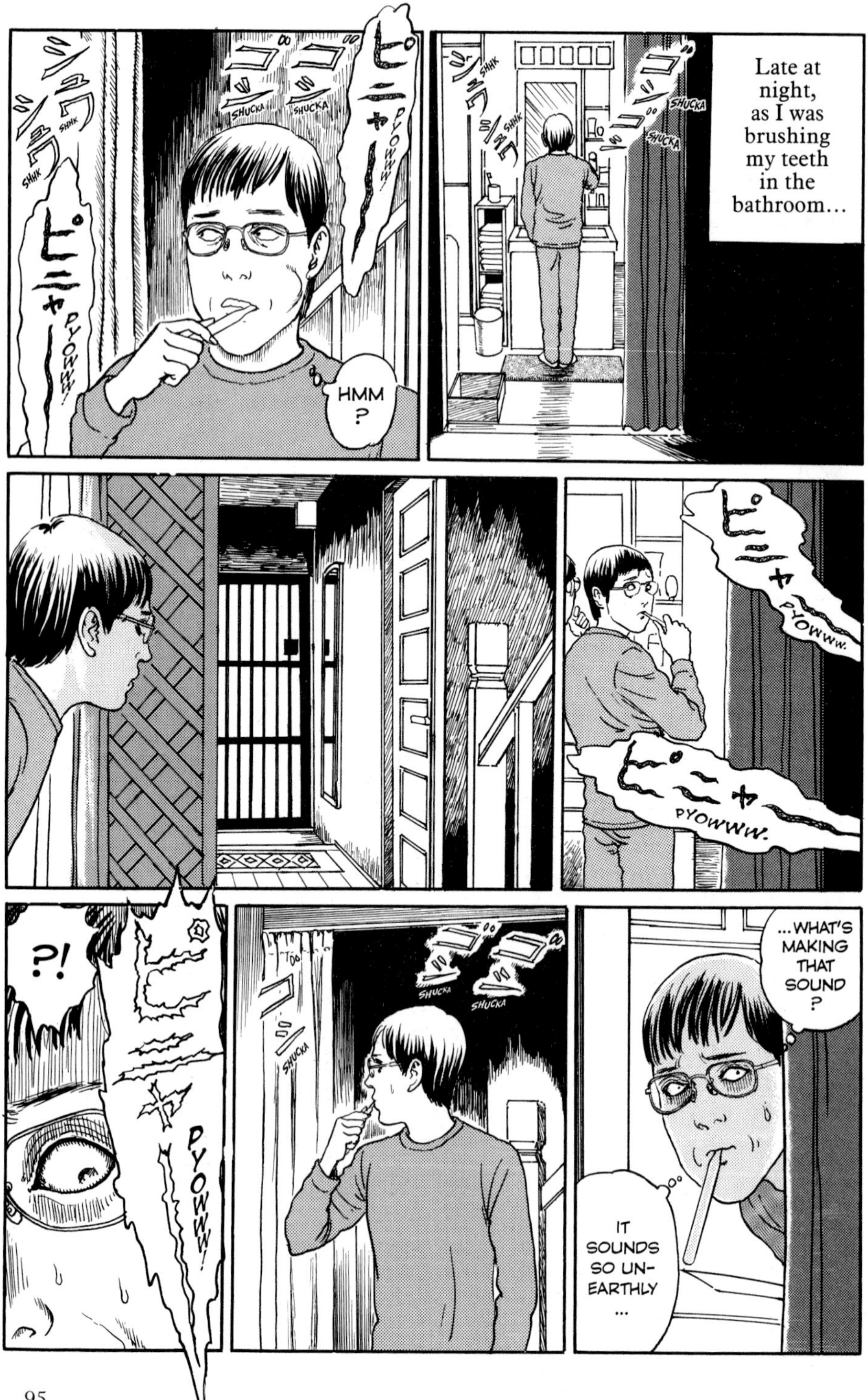

Late at night, as I was brushing my teeth in the bathroom…
SHHK
SHUCKA
SHUCKA
SHUCKA
SHUCKA
PYOWWW!
SHHK
SHHK
PYOWWW!
HMM ?
PYOWWW.
PYOWWW.
...WHAT'S MAKING THAT SOUND ?
IT SOUNDS SO UN-EARTHLY ...
SHUCKA
SHUCKA
SHUCKA
?!
PYOWWW!

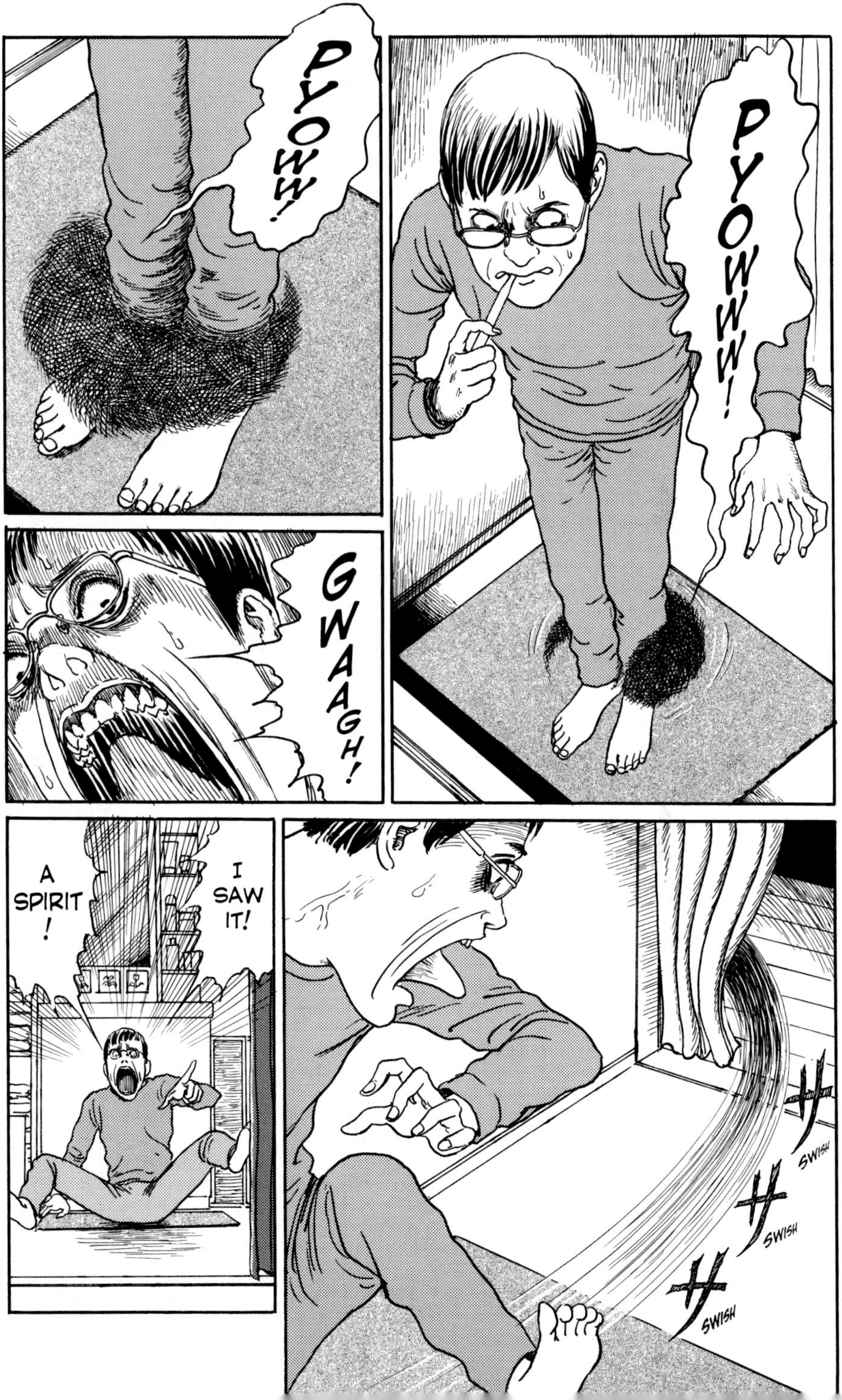
PYOWWW!
PYOWW!
GWAAGH!
SWISH
SWISH
SWISH
I SAW IT!
A SPIRIT!

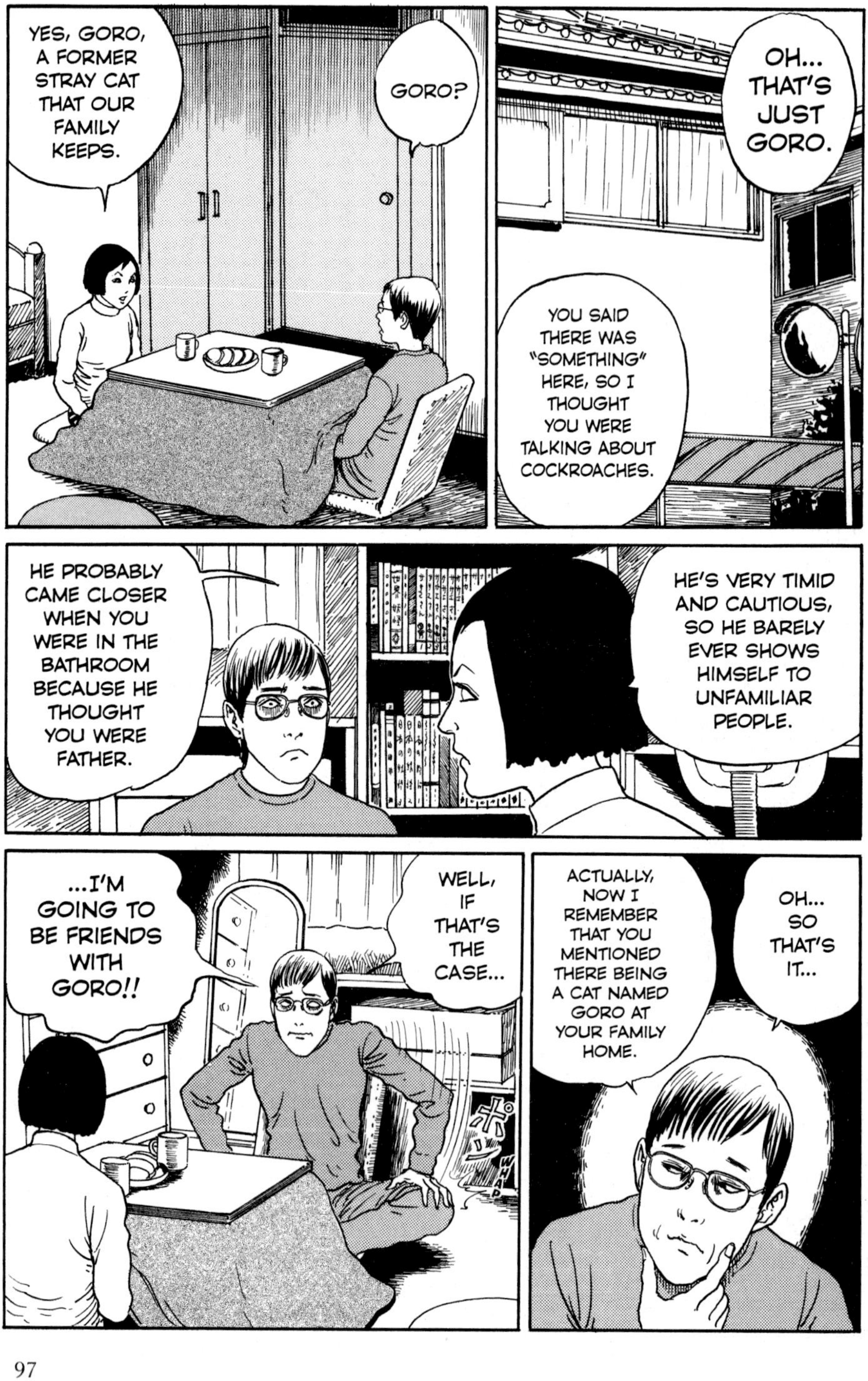
OH... THAT'S JUST GORO.
YOU SAID THERE WAS "SOMETHING" HERE, SO I THOUGHT YOU WERE TALKING ABOUT COCKROACHES.
GORO?
YES, GORO, A FORMER STRAY CAT THAT OUR FAMILY KEEPS.
HE'S VERY TIMID AND CAUTIOUS, SO HE BARELY EVER SHOWS HIMSELF TO UNFAMILIAR PEOPLE.
HE PROBABLY CAME CLOSER WHEN YOU WERE IN THE BATHROOM BECAUSE HE THOUGHT YOU WERE FATHER.
OH... SO THAT'S IT...
ACTUALLY, NOW I REMEMBER THAT YOU MENTIONED THERE BEING A CAT NAMED GORO AT YOUR FAMILY HOME.
WELL, IF THAT'S THE CASE...
...I'M GOING TO BE FRIENDS WITH GORO!!
ポン
WHAP

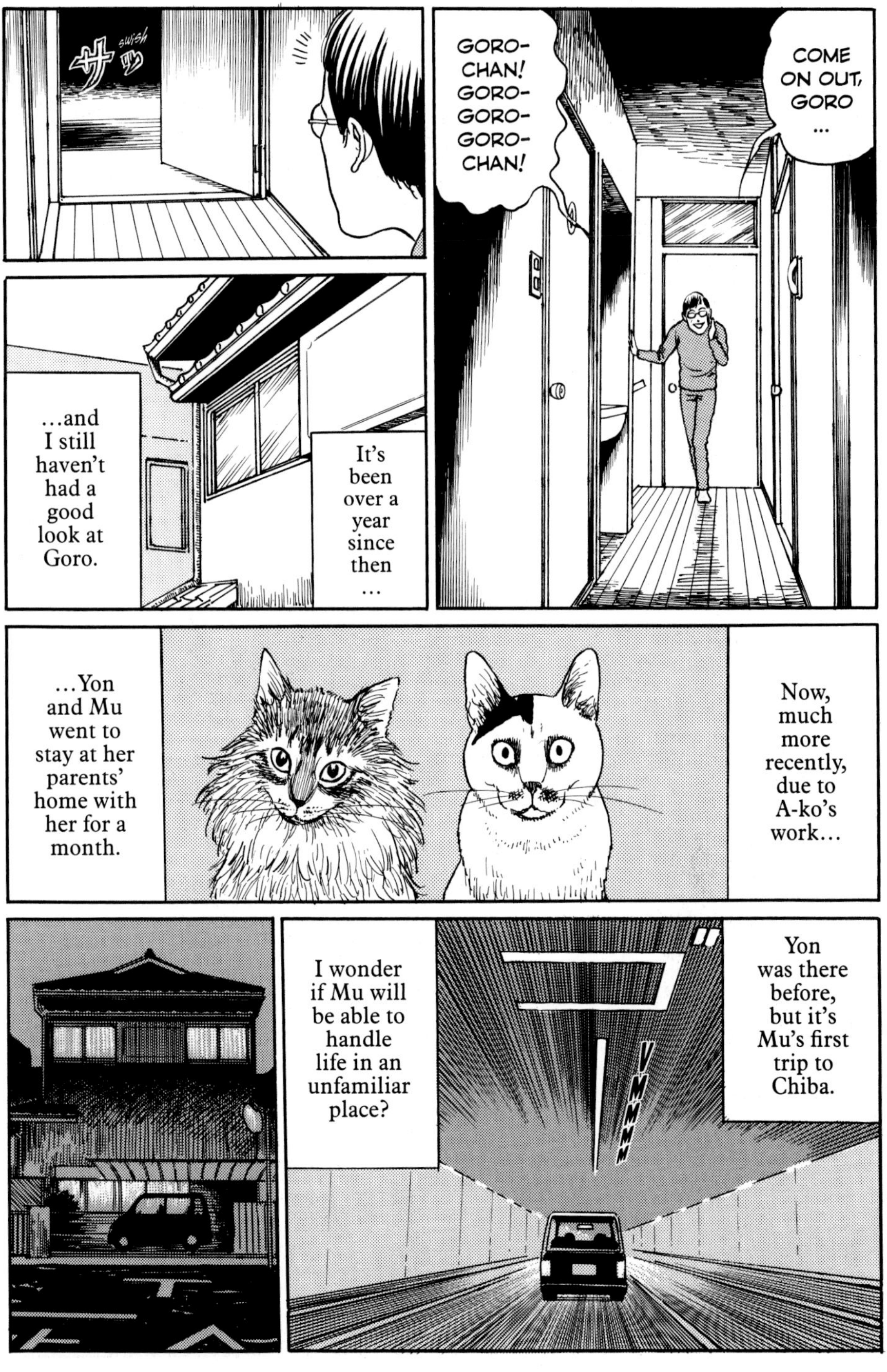
COME ON OUT, GORO ...
GORO-CHAN! GORO-GORO-GORO-CHAN!
サッ swish
It's been over a year since then ...
...and I still haven't had a good look at Goro.
Now, much more recently, due to A-ko's work...
...Yon and Mu went to stay at her parents' home with her for a month.
Yon was there before, but it's Mu's first trip to Chiba.
ブ"
VMMMM
I wonder if Mu will be able to handle life in an unfamiliar place?

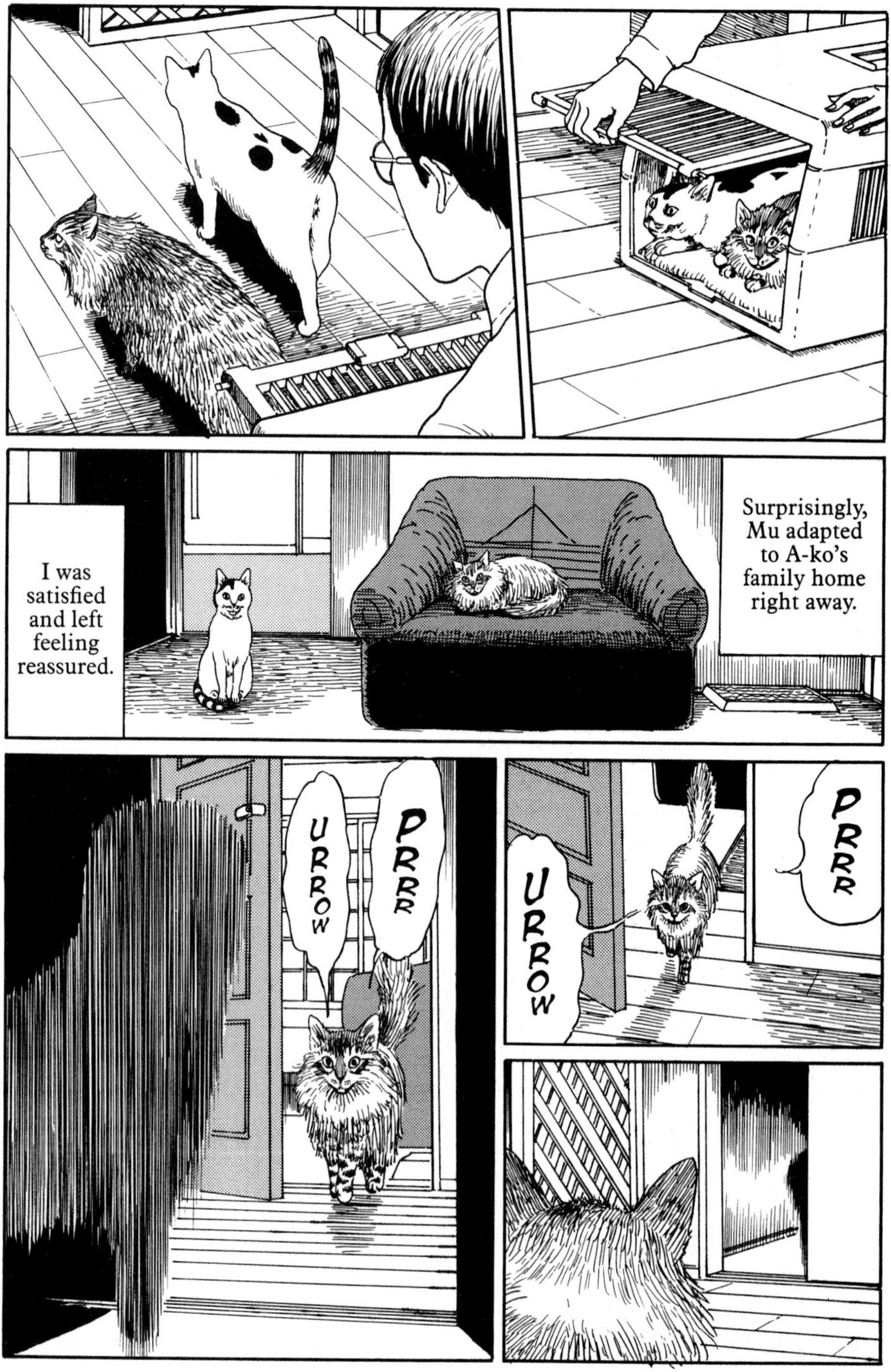
Surprisingly, Mu adapted to A-ko's family home right away.
I was satisfied and left feeling reassured.
PRRR
URROW
PRRR
URROW

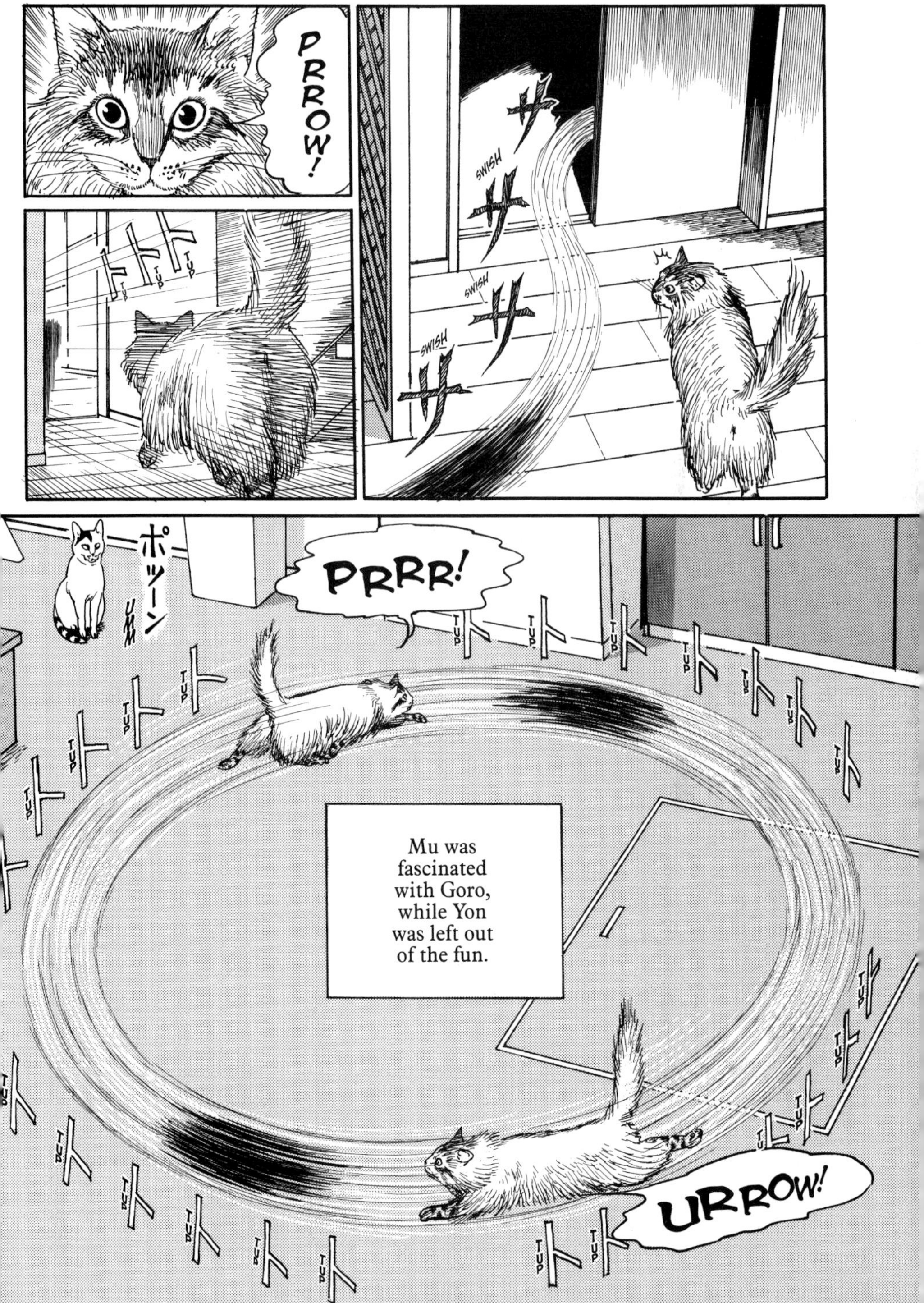
SWISH
SWISH
SWISH
PRROW!
TUP TUP TUP
ポツーン
UMM
PRRR!
TUP TUP TUP TUP TUP TUP TUP TUP
TUP TUP TUP TUP TUP TUP
Mu was fascinated with Goro, while Yon was left out of the fun.
TUP TUP TUP TUP TUP TUP TUP TUP TUP TUP TUP
URROW!

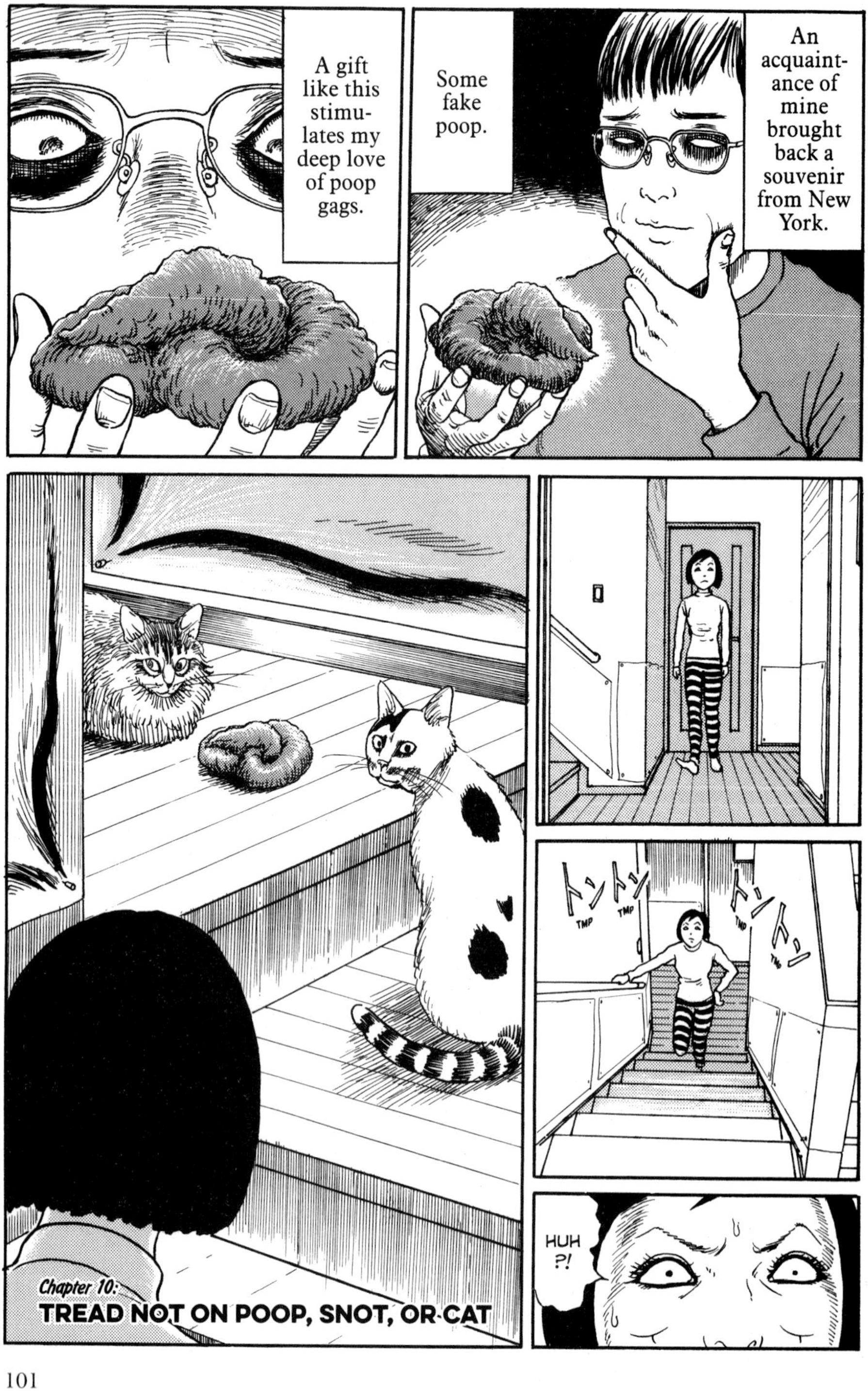
An acquaint-ance of mine brought back a souvenir from New York.
Some fake poop.
A gift like this stimu-lates my deep love of poop gags.
トントン
TMP TMP
トントン
TMP
HUH ?!
Chapter 10:
TREAD NOT ON POOP, SNOT, OR CAT

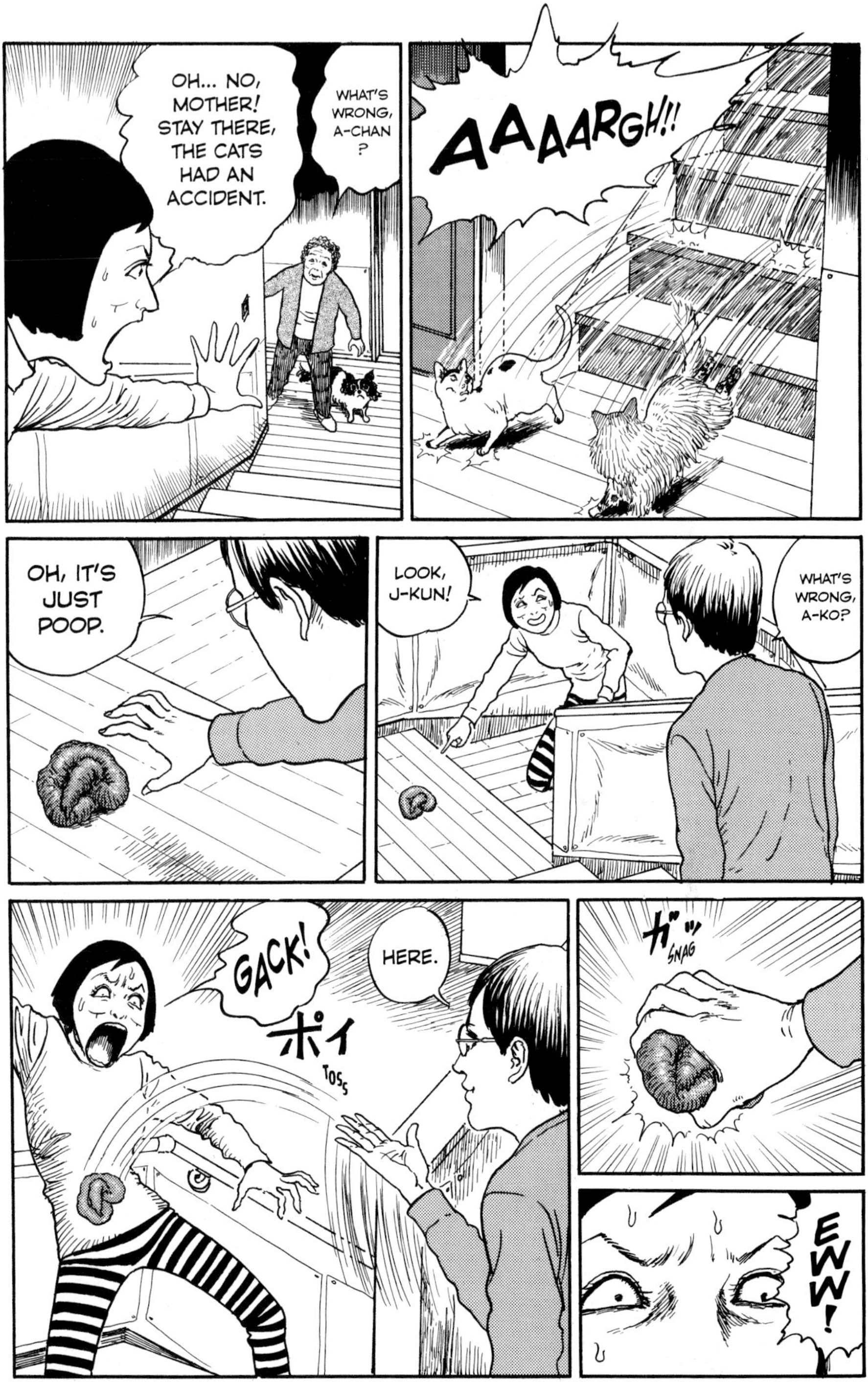
AAAARGH!!
WHAT'S WRONG, A-CHAN?
OH... NO, MOTHER! STAY THERE, THE CATS HAD AN ACCIDENT.
WHAT'S WRONG, A-KO?
LOOK, J-KUN!
OH, IT'S JUST POOP.
ガッ
SNAG
EWW!
HERE.
GACK!
ポイ
TOSS

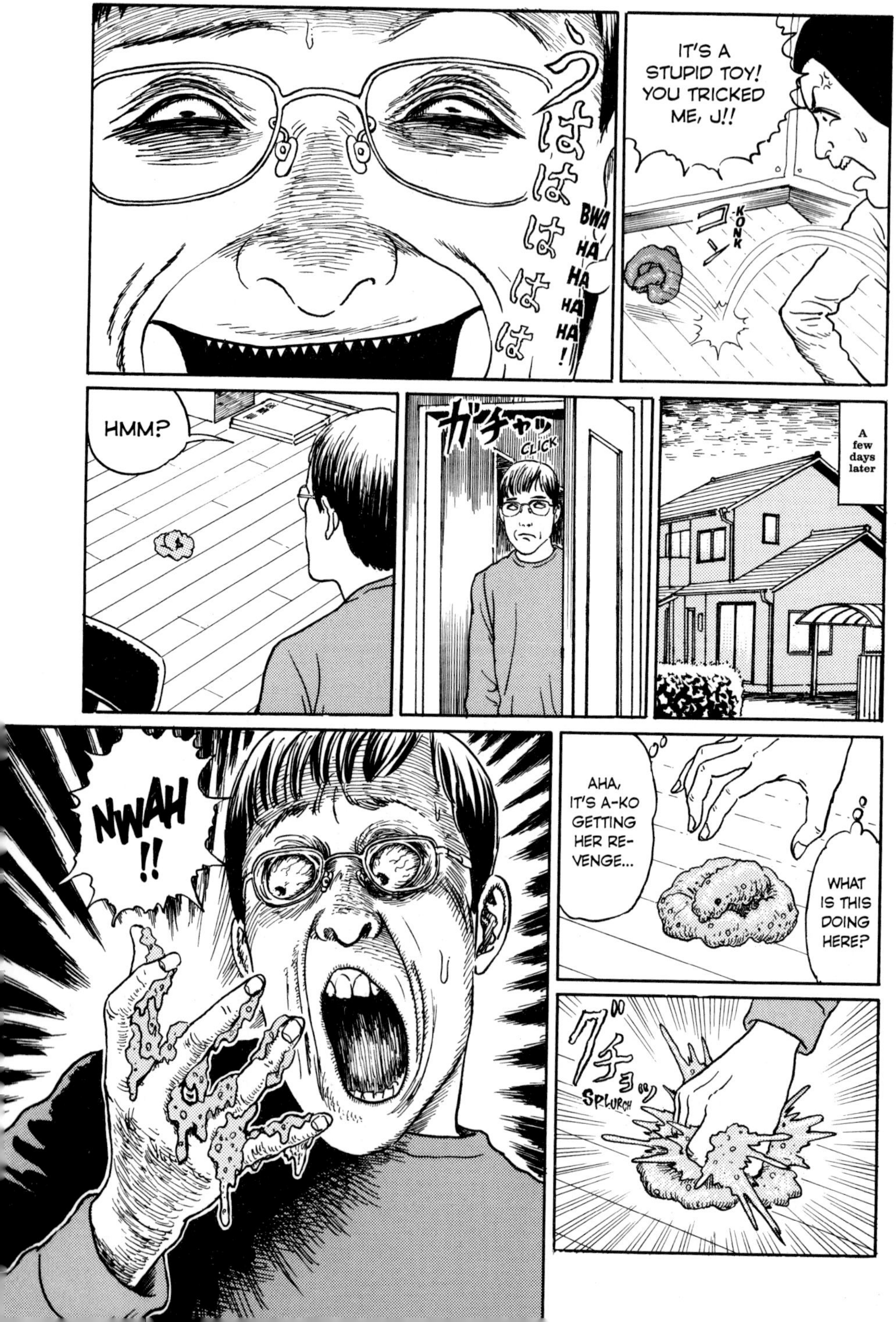
IT'S A STUPID TOY! YOU TRICKED ME, J!!
コン
KONK
うはははは
BWA HA HA HA HA!
A few days later
ガチャッ
CLICK
HMM?
WHAT IS THIS DOING HERE?
AHA, IT'S A-KO GETTING HER RE-VENGE...
クチョ
SPLURCH
NWAH!!

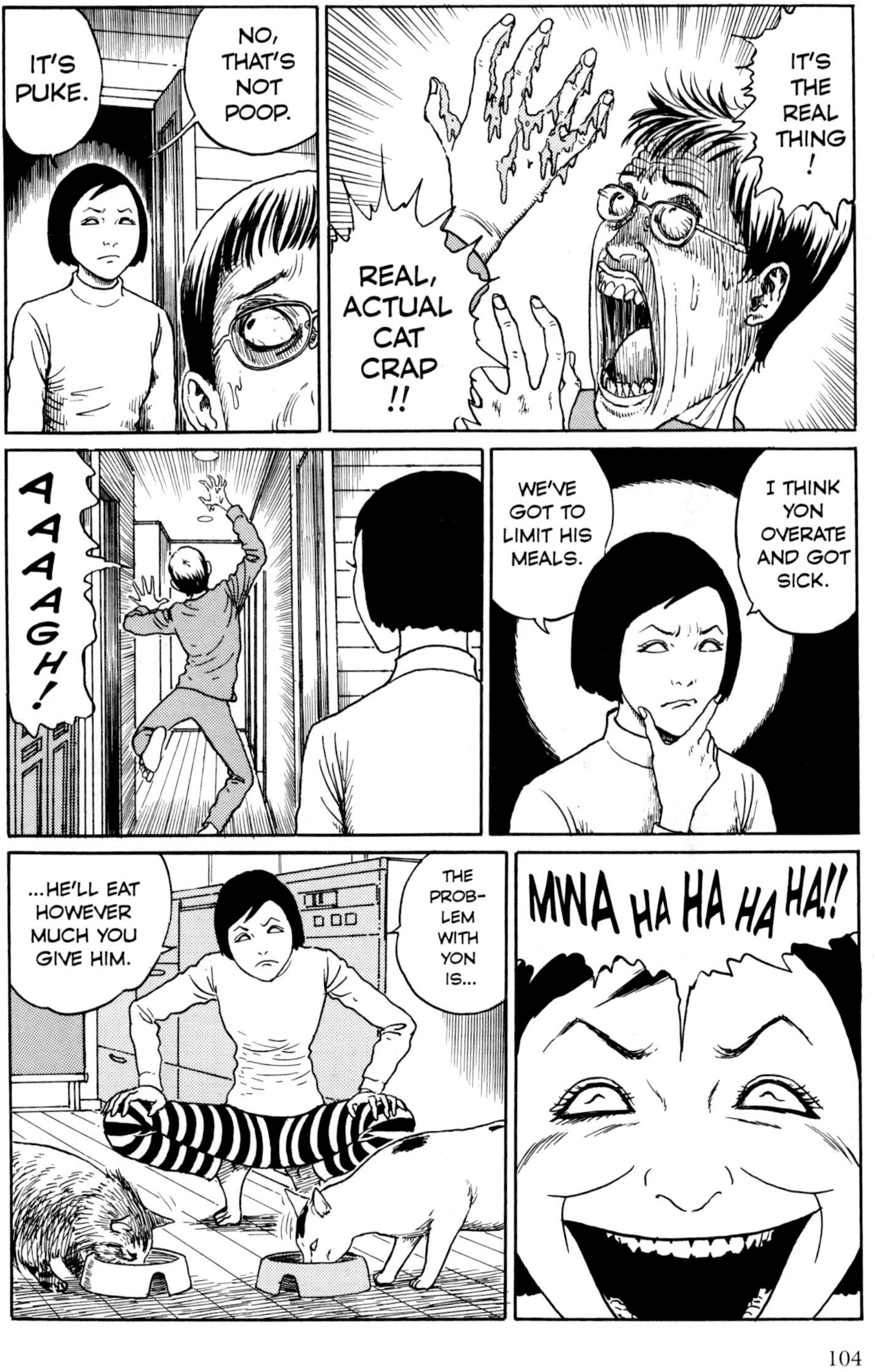
IT'S THE REAL THING!
REAL, ACTUAL CAT CRAP!!
NO, THAT'S NOT POOP.
IT'S PUKE.
I THINK YON OVERATE AND GOT SICK.
WE'VE GOT TO LIMIT HIS MEALS.
AAAAAGH!
MWA HA HA HA HA!!
THE PROBLEM WITH YON IS...
...HE'LL EAT HOWEVER MUCH YOU GIVE HIM.

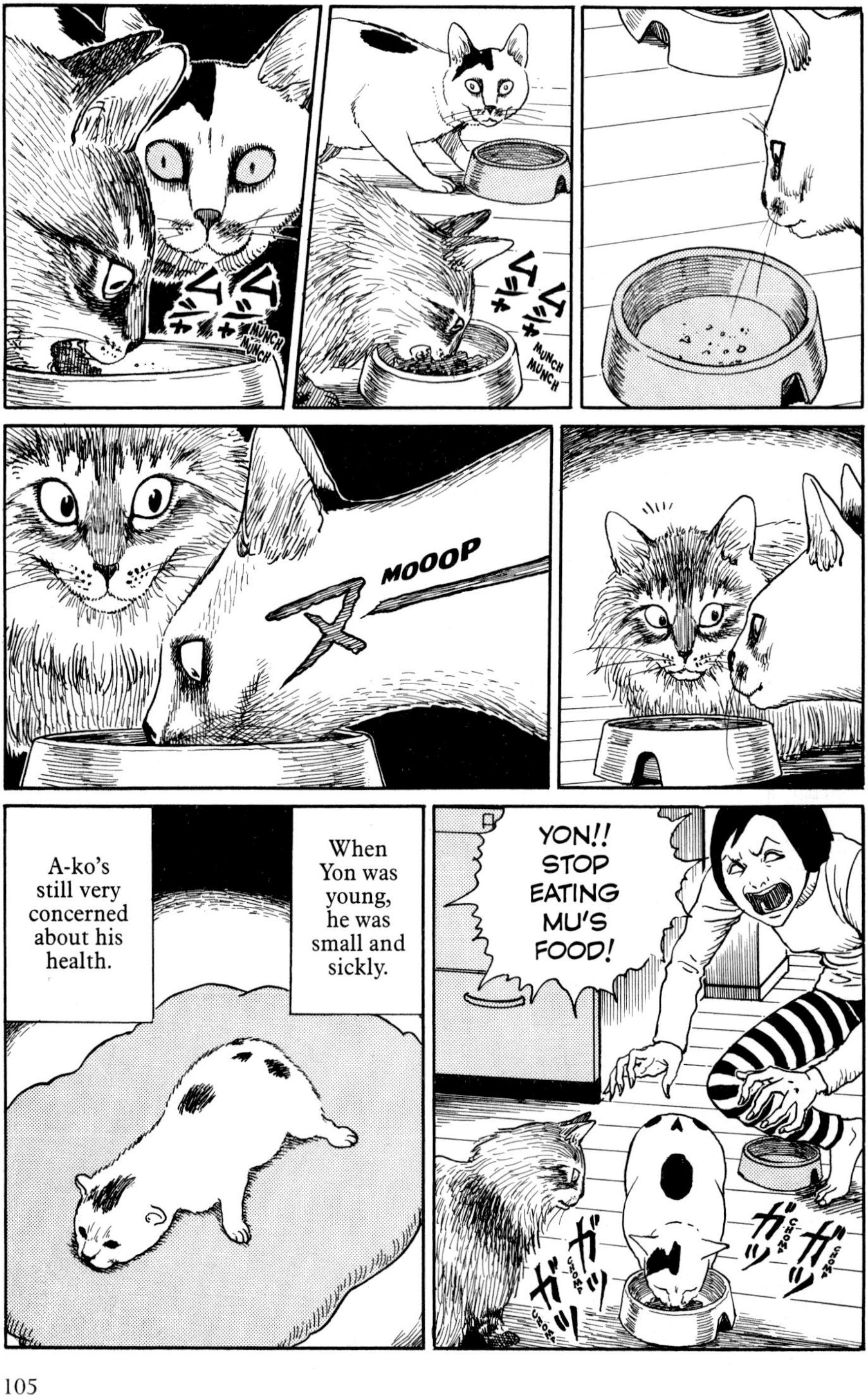
MUNCH MUNCH
MUNCH MUNCH
MOOOP
YON!! STOP EATING MU'S FOOD!
CHOMP
CHOMP
CHOMP
CHOMP
When Yon was young, he was small and sickly.
A-ko's still very concerned about his health.

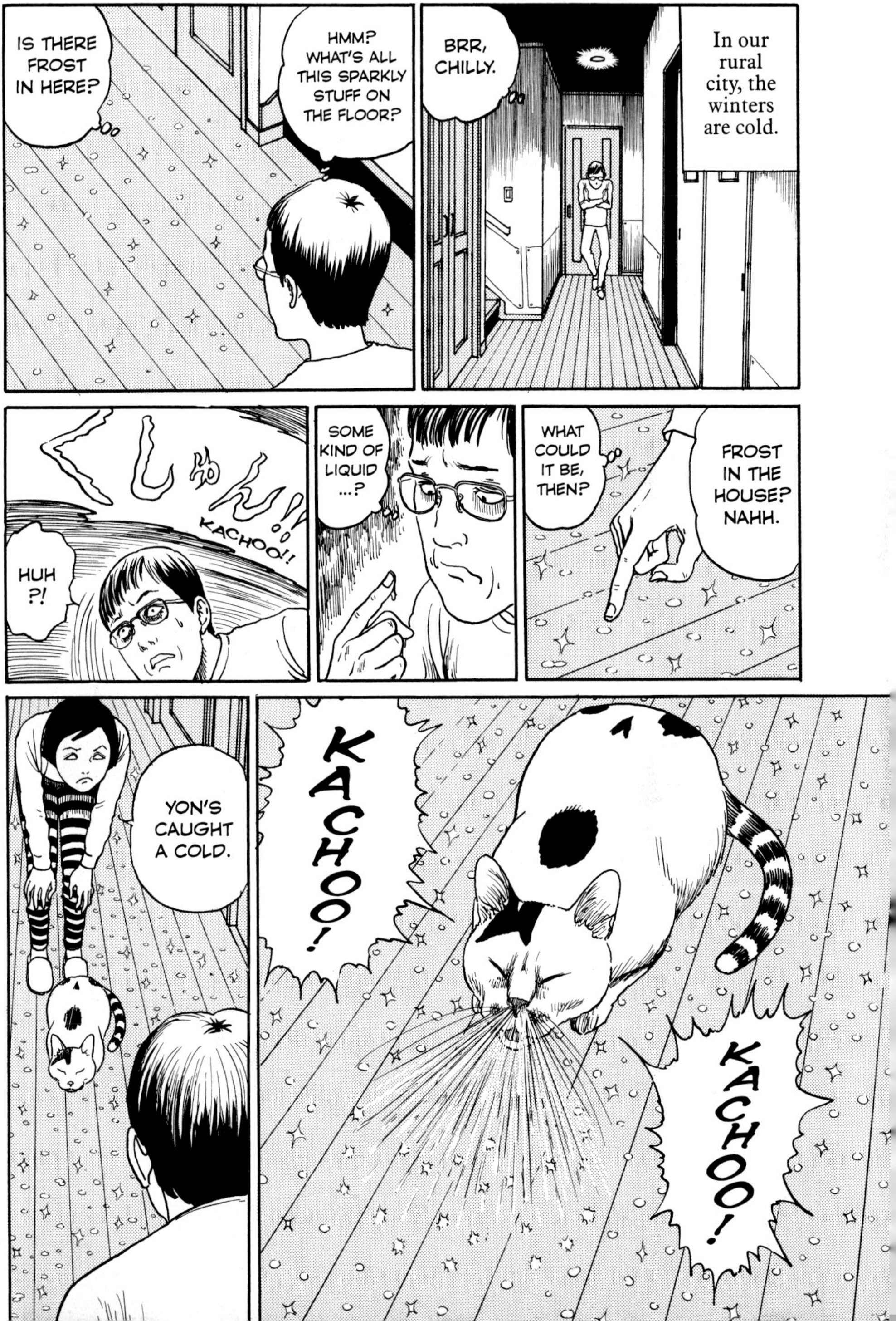
In our rural city, the winters are cold.
BRR, CHILLY.
HMM? WHAT'S ALL THIS SPARKLY STUFF ON THE FLOOR?
IS THERE FROST IN HERE?
FROST IN THE HOUSE? NAHH.
WHAT COULD IT BE, THEN?
SOME KIND OF LIQUID ...?
くしゅん!!
KACHOO!!
HUH ?!
KACHOO!
KACHOO!
YON'S CAUGHT A COLD.

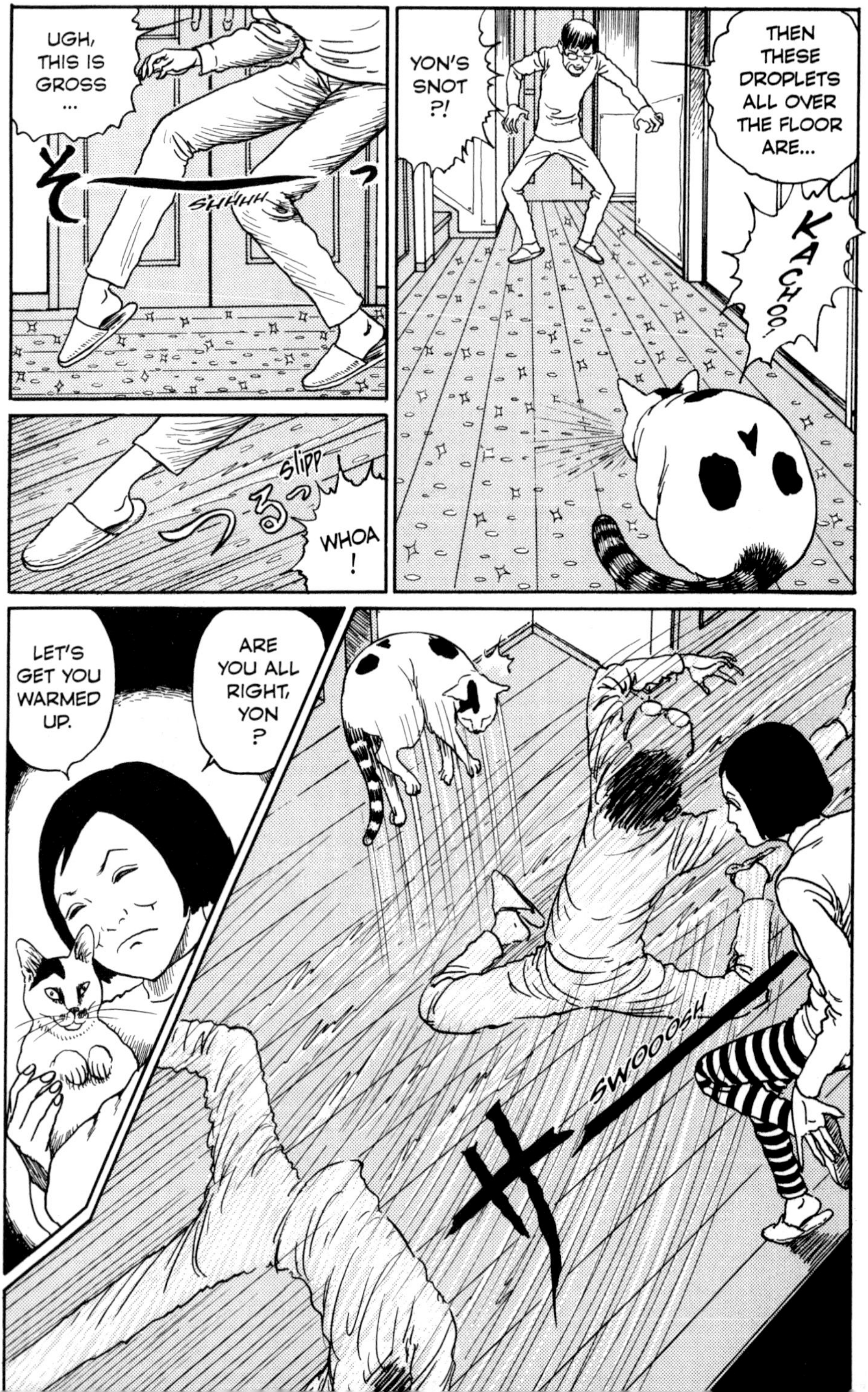

YON'S SNOT ?!
THEN THESE DROPLETS ALL OVER THE FLOOR ARE...
KACHOO!
UGH, THIS IS GROSS ...
SHHHH
slipp
WHOA !
SWOOOSH
ARE YOU ALL RIGHT, YON ?
LET'S GET YOU WARMED UP.

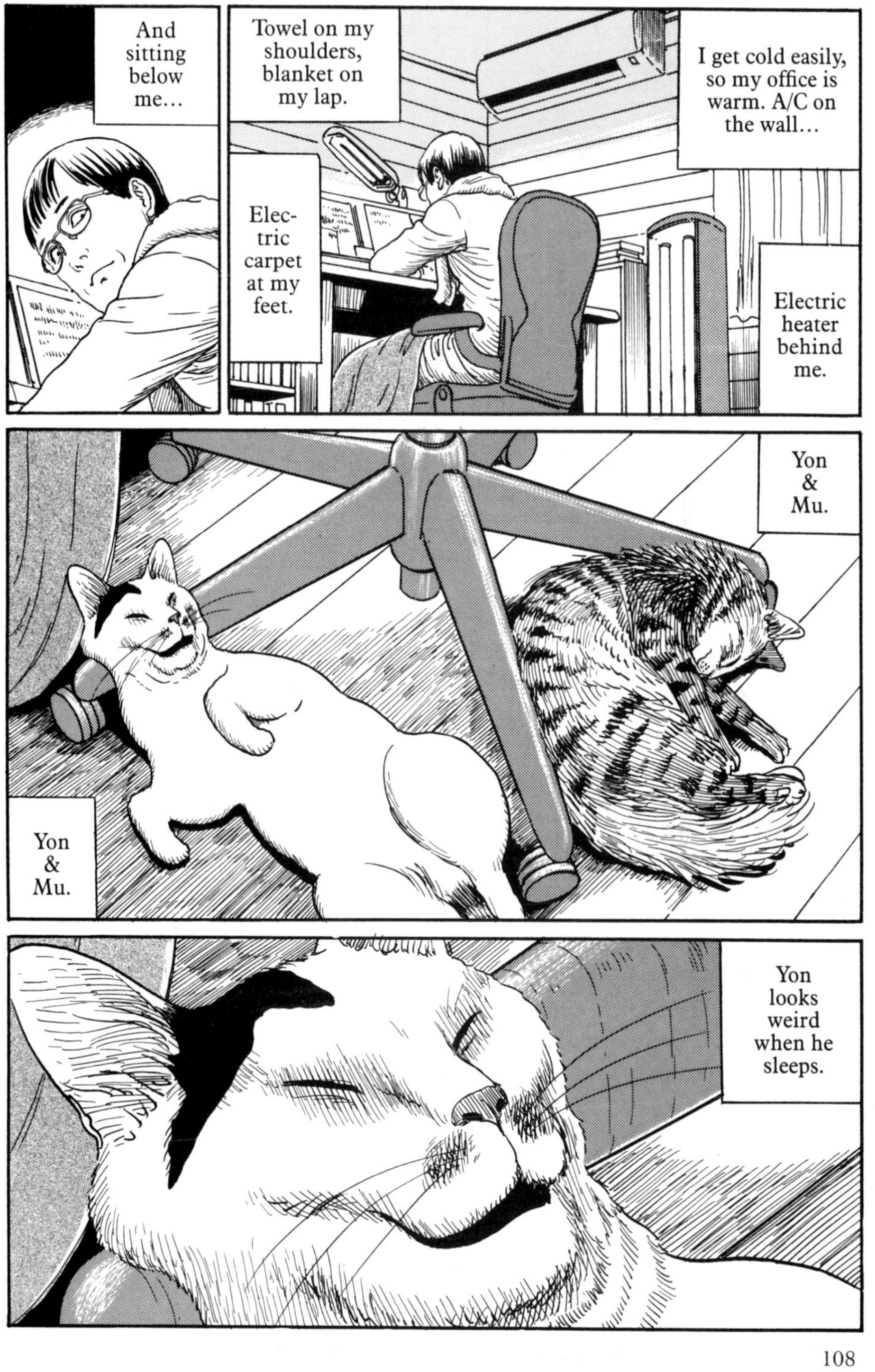

I get cold easily, so my office is warm. A/C on the wall…
Electric heater behind me.
Towel on my shoulders, blanket on my lap.
Electric carpet at my feet.
And sitting below me…
Yon & Mu.
Yon & Mu.
Yon looks weird when he sleeps.

BUT NOW I CAN'T MOVE ...
IF I MOVE THE CHAIR EVEN AN INCH...
...I MIGHT END UP RUNNING OVER YON AND MU WITH THE HEAVY WHEELS.
THEN AGAIN, YON ALREADY LOOKS LIKE HE GOT RUN OVER...
I FEEL SO CRAMPED.
I WONDER IF THERE'S A SOLUTION TO THIS...
WHAT IF I COVER THE WHEELS WITH BOWLS?
BUT THAT'LL REQUIRE SOME TRICKY MODIFICATION.
OH!!
I tried sticking the five wheels in rolls of packing tape.
It's like a water strider! I call it the "Cat-Safe Water Strider"!!

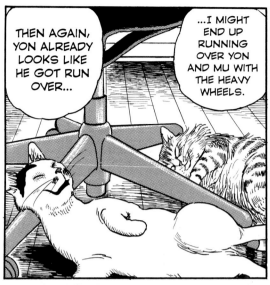

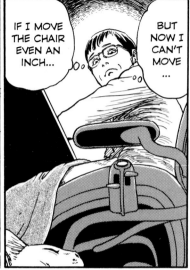

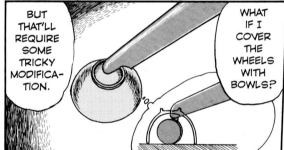

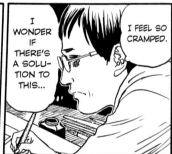

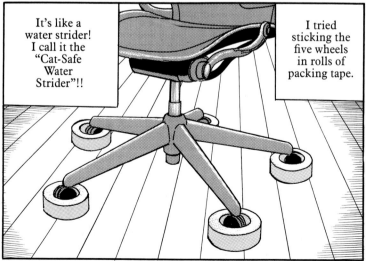

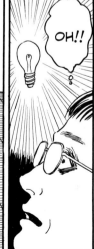

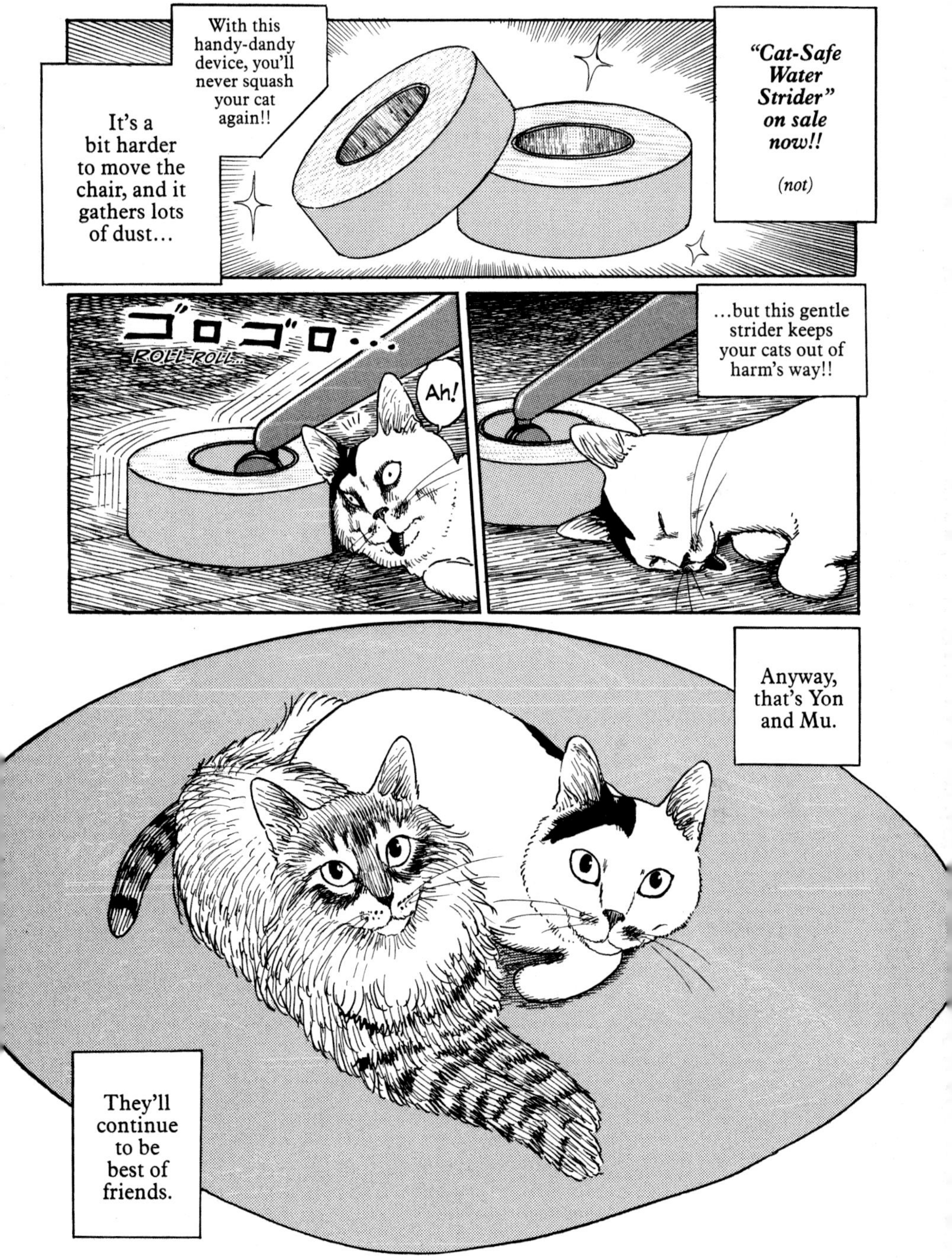
"Cat-Safe Water Strider" on sale now!!
(not)
With this handy-dandy device, you'll never squash your cat again!!
It's a bit harder to move the chair, and it gathers lots of dust...
...but this gentle strider keeps your cats out of harm's way!!
ゴロゴロ…
ROLL-ROLL...
Ah!
Anyway, that's Yon and Mu.
They'll continue to be best of friends.

The End

Question for you, J-SENSEI!

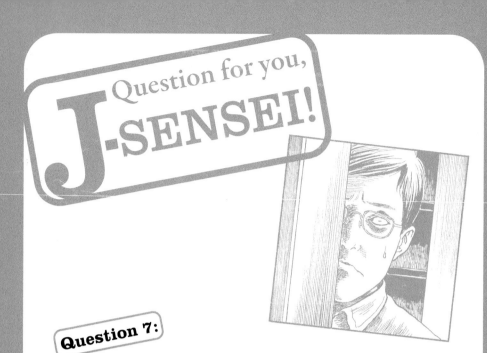

Question 7:

You are now known as a horror manga artist, but is it true that before your professional debut, you were more of a gag manga artist?

Answer:

When I drew for fun, I did both horror and comedy. I had a number of original characters who made quite a splash in my old grade-school comics: Big Dummy, Pose-Man, Little Dummy, and various other hits. Lots of my serious horror works would also start getting boring to me partway through, and would then turn comical in the latter parts.

Question 8:

This year (2009) is your 22nd as a manga artist. What are your goals for your 25th anniversary?

Answer:

I'll just keep taking things one day at a time, like I always have. But if I had to say one concrete goal, it would be to make a manga out of a novel that I wrote once for a video game. I hope my readers will continue to read my works.

Questions: Editor I-buchi   *Answers: Author Junji Ito*   *Date: January 2009*

After getting married, J and A-ko moved into a secondhand home in the same city along with their cats. It was an eccentric home, with an atrium-style living room, a large, sooty wood stove, and a very wide staircase like on a stage from a Takarazuka theater.

An atrium-style living room in this chilly, mountainous region is just the sort of layout that calls for the installation of a wooden stove. But J had no idea how to handle a wood stove. Plus, it would be dangerous to have cats leaping up onto it, and there are concerns that their children could get burned if they were to have any. Ultimately, they decided to scrap the wood stove.

When they called a wood stove vender to ask how it should be disposed of, the vendor said he would visit to show them how to use it.

“No, no, I just want to get rid of it,” J repeated. But the vendor pointed out that such stoves were lifetime fixtures worth 700,000 yen (approx. $7,000 US), and cost 100,000 (approx. $1,000 US) to take out, so why not use it just once and see what you think?

A few days later, an elderly technician came out and fixed a few broken parts without being asked, sprayed the sooty exterior black and made it look good as new. He tossed in some wood and lit it with a piece of newspaper.

The wood began to crackle pleasantly, and the room was soon full of warmth.

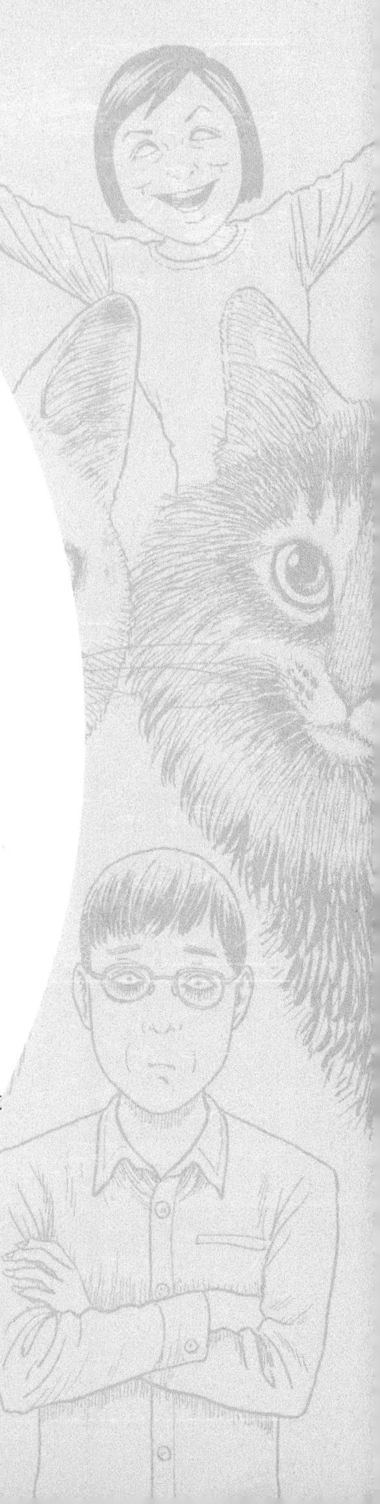

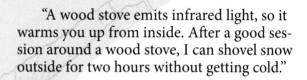

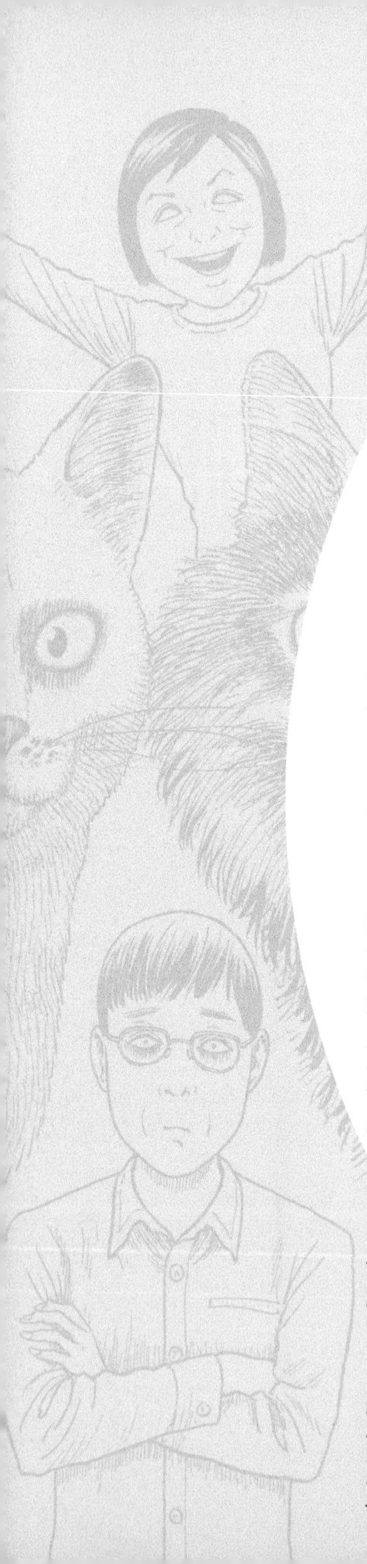

"A wood stove emits infrared light, so it warms you up from inside. After a good session around a wood stove, I can shovel snow outside for two hours without getting cold."

The elderly man seemed to be really into stoves. He plopped down happily right in front of it.

"People who love wood stoves all sit in a circle around the front of the heater and talk," he laughed. "And the top of the stove can be used to cook, so it's a hit with the ladies."

He added more wood, pleased that A-ko seemed to be taking an interest. J gave voice to one of his concerns. "We do have cats, though…"

Yon and Mu had hidden upstairs when the old fellow showed up.

"Ha ha ha. Cats don't jump up on the stove; they're too smart. I've been dealing with wood stoves for decades, and I've never once heard of a cat jumping on top of one. Huh? You're worried about kids getting burned? Ha ha ha. Well, they sell proper fences to keep them away. If you end up needing one, I can order it right away."

As the old man talked, the stove fire started to burn ever brighter, and the room was filled with a nostalgic, woody scent and comforting warmth.

Ultimately, J and A-ko decided to use the stove, and purchased a hundred bundles from the old man for the winter. Each bundle cost 500 yen (approx. $5 US), adding up to 50,000 yen (approx. $500 US) in total.

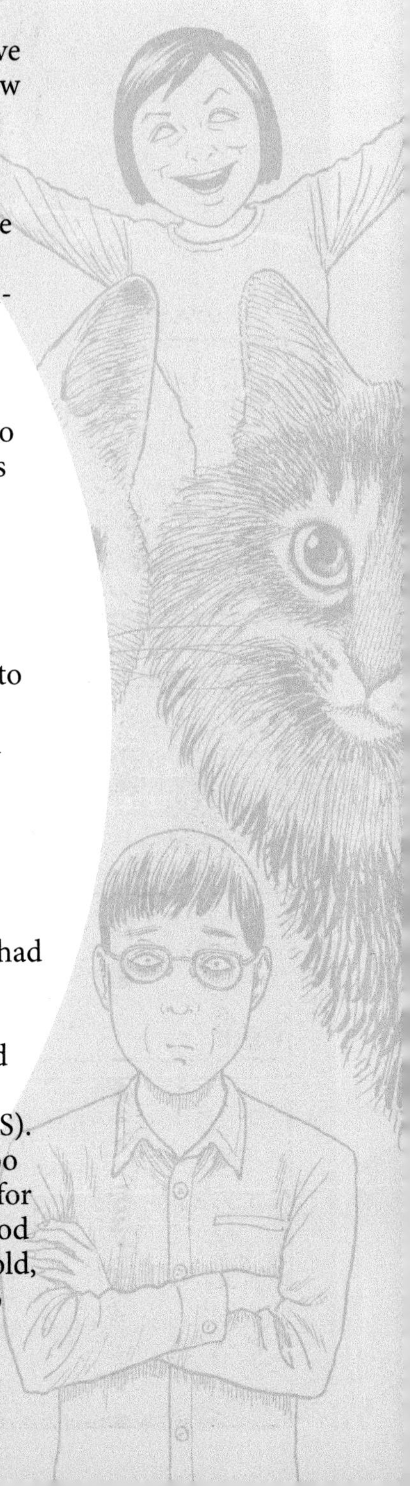

That day was the start of their wood stove life. J had never imagined that he would grow accustomed to using such a thing.

"With this new skill, I could keep warm anywhere, even in a shack during the middle of winter," J thought secretly, pleased with himself despite the fact that he had no intention of becoming a mountain-climber.

One morning, J got up late as usual and walked down to the living room, where A-ko grumbled, "Yon jumped up on the stove this morning."

"What?!"

"It was just after the last embers from yesterday went out, so it wasn't hot enough to burn him, but it must still have been pretty hot, because he danced around for a second before jumping right back off."

J imagined Yon dancing on top of the metal stove.

There was no way to tell if the old man had lied or if Yon was just a really dumb cat.

Just as J had always suspected, the wood stove was a costly item. A day's worth of wood cost at least 1,500 yen (approx. $15 US). They started to cut back, so as not to lose too much money, switching over to a gas stove for heating. In the end, they never used the wood stove to boil or cook anything, and it was sold, along with the leftover logs, to a friend who owned a bar.

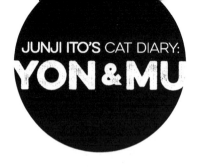

JUNJI ITO'S CAT DIARY: YON & MU

DON'T LOOK ♥

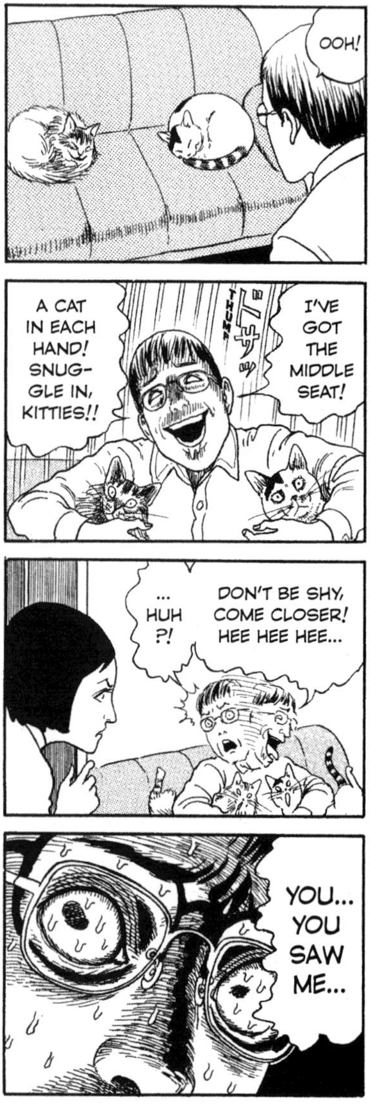
OOH!
I'VE GOT THE MIDDLE SEAT!
THUMP
A CAT IN EACH HAND! SNUGGLE IN, KITTIES!!
DON'T BE SHY, COME CLOSER! HEE HEE HEE...
... HUH ?!
YOU... YOU SAW ME...

LOVEY DOVEY LOVE ♥

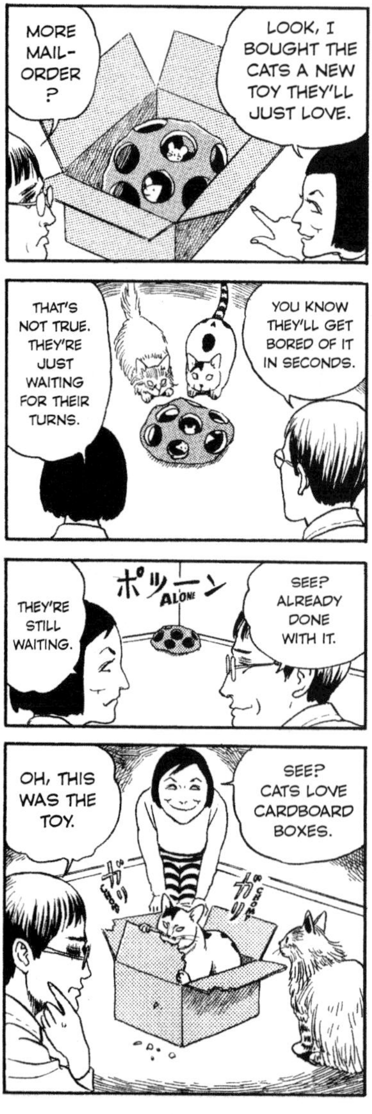
LOOK, I BOUGHT THE CATS A NEW TOY THEY'LL JUST LOVE.
MORE MAIL-ORDER ?
YOU KNOW THEY'LL GET BORED OF IT IN SECONDS.
THAT'S NOT TRUE. THEY'RE JUST WAITING FOR THEIR TURNS.
SEE? ALREADY DONE WITH IT.
ポツーン
ALONE
THEY'RE STILL WAITING.
SEE? CATS LOVE CARDBOARD BOXES.
OH, THIS WAS THE TOY.
ガリ
ガリ

PROFILE:

JUNJI ITO

Born in Gifu Prefecture, 1963. Horror manga artist.
Debuted in *Monthly Halloween* in 1987
Previously a dental technician.
Transferred to manga entirely in 1990.
His signature works include *Tomie*, the *Souichi*
series, *Lovesick Dead*, *Uzumaki*, and others.

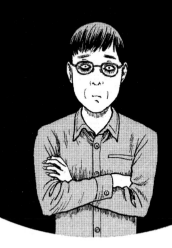

TRANSLATION NOTES

Page 3: Building a house in Japan
In the United States and other Western countries, it is typical to purchase a used house, but in Japan, this is relatively uncommon. In many cases, a family saves money with the goal of building a new house rather than purchasing an existing one.

Page 10: Yon and Mu
The word "yon" is one of the ways to say "four" in Japanese. Goro means "fifth son," and "mu" is one of the ways to say "six."

Page 39: Semi-double
A bed size that is uncommon outside of Japan. Whereas a twin size bed is usually 90 cm wide (approx. 35.4 cm) a semi-double is 120 cm (approx. 47.2 cm).

Page 52: Tsuchinoko
A legendary Japanese creature (cryptid) that resembles a very wide snake, or possibly a legless alligator. The tsuchinoko is said to be quite venomous and is able to jump several feet in the air.

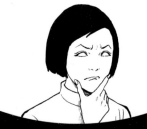

BONUS MANGA

Kodansha Comics is pleased to bring you special bonus material for the English language edition of *Junji Ito's Cat Diary: Yon & Mu*. On the following pages are a short comic and letter penned respectively by J-kun (Junji Ito) and his wife, A-ko (Ayako Ishiguro). In Japan, they were published as contributions to a book created in support of cat shelters following the Great Tohoku Earthquake of 2011. The Japanese title of the original book is *Maikeru Oshiete! Hisai Neko Ouen no Kyoukasho* (*Teach Me, Michael! A Textbook in Support of Feline Disaster Victims*).

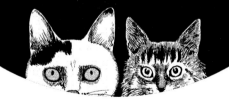

YON & MU

YON WENT TO HEAVEN

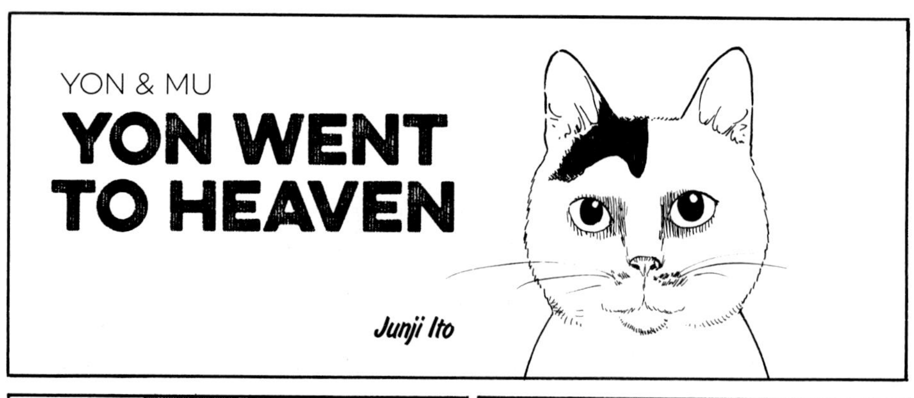

Junji Ito

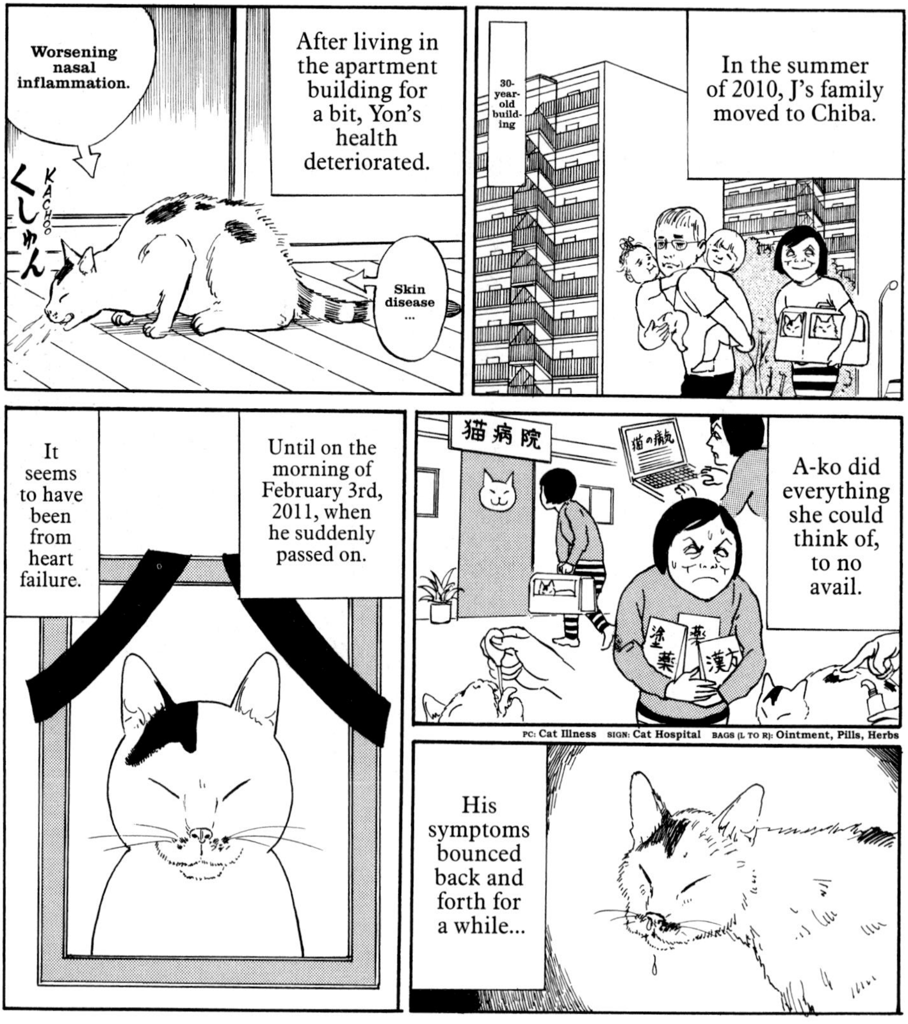
In the summer of 2010, J's family moved to Chiba.
30-year-old building
After living in the apartment building for a bit, Yon's health deteriorated.
Worsening nasal inflammation.
KACHOO
くしゅん
Skin disease...
A-ko did everything she could think of, to no avail.
猫病院
猫の病気
塗薬
薬
漢方
PC: Cat Illness SIGN: Cat Hospital BAGS (L TO R): Ointment, Pills, Herbs
His symptoms bounced back and forth for a while...
Until on the morning of February 3rd, 2011, when he suddenly passed on.
It seems to have been from heart failure.

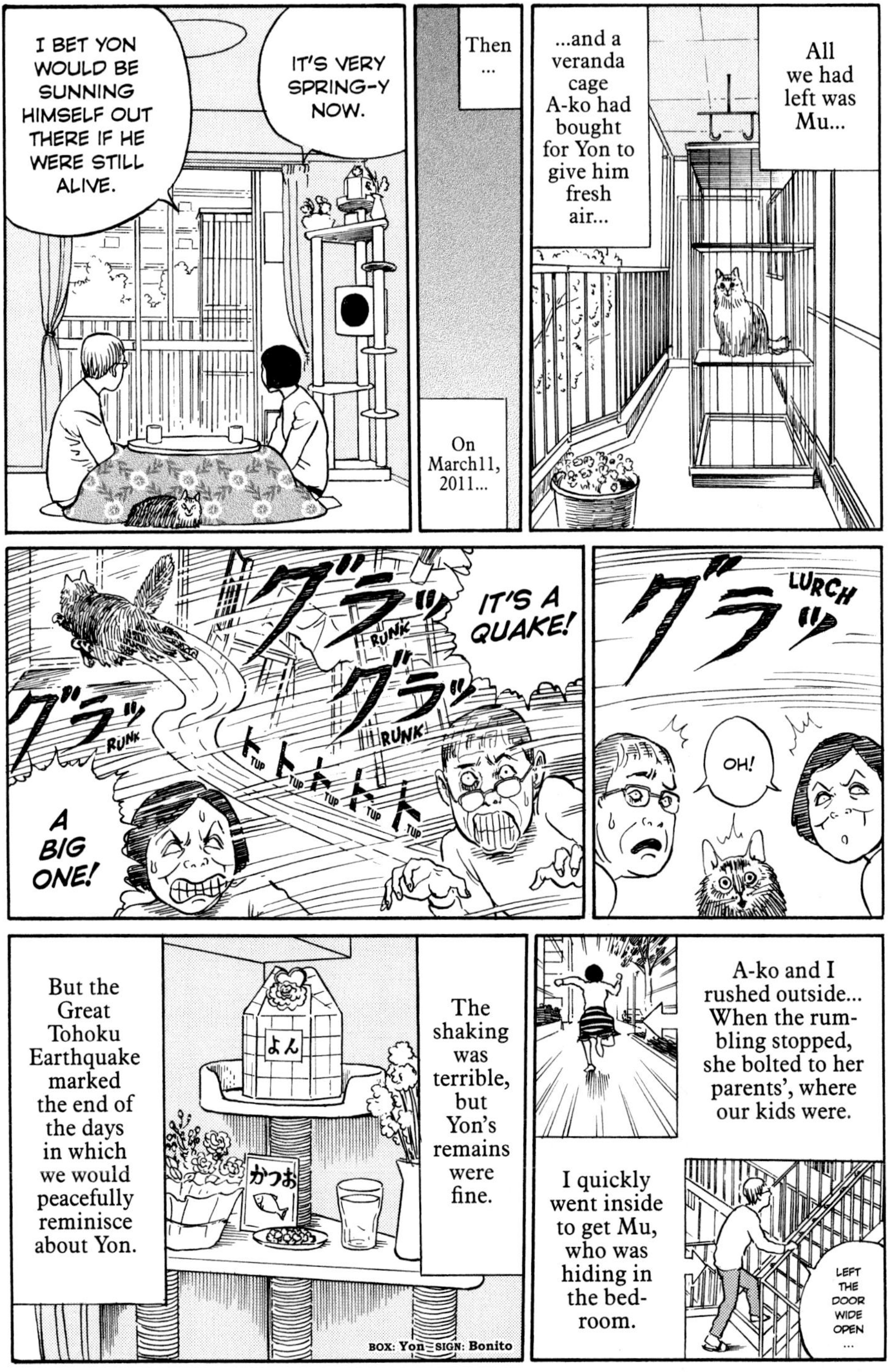
All we had left was Mu...
...and a veranda cage A-ko had bought for Yon to give him fresh air...
Then ...
On March11, 2011...
IT'S VERY SPRING-Y NOW.
I BET YON WOULD BE SUNNING HIMSELF OUT THERE IF HE WERE STILL ALIVE.
グラッ
LURCH
OH!
IT'S A QUAKE!
グラッ
RUNK
グラッ
RUNK
グラッ
RUNK
トトトトト
TUP TUP TUP TUP TUP
A BIG ONE!
A-ko and I rushed outside... When the rumbling stopped, she bolted to her parents', where our kids were.
I quickly went inside to get Mu, who was hiding in the bedroom.
LEFT THE DOOR WIDE OPEN ...
The shaking was terrible, but Yon's remains were fine.
よん
かつお
BOX: Yon SIGN: Bonito
But the Great Tohoku Earthquake marked the end of the days in which we would peacefully reminisce about Yon.

The End

As J's manga showed, Yonsuke up and died on us. For a while, he wandered around my legs, until eventually he realized, "Oh? I don't feel any pain anymore, and my body is light and breezy. I can go anywhere!" And so he flew away, over the horizon.

The next morning, I carried Yonsuke out onto the veranda, where we spent our last moment together. I put my pinky to his mouth, but he didn't suckle anymore. I was saddened by the sight of his firmly shut eyes and mouth, and I cried again.

By the end of the day, Yonsuke's remains were cremated.

I kept crying, over and over, and it was the first time I had seen J, who was right next to me, cry like that. I'm sure that if Yonsuke was there to see, he would meow with his eyes wide and rub against us, wondering what could make two grown adults behave like that. He would be helping us feel better by telling us not to cry, because it was annoying him.

"It's a wonderful thing for stuff to just be normal, don't you think?"

That was a quote a friend of mine said to me so many times, it got stuck in my brain. Those words really made sense to me after Yonsuke died. Shortly afterward, the great earthquake on 3/11 caused terrible upheaval. I was truly thankful that the people I care about were able to continue their lives the same as before. And hey, at least Yonsuke didn't have to undergo such a terrifying ordeal.

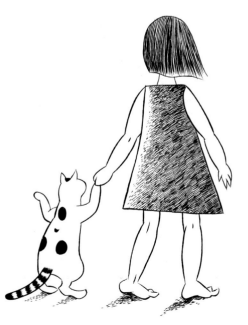

Yonsuke was the star of our household, even in manga form. No matter how creepy his face was, he was my precious little baby. Thank you for supporting me, no matter how useless I was at times.

I miss you each and every day, Yonsuke!

A-ko

ANIMAL LAND

MAKOTO RAIKU

WELCOME TO THE JUNGLE

In a world of animals
where the strong eat the weak,
Monoko the tanuki stumbles
across a strange creature
the like of which has never
been seen before -
a human baby!

While the newborn has no
claws or teeth to protect itself,
it does have the rare ability
to speak to and understand
all the different animal.

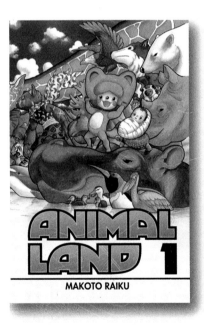

ANIMAL LAND 1
MAKOTO RAIKU

Special extras in each volume! Read them all!

RATING OT AGES 10+

VISIT WWW.KODANSHACOMICS.COM TO:

- View release date calendars for upcoming volumes
- Find out the latest about new Kodansha Comics series

KC KODANSHA COMICS

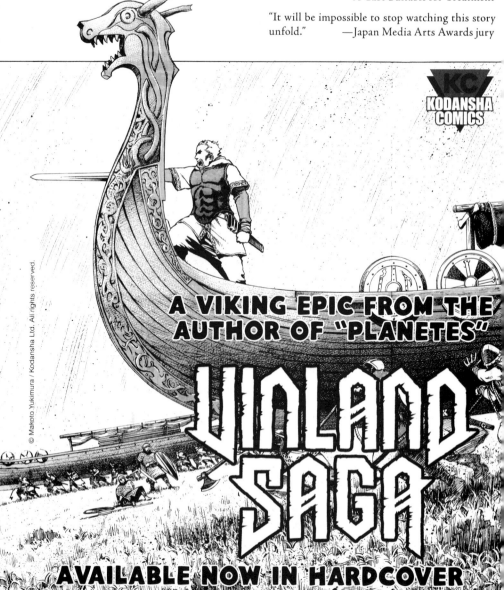

Junji Ito's Cat Diary: Yon & Mu is a work of fiction. Names, characters, places, and incidents are the products of the author's imagination or are used fictitiously. Any resemblance to actual events, locales, or persons, living or dead, is entirely coincidental.

A Kodansha Comics Trade Paperback Original.

Published in the United States by Kodansha Comics,
an imprint of Kodansha USA Publishing, LLC, New York.

Publication rights for this English edition arranged through Kodansha Ltd., Tokyo.

First published in Japan in 2009 by Kodansha Ltd., Tokyo, as *Itou Junji No Neko Nikki: Yon & Muu.*

ISBN 978-1-63236-197-4

Printed in the United States of America.

www.kodanshacomics.com

9 8 7 6

Translator: Stephen Paul
Lettering: Evan Hayden
Editing: Ajani Oloye
Kodansha Comics Edition Cover Design: Phil Balsman